D1373686

XAVIER UNIVERSITY LIBRARY
NEW ORLEANS, LA. 70125

Successful Pension Design For The Small To Medium Size Business

Robert F. Slimmon

Institute for Business Planning

IBP PLAZA, ENGLEWOOD CLIFFS, N. J. 07632

This publication is designed to provide accurate and authoritative information in regard to the subject matter covered. It is sold with the understanding that the publisher is not engaged in rendering legal, accounting or other professional service. If legal advice or other expert assistance is required, the services of a competent professional person should be sought.

—From a Declaration of Principles jointly adopted by a Committee of the American Bar Association and a Committee of Publishers and Associations.

©Copyright 1980, by Institute for Business Planning, Inc.
IBP Plaza, Englewood Cliffs, NJ 07632

All rights reserved. No part of this publication may be reproduced in any form, or by any means, without permission in writing from the publisher. Printed in U.S.A.

Library of Congress Cataloging in Publication Data

Slimmon, Robert F
   Successful pension design for the small to medium size business.

   Includes index.
   1. Pension trusts. 2. Small business--Personnel management. 3. Profit-sharing. I. Title.
HD7105.S54   658.3'253   80-13148
ISBN 0-87624-524-6

658,3253
5633s

Dedication

To my father, whose knowledge of pension plans would fill many books this size and to Meevie, whose patience and forbearance created the time and motivation to complete this manuscript.

About The Author

ROBERT F. SLIMMON is a principal of Future Planning Associates, Inc., a northeastern regional pension design, administration and consulting firm headquartered in Burlington, Vermont. A University Scholar and winner of several departmental academic awards at his Cum Lauda graduation from Princeton University in 1971, he went on to receive his M.A. in psychology from the University of Illinois in 1972.

Mr. Slimmon acquired his basic pension background in the insurance industry, receiving his CLU designation in 1975, and achieving membership in the Million Dollar Roundtable before devoting all his time to fee-based consulting activities. A member of several Estate Planning Councils, the Society of CLU's and the American Society of Pension Actuaries, Mr. Slimmon has been a frequent speaker on pension design to professional and business associations throughout the northeast.

What This Book Will Do For You

Pension and profit-sharing plans provide one of the most comprehensive planning tools available for small businessmen attempting to accumulate, manage and efficiently dispose of an estate. No other single medium can provide a complete income tax deduction for contributions, totally tax-free investment return, and a choice between 10-year income averaging and estate tax exemption. All this is available from a pension plan, without the risks generally associated with such tax favored vehicles. And yet, many small businessmen do not have qualified plans. Why?

Everyone can agree on the positive nature of these advantages. Unfortunately, putting them into practice has been very difficult. Complicated actuarial methods, the maze of government rules and burdensome regulations surrounding such key topics as integration, and the cost of covering non-key employees in a poorly-designed plan have all discouraged practitioners from recommending plans for their clients. PENSION DESIGN FOR THE SMALL TO MEDIUM SIZE BUSINESS can help.

This book will unlock the mysteries of pension design for you and your clients. It will simplify the concepts of actuarial methodology so that you can effectively use those concepts to your advantage. It will explain the critical element of plan design—integration—so that pension contributions can be slanted toward higher-paid participants. It will show you how to measure your clients' objectives, to identify the right plan for a situation, and control the on-going efficient administration of that plan. Most importantly, you will learn the *secrets* of pension design.

Most small businessmen have a limited budget for their pension plans. Before they adopt a plan, they must be shown that it will benefit primarily them. You will see how different parameters, such as age and service, can affect the budget chosen by a particular businessman. Also, they must be shown that the tax advantages of a qualified plan will not be offset by administrative and employee costs. These are the subjects of pension design.

PENSION DESIGN FOR THE SMALL TO MEDIUM SIZE BUSINESS explores in depth the myriad alternative types of pension plans. To insure an "apples to apples" comparison, as well as to keep the design process within the constraints of a budget, the book analyzes alternative plan formats with constant reference to the same employee census information and contributions. Therefore, you can see the effect of changing actuarial assumptions, plan design, integration or other factors which control pension costs and contribution allocations.

This book sets forth numerous tables, charts, forms, checklists and over forty planning tips to aid you. Where illustrations are included, you will see why certain techniques were used to accomplish a positive result for your client. You will be able to see what situation would be most suitable to a particular plan. A sophisticated IRS-approved Prototype Plan appears in the Appendix. You will be shown when and where to use it. You will see how to provide non-shareholder employees with maximum benefits at least cost to the company. You will see the advantages and disadvantages for choosing a fiduciary as well as the steps for terminating a plan.

The following questions indicate just a few of the situations for which this book offers practical answers:

- What happens when your client's financial situation changes? How do you make changes in midstream?

- Games Company's President and key man, Mr. Parker, wants to know what the comparative costs would be in terms of initial contributions of utilizing an aggressive versus a conservative set of actuarial assumptions.

- How do you plan around the Limitation on Annual Additions to get the greatest benefit for your client?

- As a sole stockholder and key man of DEF Corporation, John wants to set up a two-tiered defined-contribution plan which will provide him with the maximum annual addition. What would be the contribution rate for generating John's maximum annual addition?

- What happens when a business owner who is contemplating setting up a defined-benefit plan providing retirement income equal to 50 percent of pay has two employees each earning $75,000 annually and one of whom is 20 years older than the other?

- Compare Incorporated is considering a defined-contribution or a defined-benefit plan and has $18,727 to spend. What are the choices offered by these two alternatives?

With this book you will be able to show your clients their alternatives. You will be able to explain the long-term advantages and disadvantages of those alternatives. You will gain in-depth knowledge of the jargon and special rules which have previously made pension plans an attractive but excessively complicated subject. With this knowledge, you can provide your client with guidance in what is probably the most efficient capital accumulation and transfer vehicle available in our economy.

Contents

KEY INGREDIENTS FOR EFFECTIVELY STRUCTURING
PENSION PLANS FOR YOUR SMALL BUSINESS CLIENTS (*cont.*)

3. THE KEY TO PENSION DESIGN:
EFFECTIVE USE OF INTEGRATION ....

THE KEY TO PENSION DESIGN:
EFFECTIVE USE OF INTEGRATION (*contd.*)

**PART TWO: ALTERNATIVE PENSION PLANS:
OPPORTUNITIES, STRATEGIES AND TECHNIQUES**

SECTION A: HOW TO DESIGN DEFINED-CONTRIBUTION PLANS

CONTENTS

HOW MONEY-PURCHASE PLANS INCREASE
CREATIVE DESIGN OPPORTUNITIES (*contd.*)

HOW MONEY-PURCHASE PLANS INCREASE
CREATIVE DESIGN OPPORTUNITIES (*contd.*)

HOW DEFINED-BENEFIT PENSION PLANS
CAN BOOST PLAN EFFICIENCY (*contd.*)

CONTENTS

CONTENTS   xxi

MULTIPLE QUALIFIED PLANS FOR
MAXIMUM TAX DEDUCTIONS (*contd.*)

CONTENTS

A PRACTITIONER'S GUIDE TO OVERSEEING QUALIFICATIONS,
ADMINISTRATION AND INVESTMENT ASPECTS OF THE PLAN (*contd.*)

A PRACTITIONER'S GUIDE TO OVERSEEING QUALIFICATIONS,
ADMINISTRATION AND INVESTMENT ASPECTS OF THE PLAN (*contd.*)

PART ONE
Essential Considerations You Need to Know Before Designing a Plan For Your Client

Why Your Small Business Clients Need Qualified Plans

In this chapter we will discuss the opportunities inherent in well designed qualified plans as well as give you the ammunition you need to whet and maintain your clients' interest.

¶100   WAYS YOUR CLIENTS WILL BENEFIT FROM QUALIFIED PLANS

Most practitioners perceive qualified plans as powerful tax planning tools. However, they also find these plans to have a complicated web of complex reporting and disclosure requirements that can bog down the planning process. It's important to generate sufficient enthusiasm with the positive aspects of qualified plans to "carry" your client. The positive aspects are quite compelling. They include:

1. Income tax deductions for contributions, the bulk of which should go to key men;

2. Postponement of and increased options for handling the taxation of benefits ultimately received;

3. A "carrot and stick" motivational tool to attract and retain key employees;

4. Favorable estate taxation; and

5. Tax-free return on invested assets.

The combination of these factors provides compelling impetus for considering qualified plans.

¶101   HOW TO IDENTIFY THE RIGHT TYPE OF CLIENT

Small businesses confront monumental challenges. They are generally undercapitalized, they must compete with the broad advertising capacity of larger competitors, and they usually lack the manpower to develop a structured and sophisticated business organization. For those few small businesses that overcome these perils the most vexing problem of all awaits—taxation. Income, gift and estate taxation lurk behind every transaction. Little wonder most small businessmen value the relationship with their tax accountant or attorney highest among their professional advisors.

The first step in identifying your client requires a thorough analysis of your client's personal and business situation to determine whether he has the problems that qualified plans can conceivably solve. The answer isn't always self-evident. The following four tests will help.

¶101.1   The Psychological Test—Has Your Client's Lifestyle Matured?

The self-sacrifice and self-discipline that are prerequisites for a small business's success create an interesting psychological dilemma. When a small businessman achieves financial success he is often torn between spending his new-found wealth to make up for past abstinence, and continuing the frugal instincts which contributed to his success. Frequently, these clients develop a "you can't take it with you" attitude which leads to a substantially more expensive lifestyle—larger home, larger cars, more vacations, and so on.

The problem is commonly compounded by high educational expenses which seem to mature at the same time as the business. Both these factors tend to create cash flow problems at the same time heavy taxation creates the greatest incentive for plan implementation.

Your client will not be a good prospect for *any* sort of qualified retirement plan unless:

1. he wants to save money;
2. he can afford to save money; and/or
3. he needs to save money.

In other words, his personal financial goals must largely have been fulfilled. He must have reasonably satisfied his material needs and still have disposable cash flow. If this hasn't occurred, then no matter how cleverly you design a retirement program your time and effort will have been wasted. The primary prerequisite for setting up a pension or profit-sharing plan for a small businessman is that *he* make the long-term *personal* commitment to "stick with" his plan.

¶101.2   How Mature Is Your Client's Business?

Just as important as the business owner's personal need for cash is the business's cash flow demands. If there is going to be a plan, the company must have disposable income. Often there is no disposable income for one of the following reasons:

1. to achieve success the businessman has continually reinvested company earnings;
2. the business is capital intensive and requires substantial disposable cash for current operations;
3. the owner, to satisfy his own personal financial goals, "zeroes out" the business's income by paying himself year-end bonuses, leaving no cash in the company; or
4. the business is in a period of growth so excess cash goes to plant capacity and personnel expansion.

If some or all of the above factors are present your client may be better off without a qualified plan even though that will result in higher taxes. Sometimes it's more important to have accessible after-tax dollars than to have pre-tax dollars tied up in a plan.

¶101.3   How To Apply The Corporate And Personal Tax Test To Your Client

The single most important reason to implement a qualified retirement program in a small business is to avoid corporate and personal income taxes. Generally a qualified plan will provide an effective shelter only if your client's personal marginal income tax rate exceeds 40%. The tax rate applicable to your client's business is of lesser importance, at least in the small plan domain.

Example: Many small businessmen are impressed with the low 18½% effective tax rate applicable to their first $50,000 worth of corporate earnings. They argue in favor of paying the tax and leaving the balance in the business. If Savit Company earns $50,000 of corporate income, it pays a total tax of only $9,250. Compared to confiscatory personal rates, that seems fairly mild. And, perhaps, the $40,750 left in the business can earn a higher rate of return than alternative investment media. However, consider the alternative presented by a qualified plan assuming a comparable investment return.

Year	Corporate Income Available	Without a Plan		With a Plan	
		After-Tax Corporate Income	Cumulative Invested @ 8% Net*	Potential Pension Contribution	Cumulative Invested @ 10%
1	$50,000	$40,750	$ 40,750	$50,000	$ 50,000
2	50,000	40,750	84,760	50,000	105,000
3	50,000	40,750	132,229	50,000	165,500
4	50,000	40,750	183,624	50,000	232,050
5	50,000	40,750	239,064	50,000	305,255
6	50,000	40,750	298,939	50,000	385,781
7	50,000	40,750	363,604	50,000	474,359
8	50,000	40,750	433,443	50,000	571,794
9	50,000	40,750	508,868	50,000	678,974
10	50,000	40,750	590,327	50,000	796,871
20	50,000	40,750	1,864,800	50,000	2,863,749
30	50,000	40,750	4,616,291	50,000	8,224,701

*The 8% yield assumed would also be subject to tax.

Additional Problems May Foil Your Client's Attempt To Use His Corporation As A Tax Shelter

Apart from the attractiveness of pension plans as accumulation vehicles for surplus funds, they offer your client protection from two additional pitfalls:

1. *Accumulated earnings tax penalties* can be applied to businesses which retain earnings beyond their reasonable needs. The "trigger mechanism" for most small businesses comes at $150,000 of accumulated earnings. The penalty for retained earnings is dire—27½% of the first $100,000 and 38½% of the excess—in addition to regular corporate taxes; and

2. *The earnings will trigger a worse tax* when the owner tries to get them out of the business. Suppose your client accumulates $100,000 in his business after paying the low corporate tax rate. What does he do with the $100,000 if he doesn't need it for the operation of his business? Paying it out as salary or bonus will trigger a worse result at the personal tax rate. Collapsing the corporation through liquidation to obtain long-term capital gains rates can be difficult for small corporations but will trigger at least a long-term capital gains tax. Thus, the short-term use of the corporate shelter may lead to long-term problems.

In short, the key income tax test for small businesses should be applied to the owner and his key men, since sooner or later business earnings need to be paid out to employees. If your client's corporate or personal tax bracket is 30% or higher, he should at least consider how a well-designed plan could retrieve lost tax dollars.

¶101.4   How To Determine Whether Your Client Passes The Estate Tax Test

Pension plans can be handy tools for estate planners, since certain death benefits from pension plans are exempt from federal estate tax. Many small businessmen are, from an estate planner's point of view, illiquid. Their business represents the bulk of their net worth and there's no cash for estate settlement costs. If that's the case with your client, or if his marginal estate tax rate exceeds 30%, a qualified plan will probably provide an ideal vehicle for tax-free estate accumulation. Further, due to the liquidity of most pension plan death benefits in small corporations, careful planning may create an asset—the pension fund—which is simultaneously free of estate tax and liquid. That's a hard combination to beat.

¶101.5   A Checklist For Profiling The Ideal Prospect

Your client is a good candidate for a qualified plan if he:

☐ is taking enough salary to satisfy his personal needs comfortably;

☐ doesn't have any major "cash crunch" on the horizon such as college expenses for which no funds have been set aside;

☐ is worried about the impact of estate taxes on his accumulated assets;

☐ is subject to a high personal tax rate;

☐ is subject to a high corporate tax rate;

☐ is conscious enough of his goals to establish a reasonably long-term "game plan" and has the self-discipline to stick with it;

and if his business:

☐ generates cash in excess of operational requirements;

☐ has adequate cash reserves to weather periodic economic slowdowns; and/or

☐ doesn't anticipate major structural, operational, or personnel changes which cash reserves or bank financing wouldn't adequately cover.

If your client passes this simple "screening test" you ought to tell him what a qualified plan can do. Better that you explain the pros and cons and have him reject the idea than to risk his finding out about the opportunities from someone else.

¶102   USING PENSION PLANS TO ACHIEVE YOUR
          CLIENT'S GOALS—A COMPARISON OF TWO
                      ALTERNATIVES

The tax advantages of qualified plans are generally well known and understood. However, because they are so important they warrant repetition.

For comparative purposes let's assume your client has a pre-tax sum of $10,000 for investment. He's in the 50% income and 40% estate tax brackets. He considers the following options:

1. a pension plan invested in a long-term guaranteed interest contract yielding 9%; or
2. a portfolio of tax-free municipal bonds yielding 7%; or
3. a portfolio of stocks and bonds with an aggregate yield of 12%; half taxable at long-term capital gains rate (25%), and half taxable at ordinary income rates.

Your client asks you to evaluate these alternatives, primarily from the tax perspective.

¶102.1   How Pension Plans Can Double Your Client's Investable Dollars

If your client wants to buy municipal bonds or a stock/bond portfolio, his first check will be to the IRS. These purchases can only be made from after-tax dollars. Thus the $10,000 will be whittled down to $5,000 before any investment can occur. On the other hand, contributions to qualified plans are deductible; therefore, no tax need be paid on the $10,000 deposit.

Here's a simple comparative illustration:

Item	Municipal Bonds	Stock/Bond Portfolio	Pension Plan
Pre-tax dollars to invest	$10,000	$10,000	$10,000
Less: Income Taxes payable	(5,000)	(5,000)	(00)
Net Available for Investment	$ 5,000	$ 5,000	$10,000

That means your client will have, with the pension alternative, twice as many dollars to invest. Over a twenty-year period he will have invested $200,000, as opposed to $100,000 under either the municipal bond or stock/bond portfolio alternatives. That type of leverage may command his interest.

¶102.2   How To Double Your Client's Yield

Tax-exempt bonds appeal to high bracket taxpayers because their yield is exempt from federal income tax. High bracket taxpayers accept a slightly lower rate of return or "spread" since, after considering taxes, they represent a better net yield than that available under higher return but taxable investments. Alternatively, a portfolio of stocks and bonds is attractive because some of the appreciation will be taxed at the long-term capital gains rate, which is substantially lower than that used for ordinary income. However, investments in qualified pension trusts are exempt from current taxation. Thus, pension plans may offer the best of both worlds—high rate of return with no tax. Over a long period of time, tax-free compounding is the most significant aspect of pension plans.

Following through with the simple analysis in ¶102.1, let's see how your client fares under the three alternatives compared

Item	Municipal Bond	Stock/Bond Portfolio	Pension Plan
Amount invested (see ¶102.1)	$5,000	$5,000	$10,000
Rate of Return	× 7%	× 12%	× 9%
First Year Earnings	350	600	900
Less: Ordinary Income Taxes Payable	(0)	(150)	(0)
Less: Long-term Capital Gains Taxes Payable	(0)	(75)	(0)
Total Taxes	(0)	(225)	(0)
Net Income	$ 350	$ 375	$ 900

The long-term effect of this tax-free compounding, combined with larger amounts available for investment because of tax deductibility of pension contributions, really adds up. Consider the cumulative effects of our analysis after ten, twenty or thirty years:

Time Period	Municipal Bond	Stock/Bond Portfolio	Pension Plan
10 Years	$ 73,918	$ 76,041	$ 165,603
20 Years	$219,326	$232,763	$ 557,645
30 Years	$505,365	$555,772	$1,485,752

Pointing out to your client how he can double or triple his accumulated assets simply by using the tax-deductible medium afforded by pension plans, will probably enhance your professional position. However, a logical question from your client might be, "If this is true there must be some devastating tax when I *take the money out.*" That's a good question.

¶103   WHAT ARE THE TAX EFFECTS WHEN TAKING MONEY OUT OF PENSION PLANS

Your client will receive the benefits he has accumulated in the plan in most cases either at his retirement or his death. Thus, it is important to consider the ultimate tax effects at distribution time. Surprisingly these results continue the trend of favorable taxation for qualified retirement plans. The following discussion will show you the alternative distribution methods available and how they work.

¶103.1   Ten-Year Income Averaging And Its Tax Effect

Assuming your client takes a lump-sum distribution of his account at retirement, 10-year income averaging may prove to be the most favorable of all distribution methods. Ten-year income averaging is really very simple. Merely compute the tax on one tenth of the total distribution as if no other income were received. That tax is then multiplied by 10. The product becomes the total tax on the distribution. Ten-year income averaging can yield very favorable results.

Consider the following taxes applicable to lump-sum distributions under 10 year income averaging:

Amount of Distribution	Total Tax	Net Distribution	Effective Tax Rate
$100,000	$13,870	$86,130	14%
300,000	79,620	220,380	27%
500,000	176,460	323,540	35%

If you followed through the illustrations of ¶102.2 and ¶102.3, you can see that pension plans still come out way ahead.

Item	Municipal Bond	Stock/Bond Portfolio	Pension Plan
20-year lump-sum available	$219,326	$232,763	$557,645
Tax applicable to lump-sum	N/A	N/A	205,280
Net Available after Taxes	$219,326	$232,763	$352,365

That should answer your client's well conceived question about onerous taxes at distribution time.

¶103.2 Periodic Payments Provide One Alternative

Rather than a lump-sum distribution, a retiring participant may elect a series of periodic payments over a time frame not exceeding his life expectancy. If periodic payments are elected as the distribution method, the payments are simply added to the retired participant's other income as they are received. Since most of your clients, as small businessmen, will have accumulated substantial other assets prior to their retirement, they are likely to have additional income. If that's the case, then the periodic payments may be thrown into a higher marginal bracket. Generally, that results in a total tax higher than the one computed under 10-year income averaging.

Example: Sam Jones has a choice between taking a $250,000 lump sum distribution subject to 10-year income averaging or $25,000 per year for as long as he lives. Sam has $20,000 of other income from securities he has accumulated. The single tax on a lump-sum distribution would be $59,520. Having paid the tax Sam would have $190,480 left over which, if invested at seven percent would return $13,334 per year forever without touching principal.

Alternatively, if Sam adds $25,000 per year of periodic payments to his existing $20,000 income he will increase his income taxes by $10,696. That means his net income from the periodic payments is $14,301 per year. When he dies there will be nothing left.

Caution: Never assume that the results of a comparison like the one above will always come out the same. Most of your clients will be well worth the time it takes to analyze the alternatives thoroughly. Frequently, unusual personal circumstances affect the decision about what distribution method to use.

¶103.3 Choosing Estate Or Income Taxation At Death

Keeping in mind the marginal estate tax bracket of our hypothetical client, it is easy to see why qualified plans provide an exceptional opportunity. If they are payable to a named beneficiary over two or more taxable years, death benefits from qualified retirement programs can be free of federal estate tax. Alternatively, death benefits from plans can be taken in a lump-sum and included in the estate thereby made subject to 10-year income averaging. Thus, estate planning possibilities remain quite flexible. You can choose the favorable 10-year income averaging or the estate tax exemption.

Planning Tip: Most commentators agree that the ultimate choice between estate taxation and 10-year income averaging can be made by the beneficiary. That leads to a very unique opportunity for post-mortem planning. You should make sure your plan specifies that the beneficiary can make the choice of the form of plan distribution.

Example: Assume that after 20 years of accumulation under municipal bonds, stock/bonds portfolio, or pension plan, your client dies. Here's what happens:

Item	Municipal Bond	Stock/Bond Portfolio	Pension Plan
Balance Paid to Beneficiary	$219,326	$232,763	$557,645
Less: Applicable Estate Taxes	(87,730)	(93,105)	(0)
Net to Beneficiary	$131,596	$139,658	$557,645

While your client may be less excited about the estate planning opportunities (since he needs to die to realize them), qualified plans appear to be a "best-of-all worlds" situation. Money that was never taxed, accumulated over a period of years without tax on the yield is passed to the beneficiary without estate taxes. While the beneficiary must pay income taxes on the proceeds received, proper testamentary planning should minimize the applicable tax rates.

¶103.4   How To Decide Whether To Elect Estate Tax Exemption Or Ten-Year Income Averaging

Apart from personal considerations unique to a particular client, the following chart shows the approximate relative tax effects of the alternative mode of estate distribution under qualified plans.

A Lump Sum of	Or Monthly Income of	Income & Estate Tax On Lump	Income Tax @ 15 yrs. On Monthly
$ 100,000	$ 899	$ 33,870	$ 80,910
200,000	1,798	81,770	161,820
300,000	2,697	139,620	242,730
500,000	4,495	276,460	404,550
750,000	6,743	451,460	606,870
1,000,000	8,990	626,460	809,100

MARGINAL TAX RATES ESTATE 20%, INCOME 50% / If Distribution Is:

MARGINAL TAX RATES ESTATE 50%, INCOME 50%		MARGINAL TAX RATES: ESTATE 50%, INCOME 20%	
Income & Estate Taxes On Lump	Income Tax @ 15 yrs. On Monthly	Income & Estate Taxes On Lump	Income Tax @ 15 yrs. On Monthly
$ 63,870	$ 80,910	$ 63,870	$ 32,364
141,770	161,820	141,770	64,728
229,620	242,730	229,620	97,092
426,460	404,550	426,460	161,820
676,460	606,870	676,460	242,748
926,460	809,100		

Caution: Post-mortem estate planning is a very flexible tool if it doesn't thwart the plans made by the deceased. There may be specific reasons for your client to elect, in advance, one form of qualified plan distribution over another. His reasons may reflect personal attitudes as well as sound tax planning. After his death, the beneficiary may not perceive his or her situation in the same fashion and, if too much opportunity for post-mortem planning is available, there may be an inherent conflict of interest between the estate and its various beneficiaries.

Very few options this attractive, if any, are available to your clients. But every silver lining has a cloud. Obviously there are difficulties associated with qualified plans. It's your responsibility to point them out as well as the advantages.

¶104   WHAT ARE THE TRADITIONAL PROBLEMS WITH QUALIFIED PLANS?

Clients and practitioners frequently raise several common issues blocking or forestalling implementation of qualified plans. These include:

1. Communication limitations imposed by the special jargon applicable to qualified plans;
2. The financial and legal liability associated with qualification and administration of the plan; and
3. The cost of covering non-key employees.

Let's examine each of the three common complaints separately.

¶104.1   How To Overcome The Problem Of Pension Jargon

The pension business, like many other professional services, involves a special group of words or terms uniquely applicable to the pension field.

Phrases such as "actuarial equivalency," "funding standard account," and "limitation on annual additions" make plans seem overly complicated and, therefore, undesirable. To some extent that's true, since most pension functions can be explained in simple layman's language.

The fact is that many clients will not "buy" what they cannot understand and the time involved in making those explanations often does not justify the reward. However, the opportunities inherent in the illustrations of ¶101 clearly warrant aggressive pursuit. The easiest solution is to present plans to your clients with numeric rather than verbal illustrations. Attract your client's interest with the tax advantages before introducing him to the peculiar jargon he must ultimately be exposed to.

¶104.2   How To Solve The Legal And Financial Burden Of Qualification, Reporting And Disclosure

Pension plans require constant attention. The design process can take several months. Preparation of documents for submission to the Internal Revenue Service to obtain a Letter of Determination involves substantial clerical and supervisory time. Dealing with the Internal Revenue Service to make the necessary amendments to obtain such a letter is an unpredictable time burden. Ongoing reporting and disclosure is very time consuming. All of the above require constant monitoring because the government frequently revises its procedures and regulations. Further, if you provide only part of the services required and some other "link-in-the-chain" breaks down, your client may look to you as the responsible party.

These are legitimate concerns both from the client's perspective (he must understand the ongoing services and charges that will be associated with maintenance of his plan) and also from your prospective (you may not feel qualified or want to make the time commitment involved in proper handling of plans).

The Solutions: If you feel strongly that the opportunities inherent in well designed pension plans are too great to ignore, you must do one of two things:

1. Make an affirmative commitment to be in the pension business, meaning that you or a member of your firm must devote most of his or her energies to the qualification and administrative problems associated with your plans; or

2. Develop a qualified plan "team" of advisors who, between them, can provide sufficient:
   a) Expertise;
   b) Continuity; and
   c) Sound financial structure to handle your client's needs. The "team" may well involve an attorney, accountant,

investment advisor, and others. Critical to the success of any team, however, is the orderly and effective delegation of responsibilities, objectives, timetables and monitoring systems.

¶104.3   Who Should Do What On The Pension Team?

A typical planning team will see the attorney, accountant, and the investment advisor involved in the following tasks:

1. *Attorney:* Ultimate responsibility for drafting initial plan documents including:

    a) Plan and Trust;
    b) IRS Submission Forms;
    c) Summary Plan Description;
    d) Notice to Interested Parties; and
    e) Notice of Participation.

    The attorney should also be responsible for overseeing the qualification process with the IRS including proposed and finalized amendments. Finally, the attorney should be involved in the initial planning process, such as, helping to decide what form of plan best fits the client's unique circumstances.

2. *Accountant:* Best qualified to comment on and illustrate the effects of the tax aspects and cash flow demands of a qualified plan. The accountant should also have input into all documents and submission materials prepared by the attorney and should be closely involved in budgeting and monitoring the cash flow required by the plan within the client's business.

3. *Investment Advisor:* Ultimate responsibility for selecting the investment or combination of investments best suited to fulfilling the corporate objectives contained in the plan. The investment advisor or trustee has considerable ongoing responsibility to keep abreast of changing economic conditions and insure that the goal can be met most efficiently by the funding policy utilized.

More important than any other aspect of delegation is the appointment of a team "captain." By far the largest source of dissatisfaction generated relative to qualified plans is occasioned by one team member thinking that the other had been assigned a particular task. Constant communication among the team members together with a clear understanding of who is the "captain" will make the pension planning process simple, profitable, and effective.

¶104.4   The Cost Of Covering Non-Key Employees—Major Stumbling Block To Implementation

Most small businessmen, given the examples presented earlier in this chapter, would opt to put $10,000 a year into a qualified plan if the entire $10,000 went into their account. Unfortunately, even after the exclusions for age, service, and the 70%-80% test, there will still be employees left over who must be covered. Many small businessmen balk at providing pension coverage for employees they already feel are overpaid and who, they feel, probably have no use for pension benefits anyway. Therefore, a primary object of pension design in small closely-held businesses is to minimize the cost of including non-key employees in qualified plans.

Obviously, if your client must put one dollar in the plan for employees for each dollar he puts in for himself, he has achieved nothing in terms of his own personal financial statement. He will merely have paid one dollar to employees that otherwise would have been paid to the government. While he may prefer that, it usually does not provide sufficient incentive to establish a plan and endure the administrative burdens which follow. However, if he can put $9,000 into his own account and $1,000 in other employee's accounts, he can take the position that the $1,000 paid for regular employees was simply a "cost of doing business" to obtain $9,000 worth of tax advantages for himself. In fact, this is the most common result of the planning process.

This book will show you how you can help your client minimize that "cost of doing business." Most of your clients will tolerate or even appreciate a modicum of benefit/contribution for regular employees who have been with the firm for a certain period of time. Your job, as a pension planner, is to aggressively use the opportunities available to help your client fulfill that goal.

¶105   **HOW SUCCESSFUL PENSION DESIGN FOR THE SMALL TO MEDIUM-SIZED BUSINESS CAN HELP**

The purpose of this book is to provide you with enough knowledge to be an effective advocate for your client. That means you must be able to discuss, analyze, and improve on plan design, as well as effectively monitor administrative performance. While constant interfacing with clients and the IRS can ultimately provide a real "education," this book will help strip away some of the shrouds which have prevented many clients from availing themselves of the incredible tax advantages offered by qualified retirement programs. You should be conscious of three factors that will affect your performance as a pension practitioner. These factors can be expressed as questions and form the basis for what follows.

¶105.1   What Are The Concepts That Make Pensions Work And How Do They Affect Your Client?

To protect yourself from the "jargon" associated with the pension industry, you need to understand it and use it for the advantage of your clients. Furthermore, you must understand and use the various assumptions and factors which affect your choice of a pension design. For instance, you must understand why an older key employee would probably prefer a defined-benefit plan over a profit-sharing plan. This book will discuss, in great detail, how various factors such as age, service, interest rates, and actuarial assumptions can greatly affect and predetermine what type of plan will serve your client's needs.

¶105.2   How You Can Use Creative Design To Multiply Plan Effectiveness

Since the most common and significant objection raised by clients is the cost of covering non-key employees, it stands to reason that a thorough knowledge and understanding of alternate pension forms, designs, and assumptions will help you minimize those costs. The job of the pension designer is to:

- *Identify* the client's philosopical and budgetary objectives;
- *Review* census information to minimize coverage of employees who might be excludable for one reason or another;
- *Test* various alternative plans to find the one that conforms most closely to the objectives identified; and
- *Explain* how that design will affect your client, both personally and within his business.

This book provides a significant number of detailed comparative analyses of alternative plan formats and requirements that should put you in a position to carry out the planner's job.

¶105.3   How To Control Office Procedures To Simplify Qualification And Administrative Burdens

If you are going to design qualified plans, you need to be able to implement and administer them. In the absence of well conceived procedural routines, all of your "profit" from designing a clever plan will be absorbed by overhead. This book includes, wherever possible, checklists and actual examples of time and money-saving procedures that will allow you to effectively monitor the ongoing administrative process without an undue commitment of your time and energy. However, as noted earlier, success of a pension operation is primarily dependent on a personal commitment to be involved in a large number of plans. Since qualification and administrative services are largely repetitive in nature, no matter how efficient and clever your office procedures may be in theory, they will not work in practice unless there is a constant flow of new and old plans through the cycle.

¶106 SUMMARIZING YOUR OPPORTUNITIES

Qualified retirement programs present one of the most creative and most demanding opportunities available for your clients. They combine uniquely attractive income tax advantages with potentially burdensome reporting and disclosure costs. They offer income tax-free appreciation of assets as long as very complicated and ever changing rules are followed. They offer exceptional estate planning opportunities at the same time they may require expensive coverage of certain non-key employees. All of which leads to the conclusion that pension plans are great if you can survive the regulatory and semantic maze that has developed over the last 20 years, particularly since the 1974 enactment of ERISA.

More and more practitioners are dropping out of the pension field. That creates an exceptional opportunity for the individual willing to make the personal commitment necessary to fill the vacuum created. Those who do fill that vacuum will have an opportunity to provide one of the most attractive and socially worthwhile vehicles available to a client who, as a result, can only be deeply appreciative.

2

Key Ingredients
For Effectively Structured
Pension Plans For Your
Small Business Clients

The alternative plans we'll discuss in Chapters 4 through 12 present a broad and dramatic range of planning opportunities. However, all of these plans can be affected by variables inherent in the census information of the client for whom you are providing counsel. Furthermore, costs and/or benefits for virtually all types of plan can be significantly affected by the implicit and explicit actuarial assumptions applied in various projections.

The purpose of this chapter is to show you how these internal plan variables can affect your design process. You must be aware of the planning potential inherent in these variables so that you can use them to the advantage of your client.

¶200   GOAL-ORIENTED DESIGNS START WITH YOUR
CLIENT'S CENSUS INFORMATION

Most closely-held corporations have relatively few "key" individuals. Generally, the group is conspicuous for some attribute relative to other employees. For instance, the "key" group may be younger, older, have more past service, or have consistently higher income than average. These are some of the factors which affect pension design.

The single most important function and your first step in pension design is meticulous review of your client's census data to determine what attributes separate the "key" individuals from the rest of the employees. Once you identify these factors or variables, you can select from several pension plan formulas which inherently work in favor of employees sharing that particular quality. The process of census analysis significantly narrows the search for an appropriate plan and comprises the bulk of the pension planner's design work.

Some of the most significant variables are age, past service, and actuarial assumptions. It is important that you understand how those individual parameters may affect the ultimate design of a qualified plan in terms of relative contributions—our objective in pension design. Once you understand the operation of these variables, you can predict their effect and use them for your client's gain.

The following discussion isolates each particular variable to show its individual effect upon plan funding. Throughout this chapter you will find staggering opportunities for your client inherent in your choice of plan parameters and assumptions.

¶201   HOW TO LIMIT PLAN PARTICIPATION THROUGH AGE, SERVICE AND OTHER ELIGIBILITY REQUIREMENTS

ERISA recognizes the cost to employers of including "high turnover" employees in a pension plan and allows that a plan will qualify if employees are in the plan within six months after:

- the attainment of age 25; or
- the completion of a year of service.

Thus, many employees can be excluded from your calculations.

Planning Tip: You should eliminate all ineligible employees. This is the first step in the process of census review. Otherwise, you may design a plan for the wrong group.

Example: Let's say Turnover Company has 10 employees. It operates on a calendar year. The objective you have been given is to maximize the older employees' share of a $25,000 contribution. Without proper exclusions, you would design the wrong plan.

Situation 1— Forgot to Exclude	Employee	Age	Date of Employment	Situation 2— After Exclusions
Eligible	A	55	01/01/50	Eligible
Eligible	B	55	03/01/79	Ineligible—Service
Eligible	C	50	01/01/70	Eligible
Eligible	D	60	06/01/79	Ineligible—Service
Eligible	E	24	01/01/75	Ineligible—Age
Eligible	F	19	01/01/78	Ineligible—Age
Eligible	G	35	01/01/77	Eligible
Eligible	H	40	04/01/79	Ineligible—Service
Eligible	I	30	02/01/79	Ineligible—Service
Eligible	J	45	01/01/70	Eligible
41 years	Average Age			46 years
6 years	Average Service			10 years

The significance of a five year age differential or a four years of service differential, plus the fact that under "Situation 2" the $25,000 contribution will be shared by only four as opposed to 10 employees, cannot be overlooked.

¶201.1   How Employees Are Further Excluded

You should use age and service requirements concurrently with a requirement that eligible employees be employed on the last day of the plan year to actually accrue a benefit or share in the contributions. This will further reduce the "pool" of covered employees and help you:

1. maximize benefits for nonexcluded groups; and
2. minimize reporting and disclosure obligations for the high turnover group

Caution: A defined-benefit plan cannot use this technique. (See Chapters 7-10.)

¶201.2   Combining Age And Service Requirements For Effective
Plan Language

The following language may provide one of the simplest methods for using age and service requirements to your advantage:

Employees will become participants in the plan on the 1st day of the plan year nearest, forward or backward, to the later of the following events:
(a)   completion of a year of service; or
(b)   attainment of age 25.

The allocation or benefit accrual section of the plan may require that a participant be employed on the last day of the plan year to be an "active" participant. Only "active" participants need to accrue benefits for a particular plan year.

Example #1: Adams is employed on April 1st, 1978, by a calendar year company which allocates profit-sharing contributions on December 31st. He completes his year of service March 31st, 1979. The 1st day of the plan year (January 1st) nearest, forward or backward, to March 31st is January 1st, 1979. Therefore, Adams is a participant in the plan January 1st, 1979.

Example #2: Use the same facts as Example #1 except Benson is employed August 1st, 1978. He completes his year of service July 31st, 1979. The January 1st nearest that date is January 1st, 1980. Benson becomes a participant January 1st, 1980.

Example #3: Use the same facts as Example #2, but Benson quits on December 28th, 1980. Although he became a participant on January 1st, he will not receive an allocation of the 1980 profit-sharing allocation, since he failed to become an active participant.

The eligibility provisions discussed above substantially eliminate short-service employees and allow your client to spend his limited budget most efficiently. Be certain you take full advantage of the opportunity.

¶201.3   Alternative Approach Using Eligibility For Special
Circumstances

There is an alternative to bringing employees into the plan after a year of service. Your client can require three years of service prior to participation if he's willing to have 100% vesting on all contributions. That may seem attractive, but watch out because:

1. in small corporations, it may result in operational discrimination in favor of the "prohibited group" of highly paid employees; or

2. if the shorter eligibility requirements are used, vesting can be deferred for at least four years under the IRS's most restrictive (4-40) vesting schedule. Other vesting schedules (allowed by statute subject to IRS tests for discrimination) can defer participant "ownership" of accrued benefits much longer. Usually, it's better to control the plan funds through vesting, after all, if participants don't "own" employer contributions, what has the employer lost?

¶202   HOW THE 70%–80% TEST CAN BENEFIT YOUR CLIENTS

After you finish eliminating potential participants on the basis of age and service requirements (or union employees where good faith bargaining for fringe benefits can be evidenced), you can eliminate specific "classes" of employees. The plan will still qualify if, after the employees in the excluded class are subtracted, 70% of all employees are still eligible and, of those, 80% are participating. That means your client could conceivably set up a plan in which only a fraction of his employees participate.

Example: XYZ, Incorporated has 35 employees. Five are under age 25 and five have less than a year of service. Thus XYZ, Incorporated has 25 nonexcluded employees. Mr. XYZ, president of the company, is not concerned about public relations and includes a provision in his pension plan eliminating, as a class, all employees with green eyes. Seven employees fall into that class. For the remaining 18 eligible employees, Mr. XYZ requires, as a condition of participation, a mandatory employee contribution equal to six percent of salary. Three employees say no and waive participation, leaving 15 covered participants. The plan qualifies because:

—of the total employee pool 35

—some are excludable by statute (age & service) .... (10)

—leaving a reduced nonexcluded group of 25

—Of these, some fall into an excluded class 7

—leaving an even smaller eligible pool....................... 18

—Some of these eligibles refuse to participate 3

—leaving covered employees 15

—Of the 25 nonexcluded employees, 18 are eligible 72%

—of the 18, 15 participate 83%

Thus, with careful planning, a potential pool of 35 employees has been reduced, by statutory exemptions, eligiblity standards and participation requirements, to 15 participants. Only 43% of the employees participate. Whatever your client's budget, it will go a lot further if it's divided 15, rather than 35, ways.

Caution: The 70%–80% test is "continuously applied." If, the excluded classes fluctuate in size relative to the total employee group, your client will have to monitor his plan closely to avoid the potential of disqualification for discrimination.

¶202.1   How Maximum Age Requirements Can Be Effective

Your client can eliminate employees hired within five years of the normal retirement date. Therefore, defined-benefit and target-benefit plans can impose "maximum age requirements" for participation. Congress recognized that the expense of forcing employers to fully fund retirement benefits for older employees would discourage their being hired. Alternatively, these plans may define retirement date as the later of normal retirement age (usually 65) or a 10 year plan participation. Often the choice is difficult.

Example: XYZ Company has hired 10 employees between ages 55 and 65. It's retirement plan specifies 65 as the normal retirement date. All participants receive a $5,000 per year retirement benefit.

Your job is to determine which of the following would be more expensive:

1. giving full benefits at age 65 but excluding employees hired within 5 years of age 65; or

2. giving full benefits to all participants at the later of age 65 or 10 years' of plan participation.

I. NRD* @ 65, EXCLUDE WITHIN 5 YRS				II. NRD @ LATER OF 65 OR 10 YRS	
Retire. Age	Annual Contribution	Employee/Hire. Age		Retire. Age	Annual Contribution
65	3,728	A	55	65	3,728
65	4,276	B	56	66	3,682
65	4,964	C	57	67	3,637
65	5,854	D	58	68	3,520
65	7,044	E	59	69	3,520
Excluded	N/A	F	60	70	3,509
Excluded	N/A	G	61	71	3,468
Excluded	N/A	H	62	72	3,428
Excluded	N/A	I	63	73	3,389
Excluded	N/A	J	64	74	3,351
N/A	25,866	TOTAL	N/A	N/A	35,305

*Normal Retirement Date

At first blush, the exclusion for employees hired within five years of retirement date appears preferable. But it wouldn't take too much of a shift in the above illustration to change your decision. *Always* test the two alternatives.

Warning: Employees excluded because they were hired within fives years of normal retirement date are not part of the "age or length of service" group eliminated prior to application of the 70%–80% test. Therefore, if you apply the rule without being careful, you may inadvertently fail to meet ERISA's participation standards.

Example: Careless Corporation excludes from coverage employees within five years of retirement date(s). On its IRS audit, the plan is disqualified because:

of the nonexcluded employee group 10

some were excluded—hired at age 61 .... <u>4</u>

The remaining eligible employees............................. 6

Fail to meet the Requirement for 70% Eligibility 60%

¶203   HOW YOUR PLAN'S VESTING SCHEDULE CAN PERFORM FURTHER HOUSECLEANING

Even after your employee becomes a participant by escaping the swath of eligibility or class exclusions, he still is not entitled to receive benefits. For that, he must become "vested." Vesting means the degree to which an employee-participant owns the benefits which have been accrued on his behalf. ERISA specifically discusses several acceptable vesting schedules among which are:

1. "cliff" vesting under which a participant's accrued benefits must be 100% vested only upon completion of 10 years of service;

2. the five to 15 rule under which a participant becomes partially vested "25%" at the end of five years and becomes fully vested over the next 10 years (five percent each four years 6 through 10 and 10% per year thereafter); and

3. the rule of fund 45, under which a participant becomes partially vested at the earlier of:

   a) the time when the sum of his age and years of service equals 45 (or, if later, after five years of service); or

   b) completion of 10 years of service.

Any employee who terminates prior to the time vesting begins forfeits all accrued benefits. A participant who terminates when partially vested takes part of his benefits with him and forfeits the balance. Note that all the vesting schedules listed above allow your client at least an additional four years to "weed out" employees who for one reason or another won't become long standing participants.

The recovery of these forfeited funds will be used in one of two ways, depending on the type of plan adopted. The forfeitures will be used either:

- to reduce future employer contributions; or
- provide an extra allocation for those employees who remain behind (typically limited to profit-sharing plans).

Thus, to the extent your client has a continual turnover of employees with one to five years of service, he will recover a portion of his contributions and be in a position to apply those to the benefit of long standing employees. Although the three vesting schedules above are recognized by ERISA, Congress also has delegated authority to the IRS to apply more stringent vesting rules in cases where discrimination is thought to exist. The IRS has frequently made use of this authority by requesting more rapid vesting. That is true particularly with small employers. In these cases, the IRS will often request the so-called "4-40" or "Oregon-type" vesting schedules as follows:

Years of Service	Vested Percent
0-4	0%
4 but less than 5	40%
5 but less than 6	45%
6 but less than 7	50%
7 but less than 8	60%
8 but less than 9	70%
9 but less than 10	80%
10 but less than 11	90%
11 or more	100%

¶204   HOW TO USE EMPLOYEE AND PLAN VARIABLES TO YOUR ADVANTAGE

After excluding as many employees as possible from your client's census information, it's important to scan the remaining participating employees to find some attribute of the key man toward which you can orient the plan. Such factors as average age, length of service, and interest or actuarial assumptions significantly affect your choices. To make intelligent choices, you need to know what effect the various parameters will have.

¶204.1   How The Age Of Participants Determines Your Choice
Of Plans

Some pension formulas inherently favor older employees in terms of relative contributions. Some favor younger participants. That's because certain plans (defined benefit and target benefit) guarantee specific benefits at a specific age for all participants. For instance, a plan might promise each participant income of $5,000 per year at age 65. Depending on how old a particular participant is at entry, his funding costs can differ dramatically, since the number of years to retirement obviously affects employer deposits.

Participation Age	Lump-Sum at 65 To Pay $5,000/Yr. Retirement Income	Annual Deposit Required Assuming 6% Interest
25	$52,083	$ 317
35	52,083	622
45	52,083	1336
55	52,083	3728

In these plans, the funding "goal" ($52,803) never changes—time to accumulate the goal is the only variable. Depending on the amount of time, compound interest may do more or less of the work.

Other plans guarantee only that specific contributions will be made. These plans tend to favor younger participants, since deposits generally relate primarily to salary. Age is irrelevant. Benefits are simply the sum of employer contributions and fund earnings (or losses). Using the average deposit determined under the illustration above, look what happens to participant lump sums at age 65:

Participation Age	Lump-Sum at 65 If Deposit Is Invested at 6%	Annual Deposit
25	$246,195	$1500
35	125,765	1500
45	58,518	1500
55	20,957	1500

In these defined-contribution plans, benefits are the variable—deposits the constant. It's clear that employers with limited budgets should be cognizant of the results generated by the alternate philosophical approaches represented by benefit or contribution oriented plans.

> *Example:* Real-life situations provide even more graphic illustrations of the effect of your choice. The following example demonstrates the application of two different plan formulas, one of which relates primarily to relative **salary**, the second to relative **age**.

				PLAN I— Salary Approach		PLAN II— Age Approach	
Employee	Age	Average Compensation	% of Total	Annual Deposit	% of Total	Annual Deposit	% of Total
A	50	75,000	41	10,331	41	19,197	77
B	30	75,000	41	10,331	41	3,025	12
C	40	12,000	7	1,653	7	1,278	5
D	40	12,000	7	1,653	7	1,278	5
E	25	7,500	4	1,033	4	225	1
TOTAL		$181,500	100	$25,000	100	$25,000	100

Plan I results in a deposit allocation exactly proportioned to salaries, notwithstanding significant age differentials. A simple change to Plan II dramatically orients the same deposit toward older employees. This example offers dramatic proof of the necessity for your clients with limited budgets to carefully define their objectives. Then you can select the plan which most closely fulfills those objectives.

In many closely-held corporations, key individuals are older than the average age of employees in general. Assuming your client's corporate objective is to reward those key employees, then you should design a formula yielding deposits similar to those in Plan II.

¶204.2   Identifying Opportunities To Use Past Service

In addition to age, key employees in closely-held corporations will tend to have more past service with the employer than most employees. For instance, many such businesses have an owner who has worked in the business for 30 or 40 years but whose employees, because of turnover and lack of opportunity for advancement, have relatively little past service.

Example: The following schedule of deposits illustrates two divergent plan formulas. Plan I, as in our previous example, emphasizes relative salary as the key element in determining contributions. Plan II, on the other hand, is heavily weighted toward years of service with the employer.

Employee	Age	Years Past Service	Average Compensation	% of Total	PLAN I—Salary Deposit	% of Total	PLAN II—Past Service Deposit	% of Total
A	50	10	75,000	41	10,331	41	15,439	62
B	30	10	75,000	41	10,331	41	5,804	23
C	40	1	12,000	7	1,653	7	1,219	5
D	40	20	12,000	7	1,653	7	2,112	8
E	25	1	7,500	4	1,033	4	426	2
		TOTAL	$181,500	100	$25,000	100	$25,000	100

Notice that employee D, who in all previous illustrations had contributions identical to those of his equal pay, equal age counterpart, employee C, receives almost twice the deposit under this "past service" plan. Many plans emphasize service in their benefit formulas. Sometimes your client's key men will not have unusually large salaries. Alternatively, your client may feel that his budget should be oriented toward employees who have shown long-standing loyalty to the company. In either case, he would clearly prefer the past service formula utilized in Plan II. This illustration, too, underscores the opportunities which are available for the minimal effort involved in thorough census review.

¶204.3   Short-Term Planning With Interest Rates

In certain types of pension plans, your client or his actuary must specify an assumed rate of interest for the accumulation of plan assets. In effect, an actuary's job is to build a hypothetical model of plan performance and then monitor actual experience. To the extent actual investment experience fulfills the actuary's expectations, the choice of high versus low interest rates can lead to dramatic variations in the Plan's funding costs.

¶204.4   How To Use Interest Rate Assumptions To Benefit Your Client

In general, an employer whose key employees are older than the group average will derive the greatest benefit from higher interest rate assumptions. Younger employees have substantially more time than their older peers to accumulate a fund sufficient to pay their retirement benefits. The longer the funding period, the greater the effect of compound interest. As an illustration, consider the following example:

Employee	Age	Average Compensation	% of Total	PLAN I—5% Interest Deposit	PLAN I—5% Interest % of Total	PLAN II—8% Interest Deposit	PLAN II—8% Interest % of Total
A	50	$75,000	41%	$17,593	70%	$19,194	77%
B	30	75,000	41	4,203	17	3,024	12
C	40	12,000	7	1,426	6	1,278	5
D	40	12,000	7	1,426	6	1,278	5
E	25	7,500	4	352	1	226	1
TOTAL		$181,500	100%	$25,000	100%	$25,000	100%

Although the above alternatives must eventually provide identical retirement benefits, the deposits for the older key man is increased 10% by a simple change in interest assumptions. However, since pension plans generally require the employer to use overfunding occasioned by excess interest to reduce future deposits, this relative increase could be short-lived if too unreasonable an interest rate is used.

This can create a "Catch-22" in which your client may have to trade off relative contributions against tax deductions. However, by selecting moderately agressive or conservative investments, your client may control to a considerable extent the degree to which his assumed rate of interest parallels actual investment experience. Further, certain pension plans simply use the assumed rate of interest as a "target" with actual investment experience reflected in individual participant accounts.

¶204.5   Creative Planning Using Actuarial Methods And
                              Assumptions

Many qualified plans require the selection of an *actuarial method* for calculating plan deposits. An "actuarial method" simply provides the structured environment to measure the relationship between plan assumptions and actual experience. Depending upon the actuarial method used, you can also generate significant divergence in funding patterns. It's important to consider all the options.

¶204.6   How "Salary Scales" Can Shift Your Client's Deposit

Because of the rapid inflation which has dramatically affected payroll costs over the last few years, many plans assume a degree of "wage inflation" in their funding. In other words, your client may decide to "prefund" part of his anticipated future costs. Obviously, to the extent he prefunds future benefits instead of spending for currently earned benefits, more of his budget will be used for these anticipated costs. In many small plans, your client will be able to choose between using or not using salary scales. The difference can be significant.

Example: XYZ, Incorporated can't decide whether or not to use a 4% salary increase assumption and asks you to calculate the financial effect of his options.

			OPTION I: 4% SALARY INCREASE		OPTION II: NO SALARY INCREASE	
Employee	Age	Pay	Estimated Benefits @ 65	Annual Deposit	Estimated Benefits @ 65	Annual Deposit
A	50	75,000	$50,088/Yr.	$16,337/Yr.	$43,908/Yr.	$18,262/Yr.
B	30	75,000	98,100/Yr.	4,822/Yr.	43,908/Yr.	3,560/Yr.
C	40	12,000	11,856/Yr.	1,656/Yr.	7,020/Yr.	1,439/Yr.
D	40	12,000	11,856/Yr.	1,656/Yr.	7,020/Yr.	1,439/Yr.
E	25	7,500	13,356/Yr.	529/Yr.	4,392/Yr.	300/Yr.
TOTAL		$181,500	N/A	$25,000	N/A	$25,000

The difference is quite remarkable for such a small change in assumptions.

Caveat: Don't forget that in the long run your actuarial model will be replaced by actual experience. Therefore, if your actuarial model isn't reasonable, then, in the long run, you will pay the price.

¶204.7   How Much Will Retirement Benefits Cost?

Central to employer costs is the funding target. For example, how much does your client need to have at age 65 to provide a $5,000 per year retirement benefit for a plan participant? That depends on a couple of assumptions.

1. The "form" in which the benefit will be paid, such as a "life only" or "joint and 100% survivor" annuity; and
2. The assumed "cost" of whatever benefit form is chosen, such as 1971 Group Annuity Table or conservative life insurance settlement option tables.

Example: XYZ, Incorporated wants to know the funding costs associated with providing a $5,000 per year retirement income to plan participants under some different assumptions. They're quite surprised by the differences.

Retirement Income	Assumed Form of Benefit	Settlement Option	Lump Sum Required @ 65	Annual Deposit For 45-Year Old
$5,000/yr	Joint & 100% Survivor	Ins. Co. Rate	$75,758	$1,943/yr
5,000/yr	Life only	Ins. Co. Rate	60,582	1,554/yr
5,000/yr	Life only	'71 GAM Table	52,083	1,336/yr

That's a 40% difference in funding costs without any change in benefits.

Planning Tip: If your client has older key men and a limited budget, he may prefer using conservative (expensive) benefit cost assumptions. That way the limited budget will be necessarily skewed toward the key men.

Example: Games Company's president and key man, Mr. Parker want to know the effect, in terms of initial contributions of utilizing an aggressive versus a conservative benefit cost assumption. The results are worth thinking about.

Employee	Age	Pay	Option A: Conservative Costs*		Option A: Aggressive Costs**	
			Annual Ret. Benefit	Annual Deposit	Annual Ret. Benefit	Annual Deposit
Mr. Parker	50	50,000	$18,290	$ 9,561	$18,290	$ 7,217
B	40	35,000	12,803	2,749	12,803	2,075
C	40	20,000	7,316	1,571	7,316	1,186
D	30	20,000	7,316	746	7,316	563
E	30	10,000	3,658	373	3,658	282
		135,000	n/a	15,000	n/a	11,323

*Male age 65 receives $6.19 per $1,000 principal
**Male age 65 receives $8.20 per $1,000 principal

Note that making the simple change from a conservative estimate of the cost of providing future benefits to one more in keeping with current costs reduces Games Company's funding cost for identical benefits by almost 25%. Alternatively, 30% more benefits could theoretically have been provided if the contribution ($15,000), rather than the benefits, were held constant. Integrated defined-benefit plans with limited budgets can exaggerate planning opportunities even further (see Chapter 7).

¶204.8   How Actuarial Methods Can Affect Employer Flexibility

Apart from assumptions and parameters affecting cost, the actuarial methods themselves hold substantial opportunity for creative planners. For the time being, let's consider two significantly different actuarial methods that might be used in small plans, the Individual Level Premium Method and the Entry Age Normal with Frozen Initial Past Service Liability Method.*

The Individual Level Premium Method—Inflexible But Accurate

Under this actuarial method, the actuary determines a level funding cost for each participant from date of participation to date of retirement. Once the level premium is established for a particular "block" of compensation, it

*See Appendix for a case history showing the actuarial methods commonly used in small plans of a major pension software firm.

never changes. As salary changes generate benefit increases or decreases, the incremental level premium for those benefits is added to the prior level cost. In effect, your client uses a "building block" approach to funding retirement benefits. However, because of the level premium nature of the system, your client may be apprehensive—after all, he's seen a lot of ups and downs in his business. Sometimes a small business can't budget effectively for substantial, inflexible payments.

Entry Age Normal With FIPSL Can Provide A "Safety Valve" For Your Client

In this method, the actuary pretends that a business has always had a pension plan and asks the question, "If we had had this plan from the beginning, how much money would we have accumulated at this point?" Entry age normal plans effectively divide a participant's service into two components—one for past and one for future employment. Future costs are funded basically on a level premium approach. But the planning opportunity derives from the past service element. Participants have a "past service liability" (the amount determined by the actuary's question). This past service liability can be amortized by your client over anywhere from 10 to 30 years. For clients whose employee census reveals a lot of past service, the amortization provides very substantial flexibility.

> *Example:* Simplicity Corporation learns from its actuary that its future cost level funding will be $10,000 per year, and that its past service liability is $100,000. Further analysis shows the following flexibility:

(1) Future Cost Funding		(2) 30 Year Past Service Amortization		(3) 10 Year Past Service Amortization		(4) Minimum Deposit (1 + 2)		(5) Maximum Deposit (1 + 3)
	+		OR		=		OR	
$10,000/yr		$6,854/yr		$12,818/yr		$16,854/yr		$22,818/yr

> Since your client has complete discretion over his deposit (e.g., minimum, maximum, or in between) there's a lot of budgetary flexibility inherent in this example to accommodate periodic fluctuation in business conditions. You may ask why anyone would choose not to use it.

Watch Out: Entry age with FIPSL does not reduce funding, it only spreads it out. Sooner or later, all costs have to be paid. If your client has some older participating employees, and consistently funds only the minimum required deposit, he may not have enough money on hand to pay off these older participating employees.

Possible Solution: Don't give retiring employees in small plans the option to take lump-sum distributions if you're using entry age normal with FIPSL. That will preclude the major problems that might otherwise occur.

¶204.9   Comparing The Cost Of Both Actuarial Methods

XYZ, Incorporated asks you the funding requirements associated with the two actuarial methods we've discussed. He wants to spend between $20,000 and $30,000. Here's your answer:

				Level Premium	Entry Age Normal With FIPSL	
Employee	Age	Years Past Service	Pay	Annual Deposit	Minimum Deposit	Maximum Deposit
A	50	10	$ 75,000	$17,773	$14,861	$21,029
B	30	10	75,000	3,703	3,553	5,028
C	40	1	12,000	1,547	1,398	1,480
D	40	20	12,000	1,547	1,335	2,150
E	25	1	17,500	430	296	313
TOTAL			$181,500	$25,000	$21,243	$30,000

¶205   **COMBINING FACTORS TO YIELD SPECTACULAR RESULTS**

Clearly the various design parameters discussed in this chapter provide a tremendous opportunity for pension practitioners by themselves; when applied in combination, the results are even more spectacular.

Older employees tend to be favored by formulas "making up for lost time." These involve high interest rates, emphasis on past service, and actuarial methods based on current rather than prospective income. Consider the following example which compares two alternative plan formulas over our standard group. The goal is to benefit employee A who is relatively old and has a medium amount of past service. Plan I uses a simple non-specific formula. Plan II, on the other hand, orients all parameters to emphasize the unique attributes of employee A.

Employee	Age	Years Past Service	Avg. Comp.	% of Total	Plan I—Non Specific		Plan II—Orient to "A"	
					Deposit	% of Total	Deposit	% of Total
A	50	10	75,000	41	10,331	41	19,194	77
B	30	10	75,000	41	10,331	41	3,025	12
C	40	1	12,000	7	1,653	7	1,278	5
C	40	20	12,000	7	1,653	7	1,278	5
E	25	1	7,500	4	1,033	4	225	1
TOTAL			181,500	100	$25,000	100	$25,000	100

These relatively simple concepts, when applied in conjunction with the concepts of integration discussed in the following chapters are the pension practitioner's tool. The process must begin with a thorough analytical review of your client's census data to discover some unique characteristics of the key employee group. That done, you can compare the unique parameters discovered for selection of an appropriate benefit formula.

The purpose of this discussion of parameters affecting pension design has not been to learn the formulas underlying different plans. Rather, the intention was to generate awareness of significant design opportunities available even at the most simple level. Any of the factors considered above could be used in conjunction with actual plan formulas to tip the balance of contributions toward our key employee group. Though it's important to remember that "figures lie and liars figure," there are certain ranges of acceptable plan variables. Over a period of time and with employee turnover, these variables may in the long run significantly affect pension design for the closely-held corporation. The bottom line is an opportunity to save you time and provide the most efficient plan design opportunities for your clients.

3

Effective Use
Of Integration:
The Key To
Pension Design

Integration of qualified pension plans is of paramount importance. It is a tool that your client can use to give highly paid employees a larger percentage of plan benefits or contributions without fear of discrimination. Integration has historically been considered a "monster" difficult to tame. However, conceptually it is nothing more than a pension plan's recognition of employee retirement income provided by the social security system. Proper integration merely allows your client to "offset" his own plan's benefits with those provided under the social security system.

In this chapter, we will explore integration conceptually and show how these concepts can be of benefit to your client. Later chapters will show you how to apply integration rules to specific alternative plan formulas. You will learn how integration can boost any type of pension plan's efficiency for key men and, as a corollary, learn to control pension plan costs for lower-paid employees—costs that most discourage clients from adopting qualified plans.

¶300   HOW SOCIAL SECURITY FAVORS LOWER-PAID EMPLOYEES

Every employer has a pension plan whether he likes it or not—Social Security. For the calendar year 1980, for instance, employer contributions to Social Security are 6.13% of the first $25,900 of an employee's compensation. This is the taxable wage base. This contribution funds various death, disability and retirement benefits at a level determined roughly by the average of all taxable wage bases during an employee's working life.

¶301   HOW INTEGRATION SOLVES THE PROBLEM OF DISCRIMINATION IN CONTRIBUTIONS AGAINST KEY EMPLOYEES

Social Security contributions primarily benefit lower-paid employees since there are no contributions payable on account of employee compensation above $25,900. For example, if your client adopted a simple pension plan and contributed 13.774% of all participant's income, he would substantially skew plan deposits toward lower-paid employees.

Example: Consider the effects of such a plan on a typical employee group:

Employee	Age	Pay	% of Total	6.13% Social Security Deposit	+	13.774% Plan Deposit	=	Total Deposit	% of Pay
A	50	75,000	41	1,588		10,331		11,919	16%
B	30	75,000	41	1,588		10,331		11,919	16
C	40	12,000	7	736		1,653		2,389	20
D	40	12,000	7	736		1,653		2,389	20
E	25	7,500	4	460		1,033		1,493	20
TOTAL		$181,500	100%	$5,108		$25,000		$30,109	100

Employees C and D, between Social Security and the employer's private pension plan, receive a total allocation equal to 20% of their pay, while the two high paid employees receive contributions totaling just 16% of their salaries. The rationale for integration is that employers should be able to provide uniform retirement benefits or contributions over all compensation. Since Social Security is designed primarily to provide a "floor," employers can build their retirement plans with that "floor" in mind.

¶301.1   How Social Security Affects Contribution-Oriented
                                Retirement Plans

There are two ways of looking at the Social Security System:

1. in terms of the current *contributions* it mandates; and
2. in terms of the *retirement benefits* it ultimately provides.

The following graph depicts the 1980 relationship between employer deposits and income level.

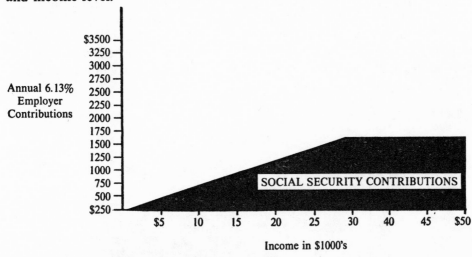

The relationship between employer contributions and income is linear up to $25,900, at which level an employee has reached the maximum. Employees earning more than $25,900 (the taxable wage base) receive no contribution for their excess pay.

¶301.2   How Integration Provides Non-Shareholder Employees
                        Maximum Benefits At Least Cost To The Company

Integration merely allows your client to extend his contributions to compensation above the "taxable wage base," in order to provide uniform deposits for all employees regardless of pay level. The following graph illustrates.

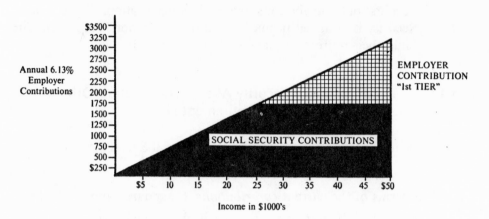

As long as this continuum between Social Security and employer-paid contributions remains linear, a pension plan is properly integrated.

To extend the concept further, an employer may provide a "two-tiered" pension plan. The first tier "makes up" for compensation not covered by Social Security. The second tier provides uniform contributions above and beyond the first tier. The combination generates a properly integrated plan.

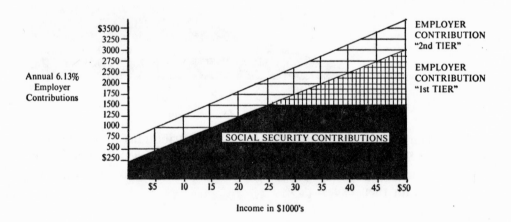

Example: Continuity Corporation sets up a defined-contribution plan, to which it contributes 9.987% of a participant's compensation *plus* seven percent of compensation in excess of $25,900. (Seven percent is the maximum "catch-up" contribution rate, deemed to create uniformity between government and employer-sponsored plan deposits.) Compare the results to those illustrated at ¶301.

Continuity Corporation
Comparing Integrated and Nonintegrated Alternatives

		"Integrated" Plan Contributions				
Employee	Pay	Social Security +	9.987% Basic Deposit +	7% Excess Deposit =	Total Allocation	% of Pay
A	$ 75,000	$1,588	$ 7,490	$3,437	$12,515	17%
B	75,000	1,588	7,490	3,437	12,515	17.0%
C	12,000	736	1,198	0	1,934	16%
D	12,000	736	1,198	0	1,934	16%
E	7,500	461	749	0	1,210	16%
TOTAL	$181,500	$5,109	$18,125	$6,874	$13,800	N/A

		Nonintegrated Alternative	
Employee	Pay	Total Deposit	% of Pay
A	$ 75,000	$11,918	16%
B	75,000	11,918	16
C	12,000	2,389	20
D	12,000	2,389	20
E	7,500	1,493	20
TOTAL	$181,500	$30,107	N/A

If your client has a limited budget, make certain he is aware of the possibilities offered by integration.

¶302   HOW INTEGRATION SOLVES THE PROBLEM OF DISCRIMINATION IN RETIREMENT BENEFITS AGAINST KEY EMPLOYEES

Similarly, discrimination in retirement benefits would occur if your client overlapped his own nonintegrated qualified plan with Social Security. This is because Social Security benefits are based only on compensation which has been subject to Social Security tax during an employee's working life. For instance, if an employer adopts a defined-benefit pension plan which promises participants retirement pay equal to 50% of their salaries, the higher paid employees receive proportionately reduced benefits, since Social Security benefits relate only to "covered compensation," a figure as low as $9,000.

Example: LMN Company establishes a 50% of pay defined-benefit plan with no "offset" for Social Security. Its key men later observe that their overall benefits provide relatively less retirement income than their lower-paid counterparts.

Employee	Age	Pay	% Of Total	Social Security Benefits @ 65	Plan Benefits @ 65	Total Benefit	% of Salary
A	50	75,000	41	$7,104/yr.	$37,500	$44,604	59%
B	30	75,000	41	8,700	37,500	46,200	62
C	40	12,000	7	7,200	6,000	13,200	110
D	40	12,000	7	7,200	6,000	13,200	110
E	25	7,500	4	5,500	3,750	9,250	123

The lower-paid employees under this approach receive substantially higher overall benefits. Assuming your client's goal is to maximize the allocation of his limited budget to those key employees, he will much prefer to utilize an integrated pension plan.

¶302.1   Understanding Integration Of Benefit-Oriented Pension Plans

The concept of integration is that your client should, if he voluntarily adopts his own qualified retirement plan, be able to recognize benefits provided by the mandatory Social Security program when computing benefits under his own plan. In other words, the government will allow your client to establish a plan which, when combined with Social Security, provides continuity of benefits to all participating employees at all income levels. In effect, your client "picks up where Social Security leaves off."

¶302.2   How To Integrate Benefit-Oriented Retirement Plans

An employee's Social Security retirement benefits are computed by a weighted formula which considers length of employment and level of compensation. The results of this computation are expressed as an Employee's "Covered Compensation." Integration under Benefit-Oriented Retirement Plans may be achieved by using "Covered Compensation."

Covered Compensation is, therefore, simply a level of pay up to which an individual participant's Social Security benefits are presumed to be provided. The government publishes Covered Compensation tables periodically in two forms:

- Table I, which provides Covered Compensation amounts for bracketed (average) ages; and
- Table II, which provides Covered Compensation amounts for individual ages.

Covered Compensation Tables I and II (published for 1978) are reproduced here:

Covered Compensation 1978
Table I

Calendar Year of 65th Birthday	Amount	Calendar Year of 65th Birthday	Amount
1978	$ 8,400	1997-1998	$13,800
1979-1980	9,000	1999	14,400
1981	9,600	2000-2001	15,500
1982-1983	10,200	2002-2003	15,600
1984-1986	10,800	2004-2005	16,200
1987-1988	11,400	2006-2007	16,800
1989-1992	12,000	2008-2012	17,400
1993-1994	12,600	2013 and later	17,700
1995-1996	13,200		

Covered Compensation 1978
Table II

Calendar Year of 65th Birthday	Amount	Calendar Year of 65th Birthday	Amount
1978	$ 8,256	1985	$10,800
1979	8,724	1986	11,052
1980	9,156	1987	11,292
1981	9,540	1988	11,508
1982	9,900	1989	11,712
1983	10,224	1990	11,904
1984	10,524	1991	12,084

Covered Compensation 1978
Table II (continued)

Calendar Year of 65th Birthday	Amount	Calendar Year of 65th Birthday	Amount
1992	12,252	2003	$15,780
1993	12,420	2004	16,068
1994	12,564	2005	16,344
1995	12,936	2006	16,632
1996	13,308	2007	16,920
1997	13,680	2008	17,160
1998	14,040	2009	17,364
1999	14,412	2010	17,484
2000	14,784	2011	17,592
2001	15,144	2012	17,664
2002	15,468	2013 and later	17,700

The following graph illustrates the relationship between Social Security Retirement Benefits and employee compensation.

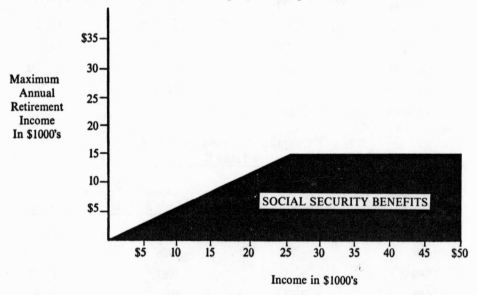

¶302.3   How To Develop A One-Tiered Plan For Further Exclusion

As with our consideration of contributions to Social Security, note that benefits, too, are provided only for limited levels of compensation. This is in keeping with the purpose of the system, namely to provide "basic" security. Integration, as it applies to pension plans which recognize Social Security benefits, simply provides employees with benefits for compensation not covered by the government system.

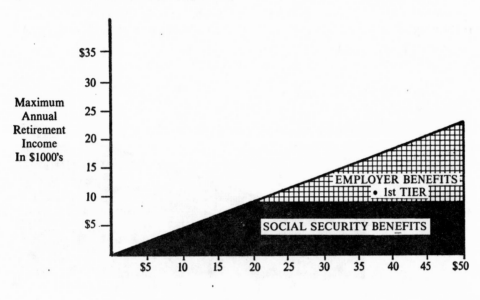

Income in $1000's

Example: There are several different integration methods for defined-benefit plans. One is called the "step rate" method. This allows your client to provide a benefit equal to 37½% of compensation in excess of the integration level. Assuming a $9,000 integration level, consider the benefits which can be provided at age 65 to employees of Simplicity Corporation:

Employee	Age	Pay	Excess Pay	37½ of Pay Excess Benefit
A	50	$ 75,000	$ 66,000	$24,750
B	30	75,000	66,000	24,750
C	40	12,000	3,000	1,125
D	40	12,000	3,000	1,125
E	25	7,500	0	0
TOTAL		$181,500	$138,000	N/A

As with defined-contribution plans, it is possible to exclude from coverage some lower-paid employees.

¶302.4   How to Develop Two-Tiered Plans Within A Budget

As with plans integrated by reference to Social Security contributions, the alternative benefit approach can generate "two-tiered" pension plans providing a "catch-up tier" of benefits for all participants. The following graph illustrates the concept of two-tiered benefit-oriented integrated plans.

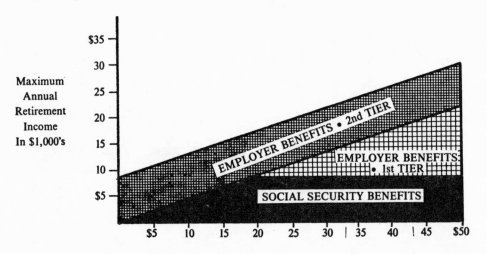

Example: John and Jim work for Level Ltd., earning $15,000 and $40,000, respectively. Each will be receiving approximately $8,000 per year from Social Security when they retire. Level Ltd. considers two alternative pension plans. The first promises retirement income equal to 50% of pay. The second, recognizing Social Security, is a two-tiered plan promising 71% of pay, reduced by 75% of the estimated Social Security payments.

PLAN I: 50% OF PAY

Employee	Pay	Level, Ltd. Plan Benefit: 50% of Pay	+	Social Security	=	Total Ret. Income	Replaced Ret. Income As % of Pay
John	$15,000	$ 7,500	+	8,000	=	$15,500	103
Jim	40,000	20,000	+	8,000	=	28,000	70
	55,000	N/A		N/A	=	N/A	

	Annual Employer Deposit	% of Total
	$ 4,837	27%
	12,900	73%
	17,737	100%

PLAN II: 71% OF PAY REDUCED BY 75% OF SOCIAL SECURITY

Employee	Pay	Level Ltd. Plan B 71% of Net Pay	– Less 75% of S.S.	= Net Plan Benefit	Social Security	Replaced Ret. Income	Replaced Ret. Income As % of Pay
John	15,000	10,650	– (6,000)	= 4,650	+ 8,000	= 12,650	84%
Jim	40,000	28,400	– (6,000)	= 22,400	+ 8,000	= 30,450	76%
TOTAL	55,000	N/A	N/A	N/A	N/A	N/A	N/A

Annual Deposit	% of Total
2,999	17%
7,998	73
10,997	100%

Observation: Proper integration is not discriminating. In fact, without integration your plan *will* discriminate against the key men. (Note under Plan I that the lower-paid employee receives substantially more retirement income as a percentage of his compensation.) If your client has a limited budget and wants it to reward key employees to the maximum, a two-tiered plan is a must.

¶303   CONTRIBUTION VERSUS BENEFIT APPROACH: PREVIEWING THE OPPORTUNITIES INHERENT IN INTEGRATION

Social Security integration is of paramount importance for designing pension plans geared toward higher-paid employees. Later chapters will show you how to apply specific integration rules to alternative plan formulas. Naturally, the combination of Social Security integration and the parameters discussed in chapter 2 can yield spectacular results. Consider the following two examples of integrated plans in which the employer's stated objective was to maximize the deposit for participants A and B. Plan I uses a "contribution" approach, Plan II, a "benefits" approach.

PLAN I: CONTRIBUTION APPROACH

Employee	Age	Years Past Service	Average Compensation	% of Total	Nonintegrated Plan Deposit	% of Total	Plan Integrated @ 12,000 Deposit	% of Total
A	50	10	75,000	41	10,331	41	11,096	44
B	30	10	75,000	41	10,331	41	11,096	45
C	40	1	12,000	7	1,653	7	1,070	4
D	40	20	12,000	7	1,653	7	1,070	4
E	25	1	7,500	4	1,032	4	668	3
		TOTAL	181,500	100	25,000	100	25,000	100

PLAN II: BENEFIT APPROACH

Employee	Age	Years Past Service	Average Compensation	% of Total	Nonintegrated Plan Deposit	% of Total	Plan Integrated @ 12,000 Deposit	% of Total
A	50	10	75,000	41	17,591	70	19,197	77
B	30	10	75,000	41	4,203	17	3,878	16
C	40	1	12,000	7	1,427	6	866	3
D	40	20	12,000	7	1,427	6	866	3
E	25	1	7,500	4	352	1	193	1
		TOTAL	181,500	100	25,000	100	25,000	100

Observation: Apart from the opportunities, in general, inherent in integration for high paid employees, Plans I and II predict further creative challenges. Consider Employees A and B. A and B differ only in terms of age (and therefore future service). Under Plan I, integrated by reference to contributions to Social Security, A and B receive *equal* shares, totalling almost 90% of the total company deposit. Under Plan II, integrated by reference to Social Security benefits, A and B still receive about 90% of the company deposit, but their relative shares are dramatically altered. The distinction between Plans I and II, therefore, is more than an exercise in Social Security integration. It foreshadows two totally different approaches to pension design.

Social Security integration, and the variables discussed in Chapter 2, are powerful tools that will help you "build" a plan consistent with your clients' objectives. While complex, they are so essential that they must be used aggressively. And, their complexity is not conceptual, but rather mechanical. With an awareness of the effects of integration and other basic plan variables, you can always check the specific rules as they apply to a particular client. The result—powerful design capacity—is well worth the effort.

PART TWO
Alternative Pension Plans: Opportunities, Strategies and Techniques

SECTION A
HOW TO DESIGN
DEFINED-CONTRIBUTION PLANS

4

How Defined-Contribution Plans Should Be Set Up For Maximum Results

In Chapters 1 through 3 we discussed general variables applicable to all types of qualified plans. With that background, it is time we consider more specific programs.

There are two major families of qualified retirement programs—the defined-contribution family and the defined-benefit family. Defined-contribution plans, as the name implies, are tied to specific rates of contribution which are defined in the plan instrument. This family includes profit-sharing and money-purchase programs.

In Chapters 4 through 6 we'll detail the operations of defined-contribution plans.

Chapter 4 sets the groundwork by:

- explaining what defined-contribution plans are;
- examining how they operate;
- considering their pros and cons;
- establishing who they benefit most or least; and
- emphasizing which employers should adopt them.

This information applies to all defined-contribution plans.

**¶400   WHAT IS A DEFINED-CONTRIBUTION PLAN AND
HOW DOES IT WORK**

The Internal Revenue Service requires that pension plans have "definitely determinable benefits." Normally, one would construe "definitely determinable benefits" to mean a specific promise for some dollar amount of future benefits. In fact, one family of pension plans, the "defined-benefit" group, meets that construction. In "defined-benefit" plans, participants know exactly what their retirement income will be. For example, Guaranteed, Incorporated establishes a defined-benefit plan providing participants with a 50% of pay retirement benefit. Joe Safeway, earning $10,000, knows that, barring changes in his compensation, he will get $5,000 per year when he retires.

There is, however, a second way to meet the criterion of "definitely determinable benefits." Under this alternative approach, the employer specifies the rate or allocation method that will govern contributions. The contribution system must relate all employees on some nondiscriminatory basis, most commonly their current level of compensation. Plans that use allocations of contributions to meet the "definitely determinable benefits" requirement are called "defined-contribution plans." Defined-contribution plans define the contribution rate or allocation method that an employer applies to current employee compensation to determine deposits.

¶400.1   How Allocations To Participants Are Determined

In general, the allocation of the defined-contribution deposits is made by comparing each participant's compensation or service to that of all participants' compensation or service. Whatever percentage each participant represents of the total will generally be the percentage of contribution he receives.

> *Example:* Simplicity Corporation sets up a defined-contribution plan to which it was to contribute $25,000 to be shared equally by participants according to relative salaries.

> Under Simplicity Corporation's simple defined-contribution plan, contributions are simply shared according to relative salaries. The plan provides "definitely determinable benefits" since the allocation method is consistently applied.

SIMPLICITY CORPORATION SALARY RATIO DEFINED-CONTRIBUTION PLAN

Employee	Age	Pay	% of Total	Share of Contribution	% of Total
A	50	75,000	41	10,331	41
B	30	75,000	41	10,331	41
C	40	12,000	7	1,653	7
D	40	12,000	7	1,653	7
E	25	7,500	4	1,032	4
TOTAL		181,500	100	25,000	100

¶400.2   Definitely Determinable Doesn't Imply Guaranteed Future Benefits

While participants in a defined-contribution plan can easily compute their share of contributions, there is no way for them to determine what their benefits will ultimately be. Note that defined-contribution plans cannot guarantee even estimated benefits. Our best effort at benefit-prediction is simply a guess based on reasonable interest and compensation assumptions. However, they will still be estimates. The age of the various participants can dramatically affect benefits, as well.

Example: Simplicity Corporation wants to tell plan participants what they should expect at age 65 from their defined-contribution plan. While it's easy to calculate contributions, benefits are estimates until retirement actually occurs. Consider what happens to cumulative participants accounts in the following circumstances. The plan earns an average rate of return of 6%, 0%, and –6% (loss):

Participant	Age	Pay	Contribution	Account Balances at Age 65 If Fund Earns: 6%	0%	–6%
A	50	$ 75,000	10,331	240,564	154,965	97,873
B	30	75,000	10,331	1,151,233	361,585	143,292
C	40	12,000	1,653	90,691	41,325	20,383
D	40	12,000	1,653	90,691	41,325	20,383
E	25	7,500	1,032	159,714	41,280	14,807
TOTAL		$181,500	$25,000			

The difference in ultimate benefits occasioned by a change in interest assumptions is quite dramatic.

Warning: Never let your client promise benefits under a defined-contribution plan. Participants are entitled only to periodic employer contributions allocated by a definitely determinable formula.

¶400.3   How Age Makes A Difference

Apart from the dramatic effect of interest rates on plan benefits, participants should focus on age as a critical variable in defined-contribution plans. Since contributions will generally be the same for all participants earning the same salary, regardless of age, it's obvious that a young employee will ultimately derive the greatest benefit from the plans. That's because they receive:

- more employer contributions over their longer working lives;
- more compound interest; and
- in the case of profit-sharing plans, more reallocated forfeitures.

The result is a substantial skewing of estimated benefits toward younger participants.

> *Example:* Look at the relative estimated benefits for participants C and E of Simplicity Corporation. Even though C earns 60% more than E, E, assuming 6% interest, will end up with 70% more benefit at retirement age. Many employers balk at this orientation, even though they like the concept of equal allocations.

Planning Tip: If your client has a specific budget for his plan, make certain you ask him the following question: Which is more important—that the key men get most of the contribution, or that the allocation formula is simple. If your client is most inclined to orient his deposits toward older key men, expose him to defined-benefit as well as defined-contribution plans.

¶401   HOW TO COMPUTE PARTICIPANT ACCOUNT BALANCES

Defined-contribution plans use individual "account balances" for measurement of participant benefits. The plan administrator or his delegate must maintain a separate recordkeeping account for each participant. The account is composed of:

1. employer contributions;
2. investment earnings (or losses); and
3. forfeitures occasioned by termination of nonvested participants (profit-sharing plans only).

Since all three of the components of account balances are variable, it's easy to see why benefits cannot be guaranteed in defined-contribution plans. What isn't subject to variability is what the administrator does with contributions, gains or losses, and forfeitures. To comply with the "definitely determinable benefits" requirement, each must be governed by the defined-contribution allocation method. Usually:

1. contributions are allocated by relative salary, relative service or a combination thereof;
2. profit-sharing forfeitures are shared according to the same ratio as contributions; and
3. earnings or losses are divided by ratio of account balances.

Example: Simplicity Corporation contributes $25,000 to its profit-sharing defined-contribution plan in year one and $15,000 in year two. The plan's assets earn $2,500 in year one and lose $1,000 in year two. Forfeitures are $2,000 in year one and $0 in year two. Compensation remains constant.

Figure 4.1

SIMPLICITY CORPORATION—TRACKING ACCOUNT BALANCES

Participant	Assumed Salary	% of Total	Assumed Beginning Balance	% of Total
A	$ 75,000	41%	$10,000	33%
B	75,000	41%	8,000	27%
C	12,000	7%	6,000	20%
D	12,000	7%	4,000	13%
E	7,500	4%	2,000	7%
TOTAL	$181,500	100%	30,000	100%

Year One

Participant	Contribution $	Contribution %	Forfeitures $	Forfeitures %	Earnings $	Earnings %	Ending Balance $	Ending Balance %
A	$10,250	41%	$ 820	41%	$ 825	33%	$21,895	37%
B	10,250	41%	820	41%	675	27%	19,745	33%
C	1,750	7%	140	7%	500	20%	8,390	14%
D	1,750	7%	140	7%	325	13%	6,215	10%
E	1,000	4%	80	4%	175	7%	3,255	6%
TOTAL	$25,000	100%	$2,000	100%	$2,500	100%	$59,500	100%

Year Two

Participant	Contribution $	Contribution %	Forfeitures $	Forfeitures %	Earnings $	Earnings %	Ending Balance $	Ending Balance %
A	$ 6,150	41%	00	41%	($ 370)	37%	$27,675	37%
B	6,150	41%	00	41%	(330)	33%	25,565	35%
C	1,050	7%	00	7%	(140)	14%	9,300	13%
D	1,050	7%	00	7%	(100)	10%	7,165	10%
E	600	4%	00	4%	(60)	6%	3,795	5%
TOTAL	$15,000	100%	00	100%	($1,000)	100%	$73,500	100%

Observation: It may be instructive to track participants A and B through the above sequence. A's salary represents 41% of total payroll. Therefore, he receives 41% of Year 1's contributions (41% of $25,000 = $10,250). Also, he receives 41% of the $2,000 of forfeitures (41% of $2,000 = $820). However, his beginning account balance ($10,000) represents only 33% of the $30,000 of total participant account balances. Therefore, he receives 33% of Year 1's earnings (33% of $2,500 = $825). Observe that participant A's ending balance at the end of Year 1 ($21,895) has increased to 37% of total participant account balances. In Year 2 participant A's salary is assumed to remain constant at 41% of total payroll; therefore, he receives 41% of the total contributions (41% of $15,000 = $6,150). However, he receives 37% of the funds' second year earnings (in this case, a loss). Thus, his account balance is debited by $370, which represents 37% of the $1,000 loss. Participant B follows the same "track" except that the employee's share of both payroll and initial account balances differ.

Planning Tip: Record keeping in large defined-contribution plans can be quite time consuming. Make sure your client has the capacity, either through a service agency or his funding mechanism, to keep track of account balances. Also, be careful to limit the number of reports participants will receive during each plan year. Most professional administration firms provide one annual report which combines all contributions, gains or losses, and forfeitures occurring during the year.

Example: Here is a typical format for a participant's statement/ annual report in a defined-contribution plan.

JOHN J. DOE
ANNUAL STATEMENT OF ACCOUNT IN THE
SIMPLICITY CORP. PROFIT-SHARING PLAN

I.   Information We Used to Calculate Your Contributions and Status:

     Your Date of Birth 05/06/25
     Your Date of Employment 03/27/77
     Your Compensation for the Fiscal Year $75,000

II.   Your Account Reconciliation

     Balance at 12/31/78 $10,000
     1979 Employer Contribution $10,250
     Your Share of Forfeitures 820
     Your Share of Investment Results 825
        Total Additions $11,895
     ENDING BALANCE, 12/31/79 .... $21,895

III.   Vesting Information

     Your Completed Years of Service 3
     Your Vested Percent Earned 30%
     Your Vested Account Balance, 12/31/79 ...... $6568

¶402   HOW TO USE ANNUAL ADDITIONS TO YOUR CLIENT'S ADVANTAGE

Of critical importance to defined-contribution plans is the concept of "maximum annual additions." ERISA limits the amount allocated to participants during a particular limitation year (generally a 12-month period, usually the employer's fiscal year, during which participant records are computed and maintained). Without the limitation, employers would be able to make contributions, subsidized by taxpayers, far in excess of what Congress intended.

¶402.1   What Are The Components Of The Annual Addition?

The maximum annual addition for any participant is computed by adding the following:

   1. employer contributions allocated to the participant during the plan year; plus

2. the lesser of:

   a) ½ of a participant's contributions; or

   b) all of a participant's contributions in excess of six percent of his compensation; plus

3. reallocated forfeitures.

Annual additions are computed on a participant-by-participant basis. It isn't always possible, referring to the plan formula, to tell what each participant's addition will be. Because of the limitations described below, it's important to test employee allocations carefully.

> *Example:* Maxin and Maxout have compensation of $20,000 and $30,000, respectively. Because of integration and various other plan parameters, they receive employer contributions of $3,000 and $6,000, respectively. There are no employer forfeitures. Maxin makes a $3,000 voluntary contribution, Maxout makes a voluntary deposit of $5,000. Each participant's annual addition is computed as follows:

	Maxin	Maxout
Employer Contribution	$3000	$6000
plus forfeitures reallocated	0	0
plus lesser of:		
(a) ½ voluntary contributions; or	1500	2500
(b) the voluntary contribution in		
excess of 6% of pay	1800	4200
Net increment to annual addition	1500	2500
Total annual addition	$4500	$8500

¶402.2   How Much Is The Maximum Annual Addition?

ERISA set the limitation on annual additions at the *lesser* of:

- $25,000; or
- 25% of compensation.

That means your clients cannot have defined-contribution plans in which the sum of any participant's

- employer contributions;
- employee contributions discussed at ¶402.1; and
- reallocated forfeitures exceeds those overall 25%/$25,000 limits.

> *Example:* Maxin and Maxout (see example at ¶402.1) each meet the $25,000 limitations. Furthermore, Maxin's annual addition represents 22½% of his compensation, so he also meets the percentage test. Maxout, on the other hand, fails to meet the percentage test since his annual addition represents 28½% of his compensation. Paragraph 402.4 will discuss how this overage is resolved.

¶402.3   How Is The Maximum Annual Addition Adjusted

Early each Spring the government publishes new maximums in accordance with cost-of-living statistics. Because of significant inflation over the past several years, the original ERISA maximums have increased substantially.

Year	Maximum Annual Addition
1975	$25,000
1976	$25,825
1977	$28,175
1978	$30,050
1979	$32,700
1980	$36,875

Thus, over a six-year period, the maximum addition to defined-contribution plans has increased by over 47%!

Planning Tip: Defined-contribution plans may include language allowing automatic increases in the maximum annual addition. This language can preclude time-consuming annual amendments. Make sure it's included in your plan.

Caution: Automatic cost-of-living adjustment may be included in defined-benefit plans, but future assumed increases may not be anticipated by the plan's actuary for purposes of funding.

¶402.4   How The Maximum Annual Addition Affects
                                          Your Clients

Let's consider the application of this limitation on annual additions with an employee earning $25,000 per year who makes a voluntary contribution of $1,800 and receives forfeitures from terminating nonvested employees totalling $700.

CALCULATION OF
LIMITATION ON ANNUAL ADDITIONS

A. ASSUMPTIONS: Employee Earns $25,000
                    Employer Contribution   5,000
                    Forfeiture Allocation   700
                    Voluntary Contributions   1,800

B. CALCULATION: Maximum Annual Addition = The Lesser of:
                         (a) 25% of pay   6,250
                         (b) dollar limit 32,700 $6,250
                    Composed of
                         (a) employer deposit   5,000
                         (b) forfeitures allocated   700
                         (c) lesser of:
                              ½ of employee deposits 900
                              or excess of 1,800
                              over 6% of 25,000 1,500
                              alternate   300 300

                    SUBTOTAL: ACTUAL ANNUAL ADD $6,000

                    SAFETY MARGIN ($6,250-$6,000) $250

The employee has underutilized his maximum annual addition by $250, therefore, he has not exceeded ERISA's limits. If, in our example, forfeitures allocated to his account had been $1,000 rather than $700, then our subtotal of actual annual additions would have been $6,300, $50 in excess of 25% of his pay. The $50 excess would have to be held in a suspense account until the next limitation year.

Since the object of most defined-contribution plan designs involves maximization of annual additions for key employees, without exceeding the 25%/$36,875 limitation imposed by Congress, this "suspense account" procedure can be counterproductive. And, when integration of the defined-contribution plan is contemplated, the situation can be substantially complicated.

¶402.5   How To Plan Around The Annual Addition To Get The Greatest Benefit For Your Client

Since, as discussed at ¶402.4, annual additions in excess of allowable limits are "suspended"—they can't benefit your client's key men. Therefore, your defined-contribution plan should anticipate the effects of the annual limitation. Furthermore, your annual administrative policy should reflect each year's actual experience as it may impact on the maximum annual addition.

Here is a checklist of suggestions along these lines:

☐ don't set up a money-purchase defined-contribution plan calling for a maximum (e.g. 25%) contribution if you anticipate voluntary key man contributions in excess of 6% of pay;

☐ anticipate the skewing effect of integration for plans contributing close to the maximum. For example, suppose your integrated profit-sharing plan received a full 15% contribution and that forfeitures to be reallocated represented another 10% of the total payroll (total allocable contributions equal 25%). The effect of integration would be to give higher paid participants more than 25% of pay;

☐ in profit-sharing plans calculate the amount of forfeitures to be reallocated as a percentage of payroll and, if it exceeds 10%, reduce the employer contribution as necessary;

☐ in profit-sharing plans, consider making voluntary deposits on a "dump in" basis in a year of little or no employer contributions. For example, an employee earning $40,000 could contribute as much as $20,000 to his voluntary account without running afoul of the annual limitation on additions during a year the employer makes no deposit.

¶403   HOW TO INCREASE MAXIMUM BENEFITS TO EITHER LOWER-PAID OR KEY PARTICIPANTS USING INTEGRATION

Integration of defined-contribution plans with Social Security is quite flexible. Revenue Ruling 71-446 allows that the "integration level" of a defined-contribution plan may be either:

a) an employee's "covered compensation"; or

b) any uniformly applied dollar amount up to the taxable wage base in effect for the year of computation. For 1980, this means $25,900.

In an integrated defined-contribution plan, different deposit rates or allocation methods are applied to participant compensation above and below the integration level. The maximum "additional contribution" for pay above the integration level is 7%.

> *Example:* Consider Simplicity Corporation's effort to determine the most efficient integration level for its plan. Integrated benefits may be based either on each participant's 1978 covered compensation (Plan A) or the taxable wage base applied uniformly to all participants (Plan B). Integrated benefits are derived from "excess pay" determined under either method.

Figure 4.2
COMPUTATION OF EXCESS PAY FOR SIMPLICITY CORPORATION

				PLAN A		PLAN B	
Employee	Age	Average Compensation	% of Total	Covered Compensation	"Excess" Pay	Taxable Wage Base	"Excess" Pay
A	50	75,000	41	15,000	66,000	25,900	49,100
B	30	75,000	41	22,900	52,100	25,900	49,000
C	40	12,000	7	19,800	0	25,900	0
D	40	12,000	7	19,800	0	25,900	0
E	25	7,500	4	22,900	0	25,900	0
TOTAL		181,500	100	N/A	N/A	N/A	N/A

Figure 4.3
COMPUTATION OF "EXCESS CONTRIBUTIONS" FOR SIMPLICITY CORPORATION

				PLAN A		PLAN B	
Employee	Age	Average Compensation	% of Total	7% Excess Deposit	% of Total	7% Excess Deposit	% of Total
A	50	75,000	41	4,300	54	3,437	50
B	30	75,000	41	3,647	46	3,437	50
C	40	12,000	7	0	0	0	0
D	40	12,000	7	0	0	0	0
E	25	7,500	4	0	0	0	0
TOTAL		181,500	100	7,947	100	6,874	100

Note that there is a significant difference between the two methods. The choice would depend on whether the employer's objective was to equalize integrated benefits for all participants (in which case Plan B is preferable) or maximize deposits for the older key man (in which case Plan A is preferable).

Planning Tip: Which Integration System To Use—"Covered Comp" or Wage Base?: Since older employees will have lower covered compensation amounts, they would benefit most greatly from the use of covered compensation tables as the integration level. In most small businesses, key men are, in fact, older than the average participant so that this may be a preferable integration system. However, if annual allocations must be computed by hand, then covered compensation tables can be unwieldy, requiring an individual determination of integration level for each employee-participant. In these cases, a uniform dollar amount integration level such as the taxable wage base is probably superior. It would also be superior in cases where key employees were actually *younger* than the average age of employee participants.

¶403.1   How To Choose The Right Integration Level Using A Lower Dollar Amount

The results for participants A and B under Plan B in Figure 403.2 could have been enhanced by using a lower dollar amount for the integration level. Since use of any dollar amount up to the taxable wage base is acceptable, it's worth testing several alternatives.

Example: Simplicity Corporation decides to try several different uniform integration levels.

Employee	Pay	$15,000 Integration Level Excess Pay	7% Deposit	% of Total	$9,000 Integration Level Excess Pay	7% Deposit	% of Total
A	$ 75,000	$ 60,000	$4,200	50%	$ 66,000	$4,620	48%
B	75,000	60,000	4,200	50	66,000	4,620	48
C	12,000	0	0	0	3,000	210	2
D	12,000	0	0	0	3,000	210	2
E	7,500	0	0	0	0	0	0
TOTAL	$181,500	$120,000	$8,400	100%	$138,000	$9,660	100%

Either the $15,000 or $9,000 integration level seems quite attractive. However, it's important to consider that any integration level lower than $12,000 will begin to draw lower-paid participants into the plan and reduce efficiency.

Planning Tip: Picking the right integration level is a matter of judgment. You should keep the following in mind:

— **if you use too low an integration level and don't amend it in subsequent years, "wage inflation" will subvert your initial planning;**

— **too high an integration level can be more costly in terms of key man excess contributions lost than may be worthwhile; and**

— **using "covered compensation" as the integration level will benefit older participants, but may add a confusing element to plans whose primary attribute may be their simplicity.**

¶403.2   How To Increase Selectivity By Using A Higher Dollar Amount

Your client may use a uniform dollar amount integration level higher than the taxable wage base. However, the rate of contribution for pay in excess of the higher integration level must be reduced from seven percent. The reduction is easily determined by multiplying the normal excess contribution rate (seven percent) by a fraction, the numerator of which is the taxable wage base in effect for the year of computation and the denominator of which is the proposed higher integration level.

Example: Simple integrated defined-contribution plans may contribute seven percent of an employee's pay in excess of the taxable wage base. Thus, an employee earning $35,900 in 1980 could receive an excess contribution as follows:

Compensation	$35,900
Less: taxable wage base	(25,900)
Equals: excess contribution	10,000
Times: contribution rate	× .07
Equals: excess contribution	$ 700

If the employer decides to raise the integration levels from $25,900 to $27,900, he would have to reduce the contribution rate as follows:

$$\text{Standard Integration Level} \quad \times \quad \frac{\text{Normal Integration Level}}{\text{Proposed Integration Level}}$$

Solving, we find $7\% \times \dfrac{25,900}{27,900} = 6.5\%$

Therefore, recomputing the above example, we would have the following:

Compensation:	35,900
Less: integration level	(27,900)
Equals: excess compensation	8,000
Times: reduced contribution rate	× 6.5%
Equals: excess contribution	$ 520

Planning Tip: Your client will probably not wish to use higher integration levels unless he has either a very limited budget or a large group of employees earning just over the normal integration level.

¶404 HOW TO GET BIGGER TAX DEDUCTIBLE CONTRIBUTIONS WITH "TWO-TIERED" PLANS

Because of the seven percent maximum rate applied to excess compensation, even a very high-paid participant can't derive too great a benefit from "excess only" defined-contribution plans. For example, without adjusting the seven percent deposit rate, a participant would need compensation of $168,757 to receive an "excess only" allocation of $10,000 ($168,757 – $25,900 = $142,857 excess pay, $142,857 × 7% = $10,000). Two-tiered plans solve the problem.

¶404.1 The Mechanics Are Simple

The maximum annual addition for 1979 was the lesser of $32,700 or 25% of pay. The maximum contribution rate for pay in excess of the integration level is seven percent. Suppose Dr. Max, who earns $150,000, establishes a base plan with a contribution rate of 16.009% and an excess plan with a deposit rate of seven percent for pay in excess of $25,900. His maximum annual addition is $32,700. Under the plan, he gets:

	Base Plan	Excess Plan	Total
Eligible Compensation	$150,000	$124,100	N/A
Times Contribution Rate	× 16.009%	× 7%	N/A
Equals Contribution Amount	$ 24,013	$ 8,687	= $32,700

Two-tiered plans substantially improve plan efficiency.

Example: Money, Ltd. considers two defined-contribution plans, one integrated (formula = 16.009% of pay, plus 7% of excess pay over $25,900) and the other nonintegrated (formula = 20.331% of pay). If Money, Ltd.'s objective is to help high-paid employees, there isn't much choice:

| | | | TWO-TIERED PLAN | | | | REGULAR PLAN | |
| | | Excess | Regular | Excess | Total | % of | Total | % of |
Employee	Pay	Pay	Deposit	Deposit	Deposit	Total	Deposit	Total
A	$150,000	$124,100	$24,013	$ 8,687	$32,700	67%	$30,496	62%
B	50,000	24,100	8,004	1,687	9,691	20	10,165	21
C	25,000	0	4,002	0	4,002	8	5,083	10
D	15,000	0	2,401	0	2,401	5	3,050	6
TOTAL	$240,000	$148,200	$38,420	$10,374	$48,794	100%	$48,794	100%

Not only does the regular plan cost six percent more to provide the same benefit for employee A, but it also spends the increased deposit substantially less efficiently.

¶404.2   How To Calculate The Best Formula For Your Client

You can save time by using the following simple formula to find the two-tiered defined-contribution formula that will spend your client's deposit objective:

$$C = X \cdot T + .07 \cdot E, \text{ where:}$$

C = the contribution desired for a particular employee (or the entire company);

X = the contribution rate applied to total pay (or payroll);

T = total pay (or payroll); and

E = pay (or payroll) in excess of the integration level.

Example: As the sole stockholder and key man of DEF Corporation, John wants to set up a two-tiered defined-contribution plan which will provide him with the maximum annual addition. His compensation is $75,000. The plan will be integrated at $15,000. John's maximum annual addition is:

The lesser of:

- 25% of pay $18,750

- dollar limitation $32,700

Thus, the contribution rate which will most efficiently generate John's maximum annual addition is:

$$
\begin{aligned}
C &= X \cdot T + .07 \cdot E \\
\$18,750 &= X \cdot \$75,000 + .07 \cdot \$60,000 \\
\$18,750 &= 75,000X + 4,200 \\
\$14,550 &= 75,000X \\
19.4\% &= X\text{—Best contribution rate.}
\end{aligned}
$$

Proving, by applying the rate to John's pay:

Total Pay	$75,000	
Multiplied by Total Pay Contribution Rate	× .194	
Equals Total Pay Contribution		$14,550
Excess Pay	$60,000	
Multiplied by Pay Contribution Rate	× .07	
Equals Pay Contribution		4,200
Total Contribution		$18,750

The simple formula works equally well when applied to a firm's total payroll.

Example: Suppose, RST Company wants to spend $25,000 for a plan integrated at $12,000. The best basic contribution rate is easy to calculate:

Employee	Total Pay	Excess Pay
A	$ 50,000	$38,000
B	30,000	18,000
C	20,000	8,000
D	10,000	0
TOTAL	$110,000	$64,000

$$
\begin{aligned}
C &= X \cdot T + .07 \cdot E \\
\$25,000 &= X \cdot \$110,000 + .07 \cdot \$64,000 \\
25,000 &= 110,000X + 4480 \\
20,520 &= 110,000X \\
18.655\% &= X
\end{aligned}
$$

Checking, we see that RST Company's objective is achieved:

Employee	Total Pay	Excess Pay	18.655% Regular Deposit	+	7% Excess Deposit	=	Total Deposit
A	$ 50,000	$38,000	$ 9,328		$2,660		$11,988
B	30,000	18,000	5,596		1,260		6,856
C	20,000	8,00	3,731		560		4,291
D	10,000	0	1,865		0		1,865
TOTAL	$110,000	$64,000	$20,520		$4,480		$25,000

Planning Tip: Integrated plans generally must use total compensation of participants to determine benefits. Nonintegrated plans often exclude bonuses, overtime, or other special compensation. Sometimes more can be achieved for key men in a nonintegrated plan with a restrictive definition of compensation, particularly if key men derive most of their pay from salaries, and rank and file employees earn substantial bonuses or overtime.

¶405   SUMMARIZING THE CONSIDERATIONS FOR USING DEFINED-CONTRIBUTION PLANS

The implications of defined-contribution plans are relatively obvious. In general, they are considered a young person's plan, since younger employees will receive the maximum number of annual allocations plus the maximum amount of time for compound interest to work.

Recall the example at ¶400.1 and note that our 50 and 30-year-old employees, each earning identical salaries, can anticipate vastly disproportionate retirement funds. The younger employee expects a retirement balance at 65 of $1,151,233, some five times greater than his 50-year old counterpart.

Since most closely-held company pension plans are set up for the benefit of an older key person group, defined-contribution plans often cannot fulfill one of our basic design objectives—maximum allocation of the employer's deposit for the benefit of those key individuals.

However, defined-contribution plans are conceptually simple. They are often favored by accountants and attorneys. They lack the mystery of actuarial deposit determinations which are a component of the defined-benefit family. For internal public relations, many small businessmen prefer the contribution equalization. Thus, defined-contribution plans are very popular.

The Internal Revenue Service, in past rulings, has tried to minimize the disparities between defined-contribution and defined-benefit plans. The result is a surprising amount of flexibility for the former group, sufficient at the same time to fulfill the important criteria of conceptual simplicity and allocation of the maximum percent of contributions to key personnel.

The following two chapters describe in great detail some of the contribution/allocation methods previously approved by the Internal Revenue Service which help fulfill these dual objectives. Let us consider, then, profit-sharing and money-purchase plans.

5

Setting Up Effective Profit-Sharing Plans To Compensate Employees For Inflation

---

Profit-sharing plans are by far the most popular form of retirement programs in small to medium-size businesses. That is not without good reason. They:

- preserve flexibility in terms of contributions;
- produce an advantage from the high turnover associated with small to medium-size businesses and work to the benefit of those employees who remain behind; and
- are very simple and easily explained.

In the right circumstances, there is no question that a profit-sharing plan ought to be the first choice of your clients.

The purpose of this chapter is to show you:

1. how profit-sharing plans work;

2. who they benefit; and

3. different plan formulas you can use to accomplish different objectives.

In addition, there will be discussion of how integration with Social Security can enhance the efficiency of profit-sharing plans for key men.

¶500   WHY PROFIT-SHARING PLANS ARE SO COMMON

Internal Revenue statistics indicate that profit-sharing plans are the most common of all qualified plans, particularly in small businesses. There are several good reasons for this. You must understand the reasons in order to use them to the advantage of your client.

¶500.1   Conceptual Simplicity Allows Easy Presentation

Profit-sharing plans are conceptually the simplest of all qualified plans. Deposits are easily calculated by applying some allocation formula to your client's contribution. For example, the simplest profit-sharing allocation method is salary proportion. Each participant shares in employer contributions according to the ratio his salary bears to the salary of all participants.

Example: Simple, Ltd. uses a salary proportion allocation method to distribute its $10,000 contribution among participants:

Participant	Salary	Salary As A % of Total	Share of Contribution	Share As A % of Total
A	$30,000	50%	$ 5,000	50%
B	20,000	33%	3,300	33%
C	10,000	17%	1,700	17%
TOTAL	$60,000	100%	$10,000	100%

*In this simplest profit-sharing plan, an individual participant's share of contributions bears the same percentage to total employer contributions as does that participant's salary to total covered payroll.

The readily understandable allocation methods used in profit-sharing plans form their first significant advantage.

¶500.2   Investment Gains Benefit Participants Directly

Investment gains or losses in profit-sharing plans are also allocated pro rata to participants' accounts. If a participant's account balance at the end of the prior plan year represented 50% of the total, then he will receive 50% of any investment gains or losses during the following plan year. Note that gains and losses are allocated according to relative account balance rather than relative compensation.

Example: Distribute, Incorporated's plan earns $3,000 during a particular plan year. Here's how participants share the gain, assuming the beginning balances shown:

Participant	Beginning Balance	Beginning Balance As A %	Share Of Gain	Share Of Gain As A %
A	$25,000	66%	$1,980	66%
B	10,000	26%	780	26%
C	3,000	8%	240	8%
TOTAL	$38,000	100%	$3,000	100%

Observation: Note the important distinctions, namely that investment earnings or losses are allocated in proportion to account balances rather than compensation. Participants directly reap the reward or loss of investment experience. As we discussed in Chapter 4, these earnings have added impact for your participants.

¶500.3   The Key To Profit-Sharing Plans—Forfeiture Reallocation

Nonvested account values forfeited by terminating profit-sharing participants are reallocatd to the accounts of those participants who remain. The concept of forfeiture reallocation dramatically distinguishes profit-sharing from all other types of qualified plans, and makes them particularly attractive to younger employees. All other qualified plans must use forfeited accrued benefits to reduce deductible employer contributions. That means your client loses a valuable tax deduction, and participants lose the opportunity to profit from their longevity.

3 1303 00066 6637

Example: ABC Incorporated terminates two participants, D and E. Here's what happens, assuming the beginning balances shown:

Participant	Beginning Balance	Current Deposit	Current Deposit As A %	Share Of Forfeiture	
A	$10,000	$3,000	38%	$1,140	(38%)
B	15,000	3,000	38%	1,140	(38%)
C	10,000	2,000	24%	720	(24%)
D	2,000	0	0	(2,000)	(−67%)
E	1,000	0	0	(1,000)	(−33%)
TOTAL	$38,000	$8,000	100%	0	(0%)

Important: Do not underestimate the importance of reallocated forfeitures in many small to medium-size businesses. All other forms of retirement program require forfeitures to be used to reduce future employer contributions. Profit-sharing plans offer a highly attractive alternative that can create a powerful incentive for employees to remain. Furthermore, the reallocation of forfeitures leaves your client free to budget his profit-sharing contribution to fit his cash flow position. Many other forms of retirement plan can be disrupted by unforeseen forfeitures which preclude anticipated deductions. The reallocation of forfeitures, therefore, forms a powerful reason for small businesses, *particularly* those with unusually high turnover rates, to consider profit-sharing plans.

¶500.4   Contribution Flexibility—Keeping Abreast Of Your Client's Cash Flow

The discretion to control the amount of annual contributions, if any, certainly forms the prime rationale for profit-sharing plans' popularity. Your client can deposit up to 15% of covered payroll or nothing into his profit-sharing plan. The volatility of profits in small businesses means that ongoing substantially fixed commitments are not palatable to accountants who have too often seen the euphoria of "good years" lead a businessman to overcommitment which can be a crushing burden when bad times arrive.

Also, your client's cash needs will change from year to year even if there are ample profits. For instance, a small manufacturing company may, from time to time, need its surplus cash flow for plant expansion, purchase of new machinery (which may, from investment tax audits, have equally attractive tax consequences), or to provide a reserve against future anticipated recessionary trends. Only a profit-sharing plan provides this constant protection against unforeseen contingencies. That's very important for most small businesses.

> *Example:* Fallback Company and Leapahead Incorporated each establish retirement plans to which they expect to contribute $25,000 per year. Fallback Company uses a profit-sharing approach. Leapahead uses a plan requiring a fixed annual deposit. All goes well for three years. Then a new computer package becomes available which, at a cost of $25,000, will
>
> • substantially increase the profits of either firm in future years; or
> • have virtually the same tax impact during the year of purchase as a $25,000 plan contribution.
>
> Fallback Company skips its annual profit-sharing contribution and buys the computer. Leapahead must makes its regular $25,000 plan deposit and borrow the money for the computer, at an interest cost of $10,000 over the amortization period of the loan.

Planning Tip: Despite all the advantages of other types of qualified plans, more favorable allocations for older key men, bigger deductions, and greater design flexibility, and the value of controlling cash flow is so important to a small business that you should strongly emphasize profit-sharing plans for your client's "first step" into the realm of qualified plans. It's much easier to build from that base than it is to dismantle a more sophisticated plan when circumstances require retrenchment.

¶501   CONSIDER THESE PROFIT-SHARING LIABILITIES: EVERY SILVER LINING HAS TO HAVE A CLOUD

Profit-sharing plans have several inherent liabilities. First, they generally favor younger employees. Second, profit-sharing plan deposits are limited to 15% of covered payroll. Even in a profit-sharing plan integrated with Social Security, this 15% limitation may generate so small a contribution as to preclude a key man from receiving a substantial enough allocation to make the time, expense, and aggravation of the plan worthwhile.

¶501.1   You Should Consider Who Are The Key Men
                                      In The Firm

Defined-contribution plans and profit-sharing, in particular, inherently favor younger employees. Their relatively young age means they will receive:

- more contributions;
- more reallocated forfeitures; and
- more compound interest.

Generally, the key men of small businesses are the older, rather than the younger employees. If there's a limited budget, and the plan is primarily for the benefit of older key men, orientation toward the wrong group may create a problem.

Example: Budget Ltd. establishes a profit-sharing plan, because the key man, employee A, needs to shelter some of his income. But, he balks at the skewing of estimated retirement benefits which assume 15% employee turnover and 7½% interest:

Employee	Age	Pay	Annual Contribution	Contribution As A %	Estimated Account Value @ 65
A	50	$ 50,000	$10,000	40%	$322,888
B	35	30,000	6,000	24	766,965
C	40	20,000	4,000	16	336,151
D	30	15,000	3,000	12	572,081
E	25	10,000	2,000	8	561,892
TOTAL		$125,000	$25,000	100%	N/A

Note: Forfeitures are allocated in the same manner as employer contributions, meaning that higher paid employees will derive the greatest advantage from them. That lends further force to the argument made at ¶501.3 regarding the importance of forfeiture reallocation to the conceptual advantages of profit-sharing plans.

The prospect of a 25-year old who earns 20% of Budget, Ltd.'s key man's salary receiving almost twice as large a retirement distribution as the key man, may create an impasse.

Observation: The philosophical differences in approach representative of profit-sharing and defined-benefit plans will effectively focus on your client's competing objectives—contribution flexibility versus contribution skewing. The earlier in the design process you force this confrontation, the sooner you will finalize your client's plans. The choices are often dichotomous.

¶501.2   Fifteen Percent Contribution Limitation May Thwart
                Substantial Planning Opportunities

Frequently a small business owner will postpone the establishment of a qualified plan for years, preferring to reinvest surplus cash in his concern. By the time he's ready to take advantage of a plan, he's in his late 40s or 50s. At that point the 15% of payroll contribution limitation may preclude the use of a profit-sharing plan for estate or income tax planning. Given the inherent orientation of profit-sharing contributions toward younger employees, it would take a large deposit to generate a meaningful annual allocation for an older key man, and monumental annual allocations to generate substantive retirement income.

> *Example:* LMN Company's owner and key employee, Jim Dandy, has been told by his accountant that a qualified plan is the cheapest way to save money. He's willing to budget 15% of the company payroll but finds that doesn't give him a large enough share of deposit to accumulate meaningful dollars before retirement; or make a plan worth the effort.

Employee	Age	Pay	Share of 15% Deposit	Accumulation @ 65
Jim	50	$ 50,000	$ 7,500	$210,579
B	40	15,000	2,250	164,421
C	35	10,000	1,500	166,732
D	30	15,000	2,250	373,096
E	25	10,000	1,500	366,451
TOTAL		$100,000	$15,000	N/A

Observation: If Jim Dandy took the $15,000 contribution as a bonus and paid 50% income taxes, he'd have the same $7,500. True, it couldn't be invested tax-free at the same rate, but also he would avoid the expense and ongoing responsibility associated with a plan.

¶502   **HOW PROFIT-SHARING PLANS WORK**

The basic characteristics of profit-sharing plans are most easily demonstrated with a simple example. Suppose your client contributes $25,000 to a profit-sharing plan allocated simply according to the relationship each participant's compensation bears to the compensation of all participants. Here's what happens:

Employee	Age	Pay	% of Total	Deposit	% of Total
A	50	$ 75,000	41%	$10,330	41%
B	30	75,000	41	10,330	41
C	40	12,000	7	1,653	7
D	40	12,000	7	1,653	7
E	25	7,500	4	1,034	4
TOTAL		$181,500	100%	$25,000	100%

Observation: In this simple plan, participants' relative allocations are identical to their relative salaries. Further, the illustration highlights the most basic profit-sharing plan attribute—differences in contribution rate occur primarily because of pay. The long term implication of that observation is that young employees will ultimately derive the greatest benefit from profit-sharing plans. They will receive more allocations, more interest, and—will benefit from forfeitures.

¶502.1   How Forfeitures Hold The Long-Range Key To Profit-
                              Sharing Plans

In Chapter 4, we discussed defined-contribution plans, and in general, pointed out that profit-sharing accounting is maintained on the basis of individual accounts. To each participant's account is credited his share of employer contributions, interest, and forfeitures. In the long run, forfeitures provide the biggest boost in benefits for younger participants. The treatment of forfeitures in profit-sharing plans is unique and deserves special attention.

Forfeitures result from the termination of employees with insufficient service credit to be fully vested. With the exception of profit-sharing plans, all retirement plans must use these nonvested forfeited account values to reduce subsequent employer contributions and tax deductions for the plan. Profit-sharing forfeitures are reallocated to participants who "remain behind." Typically the reallocation is based on the same distribution method used for employer deposits. For a client with high turnover among his employees (a restaurateur or construction company owner, for example), these reallocated forfeitures can be a bonanza, amounting to as much as a 70% benefit increase.

Example: Quit Claim, Incorporated and Stable Company each adopt profit-sharing plans. Quit Claim is a small department store and experiences 90% turnover among its employees. Stable is a family-owned and operated jewelry store with virtually no turnover. Each contributes 15% to their respective plans. After 20 years, employees A and B of Quit Claim are the only participants remaining of the initial group. All others "turned over" and were replaced. All the original participants of Stable Company stayed through the 20-year period. Compare the results:

| | | Quit Claim, Incorporated | | | Stable Company | | |
Employee	Pay	Status	Annual Deposit	"Pot" @ 20 Yrs	Status	Annual Deposit	"Pot" @ 20 Yrs
A	$ 50,000	Stay	$ 7,500	$581,908	Stay	$ 7,500	$349,144
B	50,000	Stay	7,500	581,908	Stay	7,500	349,144
C	25,000	Quit	3,750	N/A	Stay	3,750	174,572
D	15,000	Quit	2,250	N/A	Stay	2,250	104,743
E	10,000	Quit	1,500	N/A	Stay	1,500	69,829
F	10,000	Quit	1,500	N/A	Stay	1,500	69,829
G	6,667	Quit	1,000	N/A	Stay	1,000	46,555
TOTAL	$166,667	N/A	$25,000	N/A	N/A	$25,000	N/A

Planning Tip: Your clients with high turnover rates may want to consider more liberal eligibility requirements than normal, choosing to control participant funds through the plan's vesting schedule. Why not contribute the full 15% deposit on a broader covered payroll? If typical employees won't be there five years down the road, your client has nothing to lose, except taxes, by excluding them from his plan.

Caveat: In years with substantial forfeiture reallocations, the sum of forfeitures and regular deposits may exceed the 25% limitation on annual additions. That's true particularly in integrated plans where deposits, and therefore forfeitures, are skewed toward higher-paid participants. Always test your client's proposed annual contribution to be sure that, in conjunction with forfeitures, no participant will run afoul of the limitation.

¶502.2   How Inflation Enhances Younger Participants'
Opportunities

If we add the reasonable assumption that employees' salaries, and
therefore your client's contribution, will increase by four percent a year, the
effect on 20-year balances is further dramatized. Consider the turnover/no
turnover situations illustrated at ¶502.1 with this four percent inflation factor
added:

COMPARING STABLE AND HIGH TURNOVER GROUPS
IN AN INFLATIONARY ENVIRONMENT

		Quit Claim, Incorporated			Stable Company		
Employee	Pay*	Status	Initial Deposit*	"Pot" @ 20 Yrs	Status	Initial Deposit*	"Pot" @ 20 Yrs
A	$ 50,000	Stay	$ 7,500	$741,718	Stay	$ 7,500	$445,030
B	50,000	Stay	7,500	741,717	Stay	7,500	445,030
C	25,000	Quit	3,750	N/A	Stay	3,750	222,515
D	15,000	Quit	2,250	N/A	Stay	2,250	133,508
E	10,000	Quit	1,500	N/A	Stay	1,500	89,006
F	10,000	Quit	1,500	N/A	Stay	1,500	89,006
G	6,667	Quit	1,000	N/A	Stay	1,000	59,340
TOTAL	$166,687*	N/A	$25,000	N/A	N/A	$25,000*	N/A

*Deposit and pay assumed to increase at four percent per year.

Observation: The effect of inflation on deposits and account balances will be
most acutely felt by younger participants. This effect is further confirmation of
a basic fact about profit-sharing plans. However, this illustration uses only a
20-year accumulation period. It is not too unusual among small businesses to
have a 45-year-old employee. Profit-sharing plans can be very attractive,
therefore, to your clients with middle-aged key men, a high turnover, or high
investment return expectations.

**Planning Tip: In Chapters 4 though 6 we will detail defined-contribution plans
and consistently conclude that this family of retirement program
inherently favors those employees who are younger than age 45.
That fact is clearly reinforced in the illustration above. If the
objective for your client's plan is to benefit key men that are older,
you may want to consider the defined-benefit program we discuss in
Chapters 7 through 10. Defined-benefit plans allow in their actuarial**

assumptions, cost reductions based on assumed turnover rates, mortality and morbidity, and increases in the integration level, an opportunity to increase benefits allocated to the older key men. The choice of a defined-contribution versus a defined-benefit plan typically hinges on the dichotomous choice your client faces— contribution flexibility (obtained with profit-sharing programs) versus orientation of contributions for older key men (obtained through defined-benefit plans).

¶503   HOW TO YIELD MAXIMUM BENEFITS FOR THE KEY MAN BY USING INTEGRATED PROFIT-SHARING PLANS

Profit-sharing plans may be "integrated" with employer contributions to Social Security. A profit-sharing deposit will not be considered discriminatory if different contribution rates are applied to compensation above and below a specified integration level. The integration level must be uniformly applied to all plan participants and either be:

1. the taxable wage base in effect at the end of the plan year considered; or
2. covered compensation, according to IRS tables.

The maximum allocation rate application to compensation in excess of the integration level is seven percent.

¶503.1   Using Covered Compensation Versus Taxable Wage Base And How It Works

As stated in ¶503, your client can pick his integration level. In Chapters 3 and 4 we detailed the conceptual aspects of integration. Now, let's see how it works in practice.

Using a uniformly-applied dollar amount integration level not in excess of the taxable wage base ($25,900 in 1979) presents the simplest alternative. Your client can deposit up to seven percent of each employee's pay in excess of the level chosen.

How it Works: Joe earns $30,000. His company's profit-sharing plan provides for deposits of seven percent of his pay in excess of $25,900. Joe receives an allocation of $287, seven percent of his excess pay.

The alternative to using a uniform dollar amount integration level is the use of "covered compensation." Covered compensation is, in concept, the projected average of the taxable wage bases to which an employee will have been subject during his working life. Since the taxable wage base has historically risen, that means older employees will have been covered, on an average, by lower taxable wage bases. Thus, covered compensation tables generate lower integration levels for older employees, and higher ones for younger employees. Often that fits nicely with the facts of most small business. Key men are usually relatively older.

How it Works: Jim and Mark each earn $30,000. They are 50 and 30 respectively. Jim's covered compensation is $15,000, and his "excess pay" is $15,000. Mark's covered compensation is $22,900, and his excess pay is $7,100. Jim will receive $1,050 in a seven percent excess plan. Mark will get $497. That's about a 50% increase for Jim, the older of the two.

¶503.2   A Comparison Of Alternative Integration Systems In A Typical Business

The upshot of the alternative integration systems is best examined with an illustration comparing the two. Therefore, using a typical employee group, consider the simplest integrated profit-sharing allocation. Plan I contributes seven percent of compensation in excess of $25,900. Plan II deposits seven percent of pay above each participant's covered compensation as determined by 1979 Table II:

			PLAN I		PLAN II	
Employee	Age	Pay	Integration Level	7% of Pay In Excess	Integration Level	7% of Pay In Excess
A	50	$ 75,000	$22,900	$3,647	$15,000	$4,200
B	30	75,000	22,900	3,647	22,900	3,647
C	40	12,000	22,900	0	19,800	0
D	40	12,000	22,900	0	19,800	0
E	25	7,500	22,900	0	22,900	0
TOTAL		$181,500	N/A	$7,294	N/A	$7,847

Either plan has the effect of drastically limiting allocation of the employer's contribution to lower-paid employees. On the other hand, if these excess only plans were used in isolation, they would reduce key man allocations.

¶503.3   How To Decide Which Integration Level To Use

As we discussed in Chapters 3 and 4, covered compensation tables provide individual integration levels for plan participants depending upon their particular ages. The older a participant, the lower his covered compensation since the average of the taxable wage basis to which he has been subject during his working life will tend to be relatively low. Alternatively, a young employee's covered compensation level will be higher since the bulk of his working life he will be subject to significantly higher taxable wage bases. There are two factors to consider in choosing one integration level over another:

1. the age distribution of your client's employees; and
2. the availability of administrative support.

Given an employee group in which key participants tend to be older than the average age of employees in general, your client should naturally favor covered compensation tables at the integration levels. Using the covered compensation tables will result in a larger allocation of the employer's contribution to those older employees. However, if key participants tend to be young, the reverse would be true. Your client ought to consider using the flat dollar amount integration level designed to generate integrated benefits above that dollar level. The dollar level would be the lowest possible to avoid bringing in a substantial additional amount of payroll.

For example, if your client's key man earns $50,000, then lowering the integration level from $15,000 to $10,000 yields him an additional $350 allocation (seven percent of the additional excess compensation occasioned by the reduction to the integration level). However if, in lowering the integration level, he must provide integrated benefits to two additional employees earning $12,500, then his advantage will be wiped out. That's because his own $350 additional allocation will be offset by a $350 additional allocation for the employees. In this example, the integration level might most efficiently be set at $12,500.

An additional factor to consider is the administrative support necessary in all but the smallest businesses to handle covered compensation integration levels. Hand calculations for more than five employees can be quite burdensome, and tend to produce more errors. Therefore, in the absence of administrative support, your client should consider using a flat dollar integration level for all employee-participants.

¶504   HOW TWO-TIERED PLANS CAN BOOST DEPOSITS
FOR KEY MEN

Most integrated profit-sharing plans use a "two-tiered" format. That is, contributions are allocated in two pieces. First, each participant receives up to seven percent of his pay in excess of the integration level. Second, whatever contribution is left over is allocated according to the ratio each participant's compensation bears to the compensation of all participants. A two-tiered profit-sharing plan won't be considered discriminatory if the rate applied to compensation in excess of the integration level is no more than seven percent.

¶504.1   How Two-Tiered Plans Work

Two-tiered profit-sharing plans utilize the most basic of integration methods. Let's consider two different contributions made to the same integrated profit-sharing plan in successive years. The first year, Volatile Company has only $5,000 to spare. In the second year it has $20,000. Assume a $15,000 flat dollar integration level.

Analysis of Year One Contributions: The first year $5,000 deposit represents less than seven percent of the eligible excess pay. Therefore, it is allocated according to the ratio one participant's excess pay bears to another.

Participant	Pay	Integration Level	Excess Pay	Excess Pay As A % of Total	Share Of Deposit	Share As A % of Total
A	$ 75,000	$15,000	$ 60,000	46%	$2,300	46%
B	75,000	15,000	60,000	46	2,300	46
C	25,000	15,000	10,000	8	400	8
D	15,000	15,000	0	0	0	0
E	10,000	15,000	0	0	0	0
TOTAL	$200,000	N/A	$130,000	100%	$5,000	100%

Observation: Volatile Company could have deposited as much as $9,100 (seven percent of the $130,000 excess pay) without allocating anything to the lower-paid employees.

Analysis of Year Two Contributions: The second year's deposit of $20,000 will be allocated in two steps:

1. first on the basis of relative pay above the integration level up to seven percent; and
2. next according to relative total pay.

Participant	Pay	Integration Level	Excess Pay	Excess Pay As A % Of Total	Share Of Deposit	Share As A % Of Total
A	$ 75,000	$15,000	$ 60,000	46%	$ 8,288	41%
B	75,000	15,000	60,000	46	8,287	41
C	25,000	15,000	10,000	8	2,063	11
D	15,000	15,000	0	0	817	4
E	10,000	15,000	0	0	545	3
TOTAL	$200,000	N/A	$130,000	100%	$200,000	100%

¶504.2   How To Determine The Best Contribution

Critical to successful integration of profit-sharing plans is pinpointing the most efficient contribution. Assume that your client's objective is maximization of relative deposits for key employees. In a year when cash is scarce, the following formula may help:

$$D = RP + .07E; \text{ where}$$

D = employer deposit
R = contribution rate for total payroll
P = total employee payroll
E = excess employee payroll

This simple formula can be solved for any number of variables including the contribution for an "excess only" allocation, or the basic allocation rate for a given contribution.

Example: Volatile Company (¶504.1) asks how much of their $25,000 deposit would be allocated to employees A and B, given an integration level of $15,000, total payroll of $200,000, and excess payroll of $130,000. First, we need the basic contribution rate:

$$\$25,000 \ + \ R \ \times \ (\$200,000) \ + \ .07 \ \times \ \$130,000$$

The basic allocation rate for total payroll is 7.95% and for excess pay, seven percent. Therefore, the allocation for employee A or B is easily determined:

Total Pay for Employee A or B	$75,000	
Multiplied by Basic Allocation Rate	.0795	
Equals Basic Allocation		$5,963
Excess Pay	$60,000	
Multiplied by Excess Allocation Rate	.07	
Equals Excess Allocation		$4,200
TOTAL ALLOCATION FOR EMPLOYEE A OR B		$10,163

Additional Example: Volatile Company wants to know the exact amount of contribution it could make to an integrated plan at $18,000 without making any deposit or allocation to participants earning below that level. Here's how it's done:

$$X \ = \ .07 \ \times \ 114,000$$
$$X \ = \ \$7,980$$

¶504.3   Comparison Of Integrated And Nonintegrated Profit-Sharing Plans

Lets summarize the opportunities inherent in proper integration by comparing integrated and nonintegrated alternatives using a $17,700 integration level and $25,000 deposit.

PLAN I—INTEGRATED

Employee	Pay	% Of Total	Excess Pay	9.354% Total Pay	+ 7% Balance	= Total Deposit	% Of Total
A	$ 75,000	41%	$ 57,300	$ 7,015	$4,011	$11,027	44.0%
B	75,000	41	57,300	7,015	4,011	11,027	44.0
C	12,000	7	0	1,123	0	1,122	4.5
D	12,000	7	0	1,123	0	1,122	4.5
E	7,500	4	0	702	0	702	3.0
TOTAL	$181,500	100%	$114,600	$16,978	$8,022	$25,000	100.0%

PLAN II—NONINTEGRATED

Employee	Pay	% Of Total	Total Deposit	% Of Total	Change As A $ Amount	As A %
A	$ 75,000	41%	$10,330	41%	–697	–6%
B	75,000	41	10,330	41	–697	–6%
C	12,000	7	1,653	7	+531	+47%
D	12,000	7	1,653	7	+531	+47%
E	7,500	4	$1,032	4	+332	+47%
TOTAL	$181,500	100%	$25,000	100%	N/A	N/A

Integration of the identical $25,000 deposit has dramatically shifted the deposit-orientation toward the higher-paid employees. Participant A, for example, receives 41% ($10,330) of the deposit under the nonintegrated approach, but 44% ($11,027) with the alternative. His deposit is seven percent higher, and the $697 difference will generate an additional "pot" of more than $30,000 in 20 years.

¶504.4   You Should Keep Deposit-Equalization In Perspective

The greater the number of participating employees or the more restricted your client's budget, the more proper integration of a profit-sharing plan becomes critical. However, even integration cannot change the fact that profit-sharing plans are for young participants. Projecting the integrated deposits of ¶504.3 to illustrative retirement dates of each participant we find:

Employee	Age	Pay	Balance @ 65
A	50	$ 75,000	$ 256,664
B	30	75,000	1,228,791
C	40	12,000	61,558
D	40	12,000	61,558
E	25	7,500	108,643
TOTAL		$181,500	N/A

Participant B will receive an estimated distribution at age 65 almost five times that of A. Even Employee E, earning 10% of Employee A's salary, could anticipate a retirement "pot" of 40% that of her boss. The difference simply reflects compound interest. The older key man just doesn't have time to make up for his age disadvantage.

¶505   HOW TO BEST COMPENSATE LONG-SERVICE EMPLOYEES WHEN USING PROFIT-SHARING PLANS

Rather than allocate participant deposits according to pure compensation ratios, you may employ a "unit" allocation system when using profit-sharing plans. The plan, for example, may credit participants with a nonmonetary "unit" for each $100 of compensation, and a "unit" for each year of service with the employer. An employee earning $75,000 who had been employed by your client for 10 years, therefore would receive 750 "units" for compensation and 10 "units" for service, for a total of 760 "units." A participant with $7,500 of pay and 30 years of service would have 105 "units." Plan contributions (such as 15% of payroll) are allocated according to the ratio each participant's units bear to the units of all participants. Unit allocations introduce the most rudimentary form of recognizing long-standing service.

Example: U. Knit, Incorporated establishes a unit profit-sharing plan and contributes $25,000:

Employee	Pay	% Of Total	Units For Yrs Of Service	+	Units For Pay	=	Total Units	Share of Deposit	Share As A %
A	$ 75,000	41%	30		750		780	$10,389	42%
B	75,000	41	05		750		755	10,056	40
C	12,000	7	25		120		145	1,931	8
D	12,000	7	01		120		121	1,612	6
E	7,500	4	01		75		76	1,012	4
TOTAL	$181,500	100%	62		1,815		1,877	$25,000	100%

¶505.1   Compare The Equal Pay/Unequal Service Participants in Unit Plans

The example at ¶505 generates a dramatic departure from profit-sharing allocations, whether integrated or not, based on compensation alone. By analyzing Participants A and B, or C and D, you can see the dramatic shift in compensation. Each of those employee pairs is characterized by equal pay but unequal past service. The result:

- A's allocation is 3.31% greater than B's;
- A's retirement "pot" will increase by $1,586 over a nonintegrated plan;

- C's allocation is 19.79% greater than D's; and
- C's retirement "pot" will increase by $18,814 over a nonintegrated plan.

Observation: The higher the compensation, the lower the effect of past service units. That's because past service is simply overwhelmed by compensation at high pay levels. Note that A's past service units represent only four percent of his total units, while C's represents 17%.

Planning Tip: Unit plans will have their most profound effects in companies with relatively low pay levels such as banks or manufacturing companies using a lot of relatively low-skilled labor.

¶505.2   Compare The Unit And Integrated Profit-Sharing Formats

Unit plans aren't a substitute for integrated ones. If your client's objective relates to rewarding highly paid key men, there isn't much comparison. Here's how unit and integrated plans work out, with an integration level of $15,000:

Participant	Pay	Past Service	Unit Allocation Amount	%	Integrated Allocation Amount	%
A	$ 75,000	30 years	$10,512	42%	$11,764	47%
B	50,000	10 years	6,873	27	7,493	30
C	25,000	30 years	3,774	10	3,221	13
D	15,000	30 years	2,426	10	1,512	6
E	10,000	5 years	1,415	6	1,009	4
TOTAL	$175,000	105 years	$25,000	100%	$25,000	100%

Observation: The real "winner" in the unit plan is employee D, who has relatively low pay and high past service. Employee B actually receives less than he would under a nonintegrated, salary-ratio plan.

Planning Tip: Unit profit-sharing plans may best be suited as "secondary" plans. If your client's primary plan maximizes integration opportunities, he may find the service emphasis of unit allocation systems philosophically attractive. Typically, a small business client will establish his first priority as rewarding higher paid employees, with secondary emphasis on loyal, long-standing service.

¶506   **WHEN AND WHERE TO USE PROFIT-SHARING
                            PLANS**

Although profit-sharing plans offer a very unique set of advantages, they also offer potential disadvantages. Determining which type of employer should adopt a profit-sharing plan is difficult to make. You should weigh for each client the advantages against the disadvantages.

1. Consider the advantages:

   a) *Total contribution flexibility.* The most unique and persuasive argument in favor of profit-sharing plans is that they retain complete autonomy over contribution amounts for your client. Small businesses, because of the nature of their competitive environment, simply can't always budget a specific contribution for a pension plan more than several years in advance. From this perspective, profit-sharing plans look very attractive.

   b) *Conceptual simplicity.* Don't underestimate the motivational force of a plan your client's employees can readily understand. Many defined-benefit programs are sophisticated and complex to explain. Profit-sharing plans, represented in simple terms of bank account type annual statements are readily understood and communicated. If any type of qualified plan can motivate small to medium-size business employees, it is the profit-sharing plan.

   c) *Forfeiture reallocations.* No other form of retirement plan allows those who "remain behind" to be the direct recipient of forfeitures from "those who left." The direct reallocation of forfeitures not only enhances participant account balances but also avoids irritating disruption of cash flow budgets which often results when forfeitures from other forms of plan must be used to reduce your client's tax deductible contributions.

   d) *Ease of administration.* Lacking the requirement for annual actuarial certification and Pension Benefit Guarantee Corporation supervision, a profit-sharing plan enjoys the advantage of administrative simplicity over its cousins. In small and medium-size business retirement plans, administrative costs represent a large percentage of annual contributions. To the extent your selection of an administratively simple plan can reduce those costs, your client and his employee-participants will benefit.

2. Then consider the disadvantages—would the minuses outweigh the pluses:

   a) *Contribution—orientation toward younger employees.* Profit-sharing plans, and all defined-contributions plans, inherently favor younger employees. Frequently, smaller businesses involve key men older than the average. Even with effective use of integration, profit-sharing plans can never even approach defined-benefit programs in terms of their ability to skew contributions toward older key men. That may be a fatal flaw for some of your clients.

b) *Fifteen percent deduction limitation.* Small business clients that have matured to the point of considering a qualified plan frequently wish to "make up for lost time" for key employees. That objective often requries a contribution greater than 15% of payroll. In those situations, a profit-sharing plan, for all its advantages, may simply not provide enough "bang" for the key men.

c) *Corollary effect on other employer-sponsored plans—25% deduction limitation.* If a profit-sharing plan is used in conjunction with another qualified plan, then the aggregate deduction claimed for both plans can't exceed 25% of payroll. Thus, if your client is concerned about providing big deductions or benefits for older key men and establishes a defined-benefit plan, he probably can't use a profit-sharing plan.

Given these facts about profit-sharing plans, you must select with care the "right" clients. Here are a few situations for which profit-sharing plans are recommended.

Businesses With Young Key Men Derive The Greatest Benefit

Young, high-paid executives of small businesses, particularly high turnover businesses, can achieve staggering results from profit-sharing plans. Every advantage benefits them, because they:

- have more time for compound interest;
- will receive proportionately more forfeitures, both because of their higher pay (forfeitures are allocated with contributions) and longer future service (more service means more opportunities for recapture); and
- will have more contributions made to their acount.

The most ideal candidate for a profit-sharing plan would have:

- a small, centralized management of young, high-paid key men;
- a large, low-paid labor force; and

- a high turnover rate among the labor force.

If your client fits this mold, profit-sharing plans will be attractive.

Businesses With Surplus Cash Should Consider Profit-Sharing Plans

Most types of pension plans, in fact, all, must use forfeited employee account values or accrued benefits to reduce employer contributions to the plan. Therefore, your clients with heavy turnover may find their hope for substantial and consistent tax deductions diminished, offsetting a substantial part of their plan's value. Profit-sharing plans can reallocate forfeitures to remaining participants and, therefore, preserve the tax deduction.

Businesses With Substantial Accumulated Profits Can Recover Some Taxes

Profit-sharing contributions can come from current or accumulated profits. Therefore, if your client effectively "zeroes out" his income in a given tax year and yet still makes a contribution to his profit-sharing plan from accumulated profits, he will create a net operating loss which may be carried back or forward to other tax years, thereby "unlocking" dollars otherwise lost. This net operating loss, when so carried back or forward, may very well allow the business's accountant to open up prior or future years' tax returns to save taxes. This possibility is particularly valuable to your small business clients, the bane of whose existence is taxation.

Caveat: All Pension Plans create the opportunity for generating operating losses. However, only profit-sharing plans give your client control—control inherent in his ability to say when and to what extent contributions will be made.

> *Example:* In 1978, Upandown Company, with a payroll of $200,000, has a taxable income of $40,000. Upandown makes the maximum profit-sharing contribution (15% of $200,000 = $30,000) and still has taxable corporate income of $10,000, on which it pays close to $2,000 in federal and state income taxes. In 1979, with the same payroll, Upandown has a profit of only $20,000. Making a 10% of pay contribution ($20,000) would wipe out any tax liability for 1979, however, Upandown makes a $30,000 deposit and, therefore, creates a net operating loss for the year of $10,000. It carries this loss back to 1978 and, as a result, recovers the $2,000 it had paid in income taxes.

Businesses That Are Growing Or Have Substantially Fluctuating Profits Can Protect Themselves

Businesses without a "track record" or businesses whose track record indicates substantial profit volatility often can't make a fixed commitment to a qualified plan, despite their attractive tax effects. Discretion over timing and amounts of profit-sharing contributions eliminates the commitment that might be too heavy an ongoing cash flow burden for a struggling or volatile company.

Even in a year of substantial profit, business conditions sometimes dictate retention of working capital, notwithstanding the attendant expense of taxation. The consensus of the accounting community is probably well-advised on this particular matter, and it may serve to offset all of the disadvantages otherwise inherent in the profit-sharing variety of plans.

¶507   SUMMARIZING THE RANGE OF OPPORTUNITIES

Thus the plan noted for its simplicity and lack of sophistication can actually become quite a manipulative tool. While inherently favoring younger employees, profit-sharing plans offer broad allocation method choices to encompass a wide range of client objectives. That range, coupled with the discretion to determine contributions on an annual basis, should weigh heavily in favor of profit-sharing plans as the first choice of most closely-held businesses.

6

How Money-Purchase Plans Increase Creative Design Opportunities

Money-purchase plans are the most direct personification of the term "defined-contribution" plan. In money-purchase plans, the employer contribution is fixed as a percent of eligible payroll. Thus, money-purchase plans add an additional element to profit-sharing plans. In addition to defining the manner in which allocations are made, the amount of contribution is also defined.

Chapter Six will show you how, when and where to use money-purchase plans. Furthermore, you will see the pitfalls you should avoid in your planning with clients.

Money-purchase plans are the simplest type of pension plan, both operationally and conceptually. They create substantially larger tax deductible potential than profit-sharing plans and often more than a small business can afford. Like profit-sharing plans, money-purchase plans are powerful accumulation vehicles for young, high paid employees. Finally, the combination of money-purchase with profit-sharing plans may provide the ideal "mix" of flexibility and tax deductability for small to medium size businesses.

¶600 KEY SIMILIARITIES BETWEEN MONEY-PURCHASE AND PROFIT-SHARING PLANS

Money-purchase plans offer substantial creative planning opportunities. To realize these opportunities you must build on the knowledge of how profit-sharing plans work. Then you can capitalize on the major differences between money-purchase and profit-sharing plans to establish your planning strategy. Here are the essential similarities.

¶600.1   The Accounting Is Simple

Like profit-sharing plans, money-purchase plans use **account balances** to form the basis of each participant's benefits. Each year, a participant's account balance will be credited with employer contributions and credited (or charged) with a pro rata share of earnings (or losses).

> *Example:* A earns $70,000 while B earns $30,000. A and B establish a money-purchase plan and contribute $10,000 (10% of total pay). An initial *account balance* is established for A in the amount of $7,000, and for B in the amount of $3,000. During the first year the plan's assets earn $1,000 interest. Since A's account balance represents 70% of the total, A receives 70% of the income ($700). B receives the balance ($300).

Every year, the account balances are updated to reflect further contributions (which are generally allocated by reference to compensation and service) and earnings (which are generally allocated according to proportionate account balances). When a participant terminates, whether by reason of death, disability or retirement, his benefit will be related to this account balance. There is no way to predict the exact value of a participant's share, since investment results will ultimately be such a large component of the account.

¶600.2   Simplicity Is Its Own Reward

As with profit-sharing plans, the simple account balance system used in money-purchase plans to measure participant benefits makes for easy employee communications. This enhances employee appreciation of the value of the plan. Employees will recognize a money-purchase benefit as something similar to a bank book to which the employer makes contributions and periodically credits interest.

Planning Tip: If you are implementing a plan because of employee pressure, don't overlook the value of simplicity inherent in money-purchase plans. Don't expect employees to appreciate something they can't understand.

¶600.3   How Money-Purchase Plans Favor Younger Employees

Specific retirement benefits are not promised under either profit-sharing or money-purchase plans. Periodic contributions are simply added to employee accounts. Very often young employees, even those earning relatively small amounts, will have higher projected retirement benefits than older, higher paid employees. It is a fact of life that defined-contribution plans favor most heavily the younger employees, for whom compound interest and a greater number of contributions will simply add up to a larger "pot" at retirement age.

> *Example:* XYZ, Incorporated contributes 10% of pay to its participating employees and earns eight percent interest on account balances. At first glance, nothing could be more fair. But consider the results.

Participant	Age	Compensation	Annual Contribution	Account Balance At Age 65
A	55	$ 50,000	$ 5,000	$ 78,227
B	40	50,000	5,000	394,772
C	25	15,000	1,500	419,672
TOTAL		$115,000	$11,500	

Planning Tip: Money-purchase plans, like profit-sharing plans, favor young employees over a period of time. Make sure your clients understand this fact. Upon considering it, many clients will opt for a program which gives older employees an opportunity to "catch-up" under a plan formula recognizing age.

¶600.4   How Simplicity Will Conserve Your Time And Benefit Your Clients

Pension plans of any type are inherently "good" things:

1. They provide tax deductible contributions;

2. Fund earnings are tax free; and

3. Certain distributions are accorded favorable tax treatment.

Often it is tempting, in an effort to orient the plan a little more heavily toward one or two key men, to use more esoteric plan designs. If a money-purchase or profit-sharing plan comes close to fulfilling the objectives set out by your client, use them. Better to use a plan everyone understands and for which ERISA reporting and disclosure requirements are less onerous, than to create a future "time liability" often associated with more complicated plans. The time you might have to spend explaining a more complicated plan again and again may not be justified by a marginal improvement in plan efficiency.

¶601   KEY DIFFERENCES BETWEEN MONEY-PURCHASE AND PROFIT-SHARING PLANS

Most similarities between money-purchase and profit-sharing plans are cosmetic—for instance, accounting and communication techniques. Many practitioners "piggyback" money-purchase plans as secondary programs on top of existing profit-sharing plans, thinking that the money-purchase plan is merely an extension of the profit-sharing vehicle. Don't be lulled into this feeling of complacency. The differences between money-purchase and profit-sharing plans are far more substantive. Use the differences to your advantage. Don't be trapped by them.

¶601.1   A Fixed Contribution May Frighten Your Clients

Money-purchase plans *are* subject to ERISA's minimum funding standards. Once your client adopts a money-purchase plan he has a fixed, measurable, ongoing contribution commitment notwithstanding fluctuations in his business. This inflexibility can limit your client's options for cash flow management and be quite troublesome in times of recession or rapid growth when cash may be in short supply.

> *Example:* Company A adopts a profit-sharing plan. Company B adopts a money-purchase plan. Each contributes $25,000 in the first plan year. In year 2 each wishes to buy a piece of machinery which, because of investment tax credits and depreciation, will have a comparable tax effect to a $25,000 pension or profit-sharing plan contribution. Each company feels that purchase of the machinery will make it more competitive and profitable in the future. Company A skips its profit-sharing contribution and uses the cash towards purchase of the machine. Company B *must* contribute again to its money-purchase plan, and find other capital sources for the machine.

Guideline: Money-purchase plans, because of their contribution requirements, are better for *mature* businesses whose expansion rate has slowed, or service-type businesses whose cash flow is extremely stable and for whom there is no particular need for internal cash generation. Generally, labor-intensive businesses or professional organizations will make the best prospects. Manufacturing companies usually ought to stay clear of money-purchase plans.

Planning Tip: Many defined-benefit plans discussed in later chapters offer more contribution flexibility than money-purchase plans. Their greater complexity may be offset by their ability to keep your client's options open.

What To Do: Make sure your client doesn't adopt a money-purchase plan solely because of one or two highly profitable years. Discuss the contribution requirement and insure that for the forseeable future adequate *surplus* cash will be available to fund the plan.

¶601.2   How The Larger Contribution Limits Of Money-Purchase Plans Can Help Minimize Your Client's Taxes

Profit-sharing contributions are limited to 15% of covered payroll; money-purchase plans, 25%. For the client whose salary is sufficient to meet his own personal needs and yet whose business still has surplus cash, this extra 10% deduction may make a big difference.

> *Example:* Doctor Z's practice nets $130,000 after expenses. Assuming income not sheltered by a qualified plan will ultimately be taxed at 50%, the 15% deduction limit available under profit-sharing plans ($19,500) is worth $9,750 per year in tax savings. The 25% ($32,500) money-purchase deduction is worth $16,250 in tax savings. The additional $6,500 tax savings available with the money-purchase plan, compounded at eight percent interest for 20 years, has a future value of $321,249. Therefore, if the cash is available, big tax savings await.

¶601.3   Avoiding Cash Flow Disruption Under Money-Purchase Plans

When a nonvested participant leaves a profit-sharing plan, the portion of the account balance he forfeits is reallocated to remaining participants. Not so with money-purchase plans. Forfeited account balances must be used to reduce future employer contributions. This distinction between the use of forfeitures in profit-sharing and money-purchase plans is the most substantive difference between the two types. It highlights a potential problem with money-purchase plans. If your client adopts a money-purchase plan for the right reasons—stable, mature cash flow coupled with the desire for a bigger tax break—he may be displeased by the disruptive effect of forfeitures.

Example: ABC Company has a profit-sharing plan. DEF, Incorporated has a money-purchase plan. Both have four participants in their plan, each of whom has a nonvested $25,000 account balance at the beginning of the plan year. Each company regularly contributes $40,000 per year to its plan. Consider the effects on the company's tax planning if one participant terminates under ABC or DEF's plans:

		Profit-Sharing ABC Company		Money-Purchase DEF, Inc.
Beginning Account Balances (4 employees)		100,000		100,000
Total Contribution	40,000		40,000	
Less: Forfeitures Applied	N/A		(25,000)	
Net Tax Deductible Contribution		40,000		15,000
Ending Account Balances		140,000		115,000

While the three remaining participants under each plan fare identically in terms of contributions, the effect on ABC and DEF is dramatically different. DEF loses in two ways. First, it must send an additional $12,500 to Washington. Second, it now has surplus cash on hand that it had planned to put into the money-purchase plan.

Planning Tips: (1) Unless it's unavoidable, use money-purchase plans only in conjunction with profit-sharing plans. The flexible contribution possibilities of profit-sharing plans will cushion the otherwise disruptive cash flow aspects of money-purchase plans. For instance, in a year where forfeitures would otherwise reduce your client's contribution under a money-purchase plan you could boost the profit-sharing plan deposit to achieve tax and cash continuity.

(2) Use the most restrictive eligibility requirements possible when you implement money-purchase plans. Try to eliminate your sources of turnover before they come into the plan.

¶601.4   Why High Turnover Companies Should Think Twice About Money-Purchase Plans

High turnover companies, like restaurants, should think twice about money-purchase plans, and then think again. For this type of client, money-purchase plans won't stack up too well against the competition. There are two good reasons.

Turnover leads to forfeitures and forfeitures lead to disruption of cash and tax planning. The inherent instability of money-purchase contributions is particularly acute in high turnover companies. The cumulative effect of tax savings lost because of forfeitures can be quite substantial.

Furthermore, the level of turnover will most directly affect longstanding key employees—the very group most plans are designed to help. That's because forfeitures, which under a profit-sharing plan would effectively be *added* to employer contributions. In money-purchase plans, they are simply a *part* of the contribution. Over a period of time the results are very dramatic.   .

Example: Profit, Incorporated has a profit-sharing plan. Money, Ltd. has a money-purchase plan. Each wants to make a $25,000 per year addition to the plan. Each plan has annual forfeitures equal to 10% of the fund balance and an eight percent rate of return. Look what happens:

Figure 6.1

	Profit, Inc. Profit-Sharing		Money, Ltd. Money-Purchase	
YEAR ONE				
Beginning Employee Balances		100,000		100,000
Gross Annual Addition	25,000		25,000	
Less: Forfeitures Applied	(10,000)		N/A	
Net Employer Deduction		15,000		25,000
Annual Fund Earnings		8,000		8,000
Ending Employee Balances		123,000		133,000
YEAR TWO				
Gross Annual Addition	25,000		25,000	
Less: Forfeitures Applied	(12,300)		N/A	
Net Employer Deduction		12,700		25,000
Annual Fund Earnings		9,840		10,640
Ending Employee Balances		145,540		168,640
Ending Balance, Year 5		210,491		293,598
Ending Balance, Year 10		310,366		578,057

---

*Note, very importantly, that if the employer's payroll does not increase as quickly as his fund earnings and turnover, then eventually forfeitures will exceed his annual $25,000 addition objective, and he will not get any tax deduction.

**Clearly, the higher the turnover, the more persuasive the arguments for a profit-sharing plan.

Observation: Try not to use money-purchase plans unless:

- You absolutely need the larger tax deduction, and even then only if:
- none of the defined-benefit plans discussed in later chapters will achieve your client's objectives; or
- you are using the money-purchase plan in conjunction with a profit-sharing plan

Planning Tip: Try not to use insurance, other illiquid or front-end loaded products in *any* high turnover situation, but particularly money-purchase plans where relative allocations for young employees (the group most subject to turnover) will be high. If such products are attractive from other perspectives, use them only for participants who have completed some specified period of service. For instance, fund an insured death benefit with term insurance for the first five years of an employee's participation and *only then* to switch to whole life.

¶602   HOW TO USE MONEY-PURCHASE PLANS EFFECTIVELY

Notwithstanding their inherent limitations, money-purchase plans offer practitioners substantially increased design flexibility. Maximum effectiveness will occur if you follow these steps:

Eliminate those clients for whom the inherent drawbacks of money-purchase plans will be most acute:

- High turnover companies
- Plans with small contributions: The combination of reporting and disclosure costs and cash flow disruption occasioned by forfeitures will likely destroy the efficiency of the plan as a tax or cash management system
- Companies with older key employees: Remember, money-purchase plans virtually always favor younger employees. If your

goal is a big contribution for older key men, scrap your plans for a money-purchase plan.

Plan—Set your objectives in advance relative to:

- probable budget
- need for flexibility
- desired orientation of plan toward key individuals

Study the options following to see whether a particular money-purchase plan can achieve your goals within the budget parameters.

¶603   USING EFFECTIVE COMBINATIONS OF MONEY-PURCHASE AND PROFIT-SHARING PLANS

Generally money-purcahse plans are used in conjunction with profit-sharing plans by clients desiring deductions in excess of 15%. These combination plans can be effective for a variety of reasons:

- bigger deduction;
- simplicity; or
- more orientation toward key men.

Here's how to use combination plans to provide the best of both worlds.

¶603.1   How To Get A Big Tax Deduction With Maximum Flexibility

The flexibility of a profit-sharing plan combined with the *larger tax deduction* under money-purchase plans may work well for your clients. Consider the adoption of a 10% of pay money-purchase plan and a variable contribution profit-sharing plan. The minimum required employer contribution would be 10% of payroll (less any forfeitures). The maximum tax deduction would be 25% of payroll (taking full advantage of the profit-sharing plan). Consider the effect on sample company, Flexible, Incorporated, which has wide variations in its profitability.

Figure 6.2: Minimum And Maximum Contributions Under Tandem Plan For Flexible, Incorporated

FLEXIBLE, INC.—MINIMUM CONTRIBUTION

Participant	Compensation	Profit-Sharing Deposit	+	Money-Purchase Deposit	=	Total Minimum Deposit
A	50,000	0		5,000		5,000
B	25,000	0		2,500		2,500
C	15,000	0		1,500		1,500
D	10,000	0		1,000		1,000
TOTAL	100,000			10,000		10,000

FLEXIBLE, INC.—MAXIMUM CONTRIBUTION

Participant	Compensation	Profit-Sharing Deposit	+	Money-Purchase Deposit	=	Total Maximum Deposit
A	50,000	7,500		5,000		12,500
B	25,000	3,750		2,500		6,250
C	15,000	2,250		1,500		3,750
D	10,000	1,500		1,000		2,500
TOTAL	100,000	15,000		10,000		25,000

The wide choice may be very valuable to your client.

Consider also how a tandem plan can overcome the problem caused by money-purchase forfeitures. If your client desires a constant tax deduction of 20% of payroll he might be tempted simply to implement a 20% of pay money-purchase plan. However, in a year of large forfeitures this tax planning may go awry. If, however, he established a 10% money-purchase plan in conjunction with a variable profit-sharing plan, he could simply vary the profit-sharing contribution up or down to reflect forfeitures which would otherwise limit his money-purchase tax deduction.

Example: Pennywise, Incorporated and Poundfoolish, Ltd. want to deduct 20% of covered payroll each year. Pennywise implements a 10% money-purchase and variable profit-sharing plan. Poundfoolish, Ltd. tries to save money by setting up a 20% money-purchase plan. Each has $100,000 covered payroll, and widely variable turnover. Consider the effects over a period of years:

Figure 6.3

	Poundfoolish, Ltd.	Pennywise, Inc.—Tandem Plans		
	Money-Purchase	Money-Purchase	Profit-Sharing	Total
Assumed Starting Balance	25,000	10,000	15,000	25,000
Total 1979 Allocation	20,000	10,000	11,000	21,000
Less: Forfeitures Applied (10%)	(2,500)	(1,000)	N/A	(1,000)
Net Tax Deductible Contribution	17,500	9,000	11,000	20,000
1979 Fund Earnings (8%)	2,000	800	1,200	2,000
Ending 1979 Balance	44,500	19,800	27,200	47,000
Total 1980 Allocation	20,000	10,000	10,000	20,000
Less: Forfeitures Applied (0%)	0	0	N/A	0
Net Tax Deductible Contribution	20,000	10,000	10,000	20,000
1980 Fund Earnings (8%)	3,560	1,584	2,176	3,760
Ending 1980 Balance	68,060	31,384	39,376	70,760
Total 1981 Allocation	20,000	10,000	13,138	23,138
Less: Forfeitures Applied (10%)	(6,806)	(3,183)	N/A	(3,138)
Net Tax Deductible Contribution	13,194	6,862	13,138	20,000
1981 Fund Earnings (8%)	5,445	2,511	3,150	5,661
Ending 1981 Balance	86,699	40,757	55,664	96,421

Pennywise, Incorporated has achieved several important objectives:

- it has maintained a 20% of payroll per year tax deduction, and therefore, saved significant *income taxes;*
- it has managed its *cash flow* more efficiently, with a common dollar outlay each year;
- the employees in Pennywise, Incorporated have substantially *more assets* in their accounts.

Furthermore, there may be years in which Pennywise or Poundfoolish wishes to contribute *more* than 20% of payroll. Poundfoolish will be out of luck unless he adopts a profit-sharing plan at that point. Even then the profit-sharing plan would not particularly enhance his flexibility, being limited in a normal year to five percent of payroll. It would seem then that everybody gains except the government when a tandem plan is utilized.

¶603.2   How "Piggyback" Plans Retain Simplicity And Hold Down Costs

Tandem money-purchase and profit-sharing plans are much simpler to explain to employees than defined-benefit plans. To the extent motivation of employee-participants was an objective to be achieved by the plans, simplicity is important. Even though the benefits under a defined-benefit approach might be more substantial, employees may prefer a plan they can readily understand.

Apart from improved employee public relations in some respects tandem plans can actually *reduce* employer maintenance costs as compared to other plan alternatives. First, more complicated alternatives, by generating more questions, will necessarily involve a greater amount of your clients' time, if only to respond. Further, neither profit-sharing nor money-purchase plans require actuarial certification and, therefore, enjoy one cost advantage over defined-benefit plans.

Finally, there is somewhat less pressure for stability in the value of plan assets with defined-contribution plans than defined-benefit plans. Participants in defined-contribution plans are guaranteed no specific benefits. Their retirement income will simply reflect an account balance to which periodic gains and losses are attributed. Defined-benefit plans, on the other hand, promise specific retirement benefits. Actuaries must periodically certify that plan investment performance appears adequate to meet such future liability. To the extent periodic asset fluctuation occurs, situations may arise in which the actuary will require a larger or smaller annual deposit.

Planning Tip: If a defined-contribution plan appears to fit the bill, start with a profit-sharing plan. Use a money-purchase plan primarily as an adjunct to the profit-sharing program.

¶603.3   Who Scores Big Gains With Tandem Plans?

Before considering specific types of money-purchase plan formulas it is important to restate who wins and loses when tandem plans are utilized. The employer achieves the following:

- he retains control over cash flow;
- he retains control over tax planning; and
- he maintains an administratively simple and highly motivating plan format.

Employees win too.

- forfeitures stay where they should in accounts of long-term employees;
- to the extent forfeitures occur employees will actually receive allocations in excess of amounts contributed by the employer; and
- since the size of profit-sharing contributions will be somewhat dependent upon overall business profitability, the employee may recognize that his efforts enhance his position.

The only loser appears to be Washington!

- it loses revenue because of larger tax deductions;
- it loses revenue to the extent forfeitures under tandem plans are reallocated to participants as opposed to reducing the employer's tax deduction; and
- it loses revenue on income earned by the more substantial trust fund balance available with tandem plans.

¶603.4   Don't Overlook These Drawbacks

With the possibilities of tandem plans come some drawbacks. Make sure you tell your clients in advance so as to avoid a potential for misunderstanding.

Watch Out For Costs: Two plans of *any* type double your clients costs *both* for determination letters *and* for annual reporting and disclosure. Your client could easily face an initial qualification bill of $2,000–$3,000, plus recurring administrative costs of $500–$900.

Planning Tip: Unless it appears certain your client will need the full 25% tax deduction, start him off just with a profit-sharing plan. Consider a second plan only when the first plan has thoroughly proven its value and the need for additional tax deduction has been clearly established.

Confusion May Reign: Even though profit-sharing and money-purchase plans are quite similar and conceptually simple, they are different. This dissimilarity may in some instances breed confusion which could lower the motivational value of the plans.

Planning Tip: Consider using a single Summary Plan Description to emphasize the commonality of the plans. Accent the size of employer contributions as opposed to the more complicated subject of forfeitures.

Limitation On Annual Additions—A Trap For The Unwary

Don't forget that in 1980 no more than $36,875 or (25% of compensation) may be added to a participant's account for *all* defined-contribution plans in any one limitation year. Reallocated forfeitures under profit-sharing plans *are included* in the definition of annual additions. Particularly in an integrated plan, your client must be careful that none of his high paid participants exceed this maximum annual addition.

> *Example:* XYZ, Incorporated implements, in Year 1, a 10% money-purchase and variable profit-sharing plan and contributes the full 15% under the profit-sharing plan. In Year 2, forfeitures of $3,000 in the profit-sharing and $2,000 in the pension plans occur. XYZ, Incorporated tries to offset the reduced tax deduction occasioned by the forfeiture in the money-purchase plan by increasing the contribution to the profit-sharing plan. If either plan is integrated, that won't work. Here's why (integration level of profit-sharing is $15,000):

Employee:	Employee A	Employee B	Employee C	Total
Compensation	$50,000	$15,000	$10,000	$75,000
I. Profit-Sharing (15%)				
a. Share of Contribution	8,317	1,760	1,173	11,250
b. Reallocated Forfeitures	2,218	469	313	3,000
c. Total Addition	10,535	2,229	1,486	14,250
II. Money-Purchase (10%)				
a. Employer Contribution	3,667	1,100	733	5,500
b. Plus Forfeitures	1,333	400	267	2,000
c. Total Addition	5,000	1,500	1,000	7,500
III. Total Allocations				
(c + f)	15,535	3,729	2,486	21,750
IV. Allocations As A				
Percent of Pay	31%	25%	25%	29%

Since, through the combination of forfeiture-reallocation and integration, plan efficiency has been boosted, Employee A receives a combined addition greater than the 25% limitation. The excess will have to be held in a suspense account.

What To Do: Use the simple formula appearing at paragraph 604.4 to find the "best" contribution to maximize benefits for your clients' key men.

¶604   HOW TO INCREASE PLAN EFFICIENCY USING INTEGRATED MONEY-PURCHASE PLANS

Like profit-sharing plans, money-purchase plans are integrated with Social Security by reference to the percentage the employer must contribute to the government system. Basically, the employer chooses an "integration level" and contributes different amounts to his money-purchase plan for employee compensation above and below this integration level. The rate of deposit for compensation above the integration level cannot exceed the rate applied to compensation below the integration level by more than seven percent.

Example: XY, Incorporated establishes a money-purchase plan to which it contributes 10% of pay below the integration level and 16% above. The plan qualifies since the "spread" for pay above and below the integration level does not exceed seven percent. If XY,

Incorporated had established a plan calling for contributions of 15% of pay up to the integration level and 23% for the excess, the plan would not have qualified. The spread, eight percent, exceeds the allowable amount.

Proper use of integration can dramatically boost plan efficiency. Many employers, however, balk at providing a somewhat lower level of benefits (contributions) to lower-paid employees, almost all of whose pay generally is below the integration level. But *not* integrating a plan would really be unfair. High paid employees are only *partially* covered by Social Security. Without the catch-up opportunity afforded by integration low paid employees would reap the most substantial benefits from a money-purchase plan. They would receive Social Security contributions on virtually all of their salaries *and* a full allocation under the money-purchase plan. High paid employees would receive only partial Social Security contributions (for 1980, only on compensation up to $25,900) plus a regular money-purchase contribution. Remember, the purpose of integration is to allow employers to provide *uniform,* continuous coverage for employees across the entire spectrum of compensation.

¶604.1   Choosing The Right Integration Level

There is quite a variety of possible integration levels. Key questions will help you choose the right one.

- Does your client wish to maximize the percentage of his contribution allocated to high paid employees?
- Does your client think there will continue to be substantial wage inflation?
- Does your client have a specific dollar amount of annual contribution in mind, or is he willing to "let the chips fall where they may" with a particular plan formula?

The answers to those key questions will make selecting one of the following integration approaches easier.

¶604.2   A Flat Dollar Amount May Fit Your Client's Needs
Perfectly

The integration level in a money-purchase plan may be any dollar amount up to the taxable wage base effective during that plan year. Thus, for plan years ending in 1980, a flat dollar integration level of $25,900 could be applied uniformly to all participating employee compensation under a money-purchase plan. Generally speaking, however, employers use a somewhat lower flat dollar amount, chosen to fit the character of the employer's payroll more exactly. For instance, if the employer has three employees earning $12,000 or less, and one key man earning $50,000, he would be far better off using $12,000 as his integration level than $25,900.

> **Example:** Wasteful, Incorporated and Frugal Company each wish to spend $10,000 on a money-purchase plan. Wasteful, Incorporated uses an integration level of $22,900; Frugal Company $12,000. Consider carefully the annual and cumulative effect of their decisions (assuming continuity of the plan and eight percent fund earnings):

Figure 6.4 (a)

WASTEFUL, INC.: $10,000 WITH $22,900 INTEGRATION LEVEL

Employee	Pay	Excess Pay	7% Excess Allocation	+	Regular Allocation	=	Total Allocation	Total Allocation As A %	Account After 20 Years
A	50,000	27,100	1,897		5,065		6,961	70%	344,033
B	12,000	0	0		1,215		1,215	12%	60,049
C	10,000	0	0		1,013		1,013	10%	50,065
D	8,000	0	0		810		810	8%	40,033
TOTAL	80,000	27,100	1,897		8,103		10,000	100%	

FRUGAL COMPANY: $10,000 WITH $12,000 INTEGRATION LEVEL

Employee	Pay	Excess Pay	7% Excess Allocation	+	Regular Allocation	=	Total Allocation	Total Allocation As A %	Account After 20 Years
A	50,000	38,000	2,660		4,588		7,248	73%	358,217
B	12,000	0	0		1,101		1,101	11%	54,415
C	10,000	0	0		918		918	9%	45,370
D	8,000	0	0		734		734	7%	36,276
TOTAL	80,000	38,000	2,660		7,340		10,000	100%	

Properly chosen, flat dollar amount integration levels can be very effective. They are readily explainable, ostensibly fair, and easily administered.

Planning Tip: Flat dollar amounts would almost always be preferred in situations where higher paid key men are, on the average, younger than most other employees. That's because the other option for integrating money-purchase plans discussed later—covered compensation tables—generate high integration levels for young employees and low integration levels for older employees. Always check to see where your key employees sit on the age continuum. (For Covered Compensation Tables, see Chapter 3, paragraph 302.2)

But Watch Out: If you permanently fix your integration level, inflation may do you in. If we assume merely a four percent wage inflation look what happens to Frugal Company's cleverly designed plan after 20 years. Note that the $10,000 plan contribution has also been adjusted to reflect inflation.

Figure 6.4 (b)

WASTEFUL, INC. AFTER 20 YEARS WAGE INFLATION
(INTEGRATION AT $22,900)

Employee	20 Yr. Projected Pay	Excess Pay	7% Excess Allocation +	Regular Allocation =	Total Allocation	Total Allocation As A %
A	$109,556	86,656	6,066	9,754	15,820	72%
B	26,293	3,393	238	2,341	2,579	12%
C	21,911	0	0	1,951	1,951	9%
C	17,529	0	0	1,561	1,561	7%
TOTAL	175,289	90,049	6,304	15,607	21,911	100%

FRUGAL COMPANY AFTER 20 YEARS WAGE INFLATION
(INTEGRATION AT $12,000)

A	109,556	97,556	6,829	8,125	14,945	68%
B	26,293	14,293	1,001	1,950	2,951	13%
C	21,911	9,911	694	1,625	2,319	11%
D	17,529	5,529	387	1,300	1,687	8%
TOTAL	175,289	127,289	8,911	13,000	21,911	100%

Clearly the plan has lost a lot of its efficiency, reflected by the lower percent of deposit for Employee A.

The Solution—Use a "Floating Integration Level"

Consider trying your plan's integration level to some published wage statistic. For instance, your plan might automatically provide that the integration level would be the taxable wage base effective for a particular plan year. Or, you might use a lower flat dollar amount pegged to increase (or decrease) at the same rate as the taxable wage base. This should help stop erosion of your plan's efficiency.

¶604.3   Capitalizing On Covered Compensation

Usually, key employees are *older* than the average age of the participants. If that's the case with your plan, covered compensation tables may provide the right integration level for you. Oversimplified, covered compensation tables provide nothing more than the average of taxable wage bases to which an employee might have been subject during his working life. For instance, an employee who will turn 65 in 1980 would have covered compensation (Table 2, 1978) of $9,156. On the other hand, an employee who will turn 65 in the year 2010 has an estimated covered compensation of $17,484. It's readily apparent that the greater the spread between ages of key and regular employees the greater the opportunity for efficiency through the use of covered compensation tables. (For Covered Compensation Tables, see Chapter 3, paragraph 302.2)

> *Example:* XYZ, Incorporated and ABC Company each establish money-purchase plans with $20,000 contributions. XYZ uses a flat $12,000 integration level; ABC, 1978 covered compensation. Consider the annual and cumulative effect of their decisions.

Figure 6.5

XYZ, INC.—$12,000 FLAT INTEGRATION LEVEL

Employee	Age	Pay	Integration Level	Excess Pay	7% Excess Allocation	+ Regular Allocation	= Total Allocation	Total Allocation As A %	Account After 20 Years
A	55	$ 50,000	12,000	38,000	2,660	8,110	10,770	54%	532,285
B	45	20,000	12,000	8,000	560	3,244	3,804	19%	188,005
C	30	20,000	12,000	8,000	560	3,244	3,804	19%	188,005
D	25	10,000	12,000	0	0	1,622	1,622	8%	80,164
TOTAL		$100,000		54,000	3,780	16,220	20,000	100%	

ABC, COMPANY—COVERED COMPENSATION

Employee	Age	Pay	Integration Level	Excess Pay	7% Excess Allocation	+ Regular Allocation	= Total Allocation	Total Allocation As A %	Account After 20 Years
A	55	50,000	11,712	38,288	2,680	8,384	11,064	55%	546,815
B	45	20,000	14,412	5,588	391	3,354	3,745	19%	185,069
C	30	20,000	17,700	2,300	161	3,354	3,515	18%	173,322
D	25	10,000	17,700	0	0	1,676	1,676	8%	82,833
TOTAL		100,000		46,176	3,232	16,768	20,000	100%	

¶604.4   Maximizing Integration For Key Men

Frequently employers approach pension plans not from the perspective of a formula but rather a contribution. For instance, your client may know he wants to spend $15,000 on a money-purchase plan, but may have no idea of how that dollar amount translates to a formula. A simple method of determining the "most effective" contribution rate to achieve your client's funding objective is provided by the following formula, solved for R:

$$C = R \times T + .07E$$

Where: C = The Employer's Desired Deposit
          R = Contribution Rate Applied to Total Pay
          T = Total Payroll
          E = Excess Payroll (Above Integration Level)

The formula works equally well for flat dollar and covered compensation integration levels. See page 121 for an illustration for a business, trying to decide whether to spend $20,000 on a plan with a flat dollar or covered compensation integration level. The objective is to maximize plan efficiency for Employee A.

Figure 6.6

			$15,000 FLAT INTEGRATION LEVEL		1978 COVERED COMPENSATION	
Employee	Age	Pay	Integration Level	Excess Pay	Integration Level	Excess Pay
A	55	75,000	15,000	60,000	11,712	63,288
B	40	35,000	15,000	20,000	12,564	22,436
C	30	30,000	15,000	15,000	17,700	12,300
D	25	10,000	15,000	0	17,700	0
TOTAL		150,000		95,000		98,024

$$C = R \times T + .07 \times E$$
$$\$20,000 = R \times \$150,000 + .07 \times \$95,000$$
$$\$20,000 = \$150,000R + \$6,650$$
$$\$13,350 = \$150,000R$$
$$.089 = R$$

$$C = R \times T + .07 \times E$$

$$\$20,000 = R \times \$150,000 + .07 \times \$98,024$$

$$\$20,000 = \$150,000 + 6,862$$

$$\$13,138 = \$150,000R$$

$$.0875 = R$$

	$15,000 FLAT INTEGRATION LEVEL				1978 COVERED COMPENSATION			
Employee	Excess Pay x 7%	Total Pay x 8.9%	Total Allocation	% Of Total	Excess Pay x 7%	Total Pay x 8.75%	Total Allocation	% Of Total
A	4,200	6,675	10,875	54%	4,430	6,563	10,993	55%
B	1,400	3,115	4,515	23%	1,571	3,063	4,634	23%
C	1,050	2,670	3,720	19%	861	2,625	3,486	17%
D	0	890	890	4%	0	875	875	5%
TOTAL	6,650	13,350	20,000	100%	6,862	13,126	19,988	100%

Note that the calculation confirms our earlier conclusion that covered compensation provides a more efficient integration level than a flat dollar amount.

¶604.5   Higher Flat Dollar Amount Integration Levels

Sometimes it may be desirable to use a flat dollar integration level higher than the taxable wage base. That's okay *as long as* you reduce the "spread" on benefits above and below the integration level. The reduction is achieved by applying the following formula.

$$\frac{\text{Maximum Integration Level}}{\text{Integration Level Actually Used}} \times \text{Maximum Integration Level}$$

Example: Smith, Incorporated is a sales organization with several high-paid employees. Smith wishes to establish a money-purchase plan integrated at $30,000. The maximum "spread" is calculated as follows:

$$\frac{\$25,900 \text{ (Max. Integration Level for 1979)}}{\$30,000 \text{ (Desired Integration Level)}} \times .07 = 6.043\%$$

Thus, Smith can use a $30,000 integration level as long as the maximum "spread" is nor more than 6.043%. Let's see what they've achieved by comparing their allocation of $10,000 with that of Jones, Inc.'s, whose plan uses $25,900 as its integration level:

Figure 6.7

SMITH, INC. (INTEGRATED AT $30,000)

Employee	Pay	Excess Pay	6.043% Excess Allocation	Regular Allocation	Total Allocation	Total Allocation As A %
A	$102,266	$72,266	$ 4,367	N/A	$ 4,367	39%
B	90,000	60,000	3,626	N/A	3,626	32%
C	85,000	55,000	3,324	N/A	3,324	29%
D	30,000	0	0	N/A	0	0%
E	30,000	0	0	N/A	0	0%
TOTAL	$337,266	$187,266	$11,317		$11,317	100%

JONES, INC. (INTEGRATED AT $25,900)

Employee	Pay	Excess Pay	Share of Excess Allocation	Regular Allocation	Total Allocation	Total Allocation As A %
A	102,266	76,366	5,346	N/A	5,346	36%
B	90,000	64,100	4,487	N/A	4,487	30%
C	85,000	59,100	4,137	N/A	4,137	28%
D	30,000	4,100	287	N/A	287	3%
E	30,000	4,100	287	N/A	287	3%
TOTAL	337,266	207,766	14,544		14,544	100%

Planning Tip: The smaller the contribution, the more important selection of the integration level.

Planning Tip: Companies with budgets so restricted that the above illustration is meaningful are probably not good prospects for anything more than a profit-sharing plan.

¶604.6   A Trap For the Unwary—Forfeitures Can Hurt High-Paid Participants

Remember, the *maximum* annual addition for any participant cannot exceed the lesser of 25% of pay or (1980) $36,875. The maximum annual addition is composed of employer contributions, reallocated forfeitures and a portion of voluntary contributions. You might be tempted to set up a 25% of pay money-purchase plan integrated with Social Security. Don't! The excess contribution for higher paid participants resulting from integration of the plan will push these participants "over the top." To the extent 25% of pay is exceeded, the balance will have to be held in a suspense account to be allocated in a later year.

Planning Tip: Use the technique discussed in ¶604.4 to "fine" a contribution formula. Then *apply* the formula to key participants' compensation. Make sure you have a "safe haven." Insure that the formula chosen *maximizes* the contribution share for your key employees. Don't necessarily go for the biggest tax deduction possible.

¶605   USING PAST SERVICE EFFECTIVELY ACHIEVES YOUR GOALS AT LOWER COST

Profit-sharing plans sometimes utilize "unit" allocation system to partially weigh contributions in favor of employees with substantial past service. That simple concept gives way in money-purchase plans to a much more elaborate and powerful planning technique—the amortization of a "past service liability." Since money-purchase plans must have definitely determinable contribution formulas, it is possible to "pretend" that an employer always had his money-purchase plan in place. Given that hypothesis one may reasonably ask what would cumulatively have been contributed to the plan in the past. Computing the answer leads to the determination of an unfunded "pot" of money—the past service liability which can theoretically be "paid off" over some future period. There are two methods of measuring and amortizing this liability.

¶605.1   Creating A Flexible Past Service Liability

The simplest approach is to assume that a money-purchase plan has always been in force. Applying the plan's contribution formula to average compensation for the number of years of an employee's past service yields a separate "pot" for each participant. Under the money-purchase plan approach this "pot" can be amortized over anywhere from 10 years to the number of years remaining until the employee's retirement. The annual amortization is subject to the discretion of the employer. Therein lies the flexibility with this approach. In a good year the employer can make his contribution for current compensation plus a large amount (based on the most rapid amortization—10 years) for past service. In a bad year he can pull in his horns and make his contribution for current compensation plus a minimum (based on the least rapid amortization system). Let's consider the latitude this provides.

> *Example:* GHIJ, Incorporated establishes a 10% of pay money-purchase plan, including years prior to implementation of the plan. The company wishes to know:
>
> * How much past service liability the plan creates; and
> * How broad a range of deposits will be created by this method.

> For purposes of our illustration, average compensation and future compensation are presumed to be the same. See page 125 for the calculation for (a) the initial amount of past service; and (b) minimum and maximum contribution.

> Obviously, this use of past service mitigates one potential problem with money-purchase plans—the disruption of cash and tax planning due to forfeitures.

Watch Out For This Drawback: Keeping track of the past service liability as it is amortized by periodic employer contributions can be an administrative nightmare. Thus, in a larger plan, if the flexibility associated with this past service liability were particularly attractive it might be better achieved simply by adding a profit-sharing plan.

¶605.2   Past Service Integration—A Tricky Boost For Your Plan's Performance

Since employers have contributed to Social Security in the past it stands to reason that they ought to be able to create a past service liability based on *integrated* allocations. This is okay *as long as* the "spread" between the contribution rates above and below the integration level does not exceed five percent for past service. The calculation of an integrated past service liability is somewhat cumbersome, but sometimes the results can be worthwhile.

Figure 6.8

GHIJ, INC. CALCULATION OF PAST SERVICE LIABILITY

Employee	Age	Past Service	×	Pay	×	Contribution Rate	=	Past Service Liability
A	55	30 yrs.		50,000		10%		$150,000
B	45	20 yrs.		30,000		10%		60,000
C	35	10 yrs.		20,000		10%		20,000
D	35	5 yrs.		20,000		10%		10,000
E	25	0 yrs.		10,000		10%		0
TOTAL				130,000				$240,000

GHIJ, INC. CALCULATION OF PLAN CONTRIBUTIONS

Employee	Pay	Future Service	Regular Future Contribution (10% of Pay)	Past Service Amortization 10 Yr Payoff	Future Service Payoff	Contribution Requirements Minimum — Columns 4 + 6	Maximum — Columns 4 + 5
A	50,000	10 yrs.	5,000	15,000	15,000	20,000	20,000
B	30,000	20 yrs.	3,000	6,000	3,000	6,000	9,000
C	20,000	30 yrs.	2,000	2,000	667	2,667	4,000
D	20,000	30 yrs.	2,000	1,000	333	2,333	3,000
E	10,000	40 yrs.	1,000	0	0	1,000	1,000
TOTAL	130,000		13,000	24,000	19,000	32,000	37,000

*Any time proper planning can enhance a client's flexibility it should be an important goal.

Example: The principals of WXY, Incorporated have been employed since they got out of college; most of their employees are of relatively recent "vintage." The company sets up a past and future service money-purchase plan. Benefits for past service are 1% of Total Pay × Years of Past Service plus five percent for pay above the integration level ($9,000); future service contributions are 1.4% of pay and seven percent of excess pay. Following is the calculation of the initial past service liability, and the minimum and maximum deposit allocations. (See page 127.) Note how heavily contributions are skewed in favor of the principals.

Planning Tip: If the facts otherwise warrant a money-purchase plan, check participant dates of employment to provide an indication of the effectiveness of past service. If the average of the years of service of the key employee group is greater than the average of the years of future service for regular employees, test a past service plan.

¶605.3   Doing It The Hard Way May Pay Off Big

The second alternative for creating a past service liability is to build a defined-benefit plan, unit benefit variety, to pay off the past service element. Complete discussion of the unit-benefit approach appears in Chapter 9. However, if you must use a money-purchase plan and if most of your key employees are relatively old, your persistence in studying the potential of a unit-benefit approach to past service under a money-purchase plan will be rewarded.

¶605.4   The Unit-Benefit Concept Made Simple

The concept of a unit-benefit plan is simply that during each year of service an employee "accrues" a specific "chunk" of retirement income. Upon retirement, the participant's benefit will be equal to the sum of these "chunks" earned during his working life. For example, an employer might establish a one percent per year of service unit-benefit plan. Under such a plan, a 45-year-old employee earning $20,000 would earn, each year, a "chunk" equal to one percent of $20,000 or $200. After 20 years of service, his cumulative "chunks" would provide him with a retirement benefit of $4,000 per year. Determining the retirement benefit therefore, is relatively easy. Computing the annual cost is more difficult.

Using the $4,000 retirement benefit as an illustration may help clarify the funding. To pay a $4,000 retirement benefit we know that we need to have approximately $40,000 on hand at age 65. Annual contributions to fund this

Figure 6.9

WXY, INC. INTEGRATED PAST SERVICE MONEY PURCHASE PLAN

	Age	Past Service	Future Service	Pay	Excess Pay	Integrated 5% Excess × Yrs.	Regular + 1% Total × Yrs. =	Total
						Past Service Liability		
A	55	35	10	$ 50,000	$ 41,000	$ 71,750	17,500	$ 89,250
B	55	30	10	40,000	31,000	46,500	12,000	58,500
C	50	25	15	40,000	31,000	38,750	10,000	48,750
D	30	5	35	40,000	31,000	7,750	2,000	9,750
E	30	5	35	30,000	21,000	5,250	1,500	6,750
TOTAL				$200,000	$155,000	$170,000	$43,000	$213,000

WXY, INC. CALCULATION OF MINIMUM AND MAXIMUM CONTRIBUTIONS

	Future Service Contributions			Past Service Contributions		Total Contributions		
	7% Excess + 1.4% Total =		Allocation	Minimum Pay to 65	Maximum Pay in 10 Yrs	3 + 4 Minimum	3 + 5 Maximum	Maximum As A %
A	$ 2,870	$ 700	$ 3,570	$ 8,925	$ 8,925	$12,495	$12,495	36%
B	2,170	560	2,730	5,850	5,850	8,580	8,580	24%
C	2,170	560	2,730	3,250	4,875	5,980	7,605	22%
D	2,170	560	2,730	279	975	3,009	3,705	11%
E	1,470	420	1,890	193	675	2,083	2,565	7%
TOTAL	$10,850	$2,800	$13,650	$18,497	$21,300	$32,147	$34,950	100%

*Note: If past services were not used, it would take a total contribution (with no flexibility) of $49,398 to generate the same $12,495 deposit for Employee A. That's a 40-50% increase in employer costs without any improvement for the key man.

benefit are like the reverse of a mortgage—the sum of contributions plus interest earnings should provide the necessary sum if systematically paid over the working life of the employee.

It is readily apparent that the primary variable in determining annual contributions is the number of years a participant has to go before retirement; a young employee will require very small contributions, since compound interest will do most of the work. An older employee, on the other hand, will require larger principal deposits. For example, the cost at six percent interest to provide the $4,000 per year retirement income is as follows for the indicated ages.

Age	Annual Deposit To Provide At Retirement Age
25	$244/yr.
35	477/yr.
45	$1,026/yr.
55	2,863/yr.

What This Can Mean To The Typical Client

The annual accrual percentage would generally be two percent or less since the sum of accruals cannot provide a benefit greater than 100% of pay. Let's see how this works out for Sample Company, Incorporated which establishes a money-purchase plan providing a past service benefit of one percent for each year of service and a future money-purchase contribution of 2.633% of pay.

Figure 6.10

SAMPLE COMPANY, INCORPORATED

Employee	Age	Service	Pay	Past Service Benefit 1% x Yrs. x Pay	Contribution	Normal Contribution— 2.633% of Pay	6 + 7 Total Deposit	Total As A %
A	55	30	$50,000	$15,000/yr @65	$11,183	$1,317	$12,500	71%
B	45	5	30,000	1,500/yr @65	401	790	1,191	7%
C	45	20	30,000	6,000/yr @65	1,603	790	2,393	13%
D	35	10	30,000	3,000/yr @65	373	790	1,163	7%
E	25	0	10,000	N/A	N/A	263	263	2%
TOTAL			$150,000		$13,560	$3,950	$17,510	100%

*This "hybrid" method of using Past Service in money-purchase plans gives a sneak preview to the power of defined-benefits plans. The ability to allocate 71% of a money-purchase contribution to a participant whose compensation represents only 33% of the total is a dramatic boost in efficiency.

Planning Tip: While the past service approach to money-purchase plans looks favorable, keep in mind that it works best for older employees. By the same token, defined-benefit plans provide far more heavily skewed contributions for this group. After you have studied the defined-benefit plans in later chapters, come back and compare them to past service money-purchase plans.

How Integration Enhances Your Creative Opportunities

As you might expect, unit benefit past service costs under money-purchase plans can be integrated with Social Security. This is so as long as the accrual rate for compensation in excess of the integration is not more than one percent greater than the accrual rate for compensation below the integration level. Thus, for example, we could provide a very sophisticated money-purchase plan with past service contributions equal to one percent of total pay plus one percent of excess pay for each year of past service, combined with a future service money-purchase allocation formula of three percent of total pay plus seven percent of excess pay. The results show exceptional efficiency if the employee facts are right. (See page 130.)

Clearly, money-purchase plans can begin to overcome the inherent limitations of defined-contribution plans for generated high deposits for older key men.

¶606   THE WHO'S, WHAT'S, WHERE'S AND WHEN'S OF MONEY-PURCHASE PLANS

Notwithstanding some of the opportunities provided by past service amortization, the use of money-purchase plans should generally be restricted to the following situations:

— businesses with a stable employee pool;

— businesses where the key employees are young; and

— situations in which simplicity is of paramount importance.

If you must use money-purchase plans *be certain* to show your client the alternatives. Better that he hear about defined-benefit plans from you and reject them then hear about them later from one of your competitors. Most small employers, when pressed, will choose a plan whose contributions are heavily weighted to their key men, even though the plan may be slightly more onerous in terms of administration and cost.

Figure 6.11

PAST SERVICE MONEY-PURCHASE PLAN—UNIT-BENEFIT (INTEGRATED AT $22,900)

	Age	Past Service	Pay	Past Service Benefits at Age 65			Past Service Contribution	Future Service Contribution	Total Contribution	Total As A %
				1% x Yrs. x Pay	1% x Yrs. x Excess Pay	Total Benefit				
A	50	15 yrs	$ 50,000	$7,500/yr	$4,065/yr	$11,565/yr	$ 4,883	$3,397	$8,280	41%
B	50	10 yrs	50,000	5,000	2,710	7,710	3,255	3,397	6,652	33%
C	40	20 yrs	30,000	6,000	1,420	7,420	1,329	1,397	2,726	14%
D	40	10 yrs	30,000	3,000	420	3,710	665	1,397	2,062	10%
E	30	5 yrs	$110,000	500	N/A	500	44	300	344	2%
Total							$10,176	$9,888	$20,064	100%

**¶606.1   Because of Their Simplicity, Money-Purchase Plans Do
Have A Cost Advantage**

The do not require actuarial certification. They do not present the potential Pension Benefit Guaranty Corporation liability associated with defined-benefit plans. Simple accounting lowers recordkeeping costs. And greater simplicity means a minimized "time liability" for you in the future— you won't have to explain money-purchase plans over and over to employees.

¶606.2   When Should Money-Purchase Plans Be Used

The recurrent dogma with money-purchase plans is to use them when key men are young. Even though the use of past service allows some "catch-up" for older key men under money-purchase plans, the fact remains that the combination of contribution frequency and compound interest will weigh heavily in favor of younger key men. Unless the average age of key employees is less than 40-years old, you should, as a general rule, steer clear of money-purchase plans.

¶606.3   What To Do When Turnover Is A Major Factor

If the tax deduction afforded by a pension plan is important to your client, and his employee group has relatively high turnover, *do not* use a money-purchase plan. If you have no choice, then make sure you do the following:

— Use the most restrictive eligibility requirements possible.
— Avoid funding media with high front-end loads.
— Plan your cash and tax flow budgets with forfeitures in mind.

In general though, turnover and money-purchase plans do not mix.

¶606.4   Your Client's Cash Flow May Hold The Key

Critical to the decision to implement a money-purchase plan will be an analysis of your client's cash flow. If it's quite erratic, he may not like the fixed commitment of a money-purchase plan. If it's quite stable, and largely taxable, he may not like the treatment of forfeitures under money-purchase plans. But in situations where a relatively young, stable group of employees form the participant group for a business with good, stable cash flow, money-purchase plans may be an attractive and inexpensive way to get a big tax deduction.

SECTION B
How To Design
Defined-Benefit Plans

7

How Defined-Benefit Pension Plans Can Boost Plan Efficiency

Defined-contribution plans offer a simple and flexible series of alternatives for your clients. However, the key objective of most small businessmen is to maximize the percentage of the plan's contribution allocated to them. Assuming the vast majority of your small to medium-sized business owners are comparatively old (over 45), then defined-contribution plans may have a fatal flaw—they inherently and inevitably favor younger participants.

Defined-benefit plans offer an alternative, albeit with increased complexity, which may achieve a contribution distribution more favorable to your client's key men. Chapters seven, eight and nine will show you:

- how to radically skew deposits toward older key men;
- how to simplify the complicated jargon peculiar to defined-benefit plans;
- when defined-benefit plans can be most effective; and
- how to overcome the most frequent objections to defined-benefit plans—the problem of a fixed contribution.

More specifically, chapter seven will set the groundwork by discussing the differences between defined-benefit and defined-contribution plans, and how to identify and take advantage of situations where defined-benefit plans offer the most efficient use of your client's funds. (Also, see Appendix B for an IRS-approved Model Defined Benefit Plan.)

¶700   IMPORTANT DIFFERENCES BETWEEN DEFINED-BENEFIT AND DEFINED-CONTRIBUTION PLANS

In defined-contribution plans, the *deposit* is "definitely determinable." That is, application of the plan formula or allocation method to eligible employees' compensation will, if the plan is properly designed, result in uniform, nondiscriminatory treatment of plan participants. Future *account values*, on the other hand, are indeterminable. They are clearly a function of several variables:

Variable Number 1—Time

The first and most important variable is time. Recall that an annual deposit of $100 for 10 years generates a future value of $1,397; $100 per year deposited for 25 years generates a future value of $5,816. However, the converse is also true if we set a specific age-related accumulation goal for all participants. For example, if two employees, aged 25 and 50, are promised a "pot" of $10,000 at age 65, the annual deposits required would be $61 and $405 in the cases of the younger and the older employee respectively. Due to a longer remaining working life, younger participants will benefit from time. Compound interest will do most of the "work." Chapters four through six concluded that defined-contribution plans inherently favor younger employees in terms of contributions. Defined-benefit plans reverse that orientation.

Variable Number 2—Plan Earnings Are Significant, Too

The second important variable in defined-contribution plans is interest. One hundred dollars per year for 20 years at four percent generates a future value of $3,097; $100 per year for 20 years at eight percent interest generates a future value of $4,942. One hundred dollars per year for 20 years assuming an annual *loss* of four percent results in a future value of $1339. However, defined-contribution plans meet the IRS qualification requirements of providing "definitely determinable benefits" since the *benefit* of plan participation is an employee's right to receive a share of *contributions*. Those benefits are "definitely determinable" simply by application of the formula. Investment results do not affect a participant's status in a defined-benefit plan.

¶701 HOW DEFINED-BENEFIT PLANS WORK: A TOTALLY DIFFERENT APPROACH TO "DEFINITELY DETERMINABLE BENEFITS"

Defined-benefit plans represent a wholly different group, conceptually and mechanically. As the name implies, the benefits of these plans are *defined* in advance, generally determined by application of the plan formula to compensation. However, the result of formula application is not a current *contribution* to the plan, but rather, a specific stated benefit which the plan commits to pay at retirement age, and toward which the plan must fund.

> *Example:* A simple defined-benefit plan formula promises all participants a retirement benefit at age 65 equal to 50% of their pay. A participant earning $10,000 prior to retirement is entitled to a pension benefit of $10,000 × 50% or $5,000 per year for life. The contribution to fund the benefit is actuarially determined. It is the amount which, together with interest, should be sufficient to pay the promised benefit. For instance, to follow our example above, suppose that the employee to whom we have promised $5,000 per year at age 65 is currently 45-years old. Annuity tables indicate that for every $1,200 per year of benefit to be paid at age 65, you will need to have a "pot" of $13,333 on hand. Therefore, to fund a benefit of $5,000 per year, the plan needs to accumulate $55,422 during the next twenty years.
>
> Thus, this plan's objective would be to put a sufficient amount of money away each year which, with assumed interest, would accumulate $55,422 in the 20 years remaining until retirement. Assuming that fund deposits consistently earn six percent, the annual deposit is $1,421.

¶701.1 Applying The Concept to A Typical Situation

Here's how the simple defined-benefit plan would work for Definitely, Incorporated. The formula calls for each participant receiving 50% of pay as a retirement benefit.

Employee	Age	Pay	50% Retirement Benefit @ 65	Annual Deposit
A	50	$ 75,000	$37,500/yr.	$15,832
B	30	75,000	37,500	3,307
C	40	12,000	6,000	1,075
D	40	12,000	6,000	1,075
E	25	2,500	3,750	238
TOTAL		$181,500	N/A	$21,527

The key to understanding defined-benefit plans lies in the relationship between Employees A and B. Although each earns the same income and is therefore entitled to the same benefit at retirement (50% of $75,000 = $37,500), the *time* available to accumulate sufficient funds to pay the promised benefit differs dramatically—15 and 35 years respectively. Thus, Employee A's annual funding deposit for those 15 years must be five times B's. The example graphically highlights the potential for rewarding older key men which makes defined-benefit plans so attractive.

¶702   WHAT IS A "FUNDING STANDARD ACCOUNT"?

Interest assumptions in defined-contribution plans were only valuable for *projecting* future accumulations, however, defined-contribution plans don't promise any future accumulations. With defined-contribution plans, your client simply makes deposits on a regular basis; a participant's benefit at retirement age is whatever he has in his plan, no more or no less.

Defined-benefit plans make a specific *promise* of future benefits. And ERISA provides that your client is "on the hook"—potentially up to 30% of his net worth—to fulfill the commitments of his defined-benefit plan. Therefore, the extent to which the plan assumptions deviate from actual experience will affect whether your plan will generate too much or too little money for the "pot" to pay future benefits. For example, suppose you assume your plan will earn six percent per year, and it actually earns eight percent. Your plan will be over-funded because of the excess interest earned. But since the "pot" is predetermined, under or over-funding isn't acceptable. There needs to be a system to compare hypothetical with actual plan experience.

¶702.1   How The Funding Standard Account Works

This introduces the concept of the "funding standard account." Conceptually, a "funding standard account" is a plan's "perfect balance." That is, the funding standard account represents the balance that should be in the plan assuming all plan variables exactly duplicate your projections. At least every three years, an "enrolled actuary" must review the plan's actual performance and compare it to the assumed performance predicted by the actuarial method and the funding standard account. To the extent that the plan is under or over-funded, the plan trustees must amortize surpluses or shortages over a specific time period.

Thus the funding standard account provides a conceptual framework for comparing a plan's assets and liabilities—its income with its outgo. Since the cost of future benefits can be expressed as a present value, it is easy to consider that, for the plan to be "in balance," some simple arithmetic must work.

THE FUNDING STANDARD ACCOUNT SIMPLIFIED

A Plan's Assets	Must Equal	Its Liabilities

Present Value of Future Contributions

+

Accumulated Assets   =   Present Value of Future Benefits

+   +

Employer Deposits   Investment Losses

+   +

Investment Earnings   Payables to Vested Terminees

Periodically an actuary reviews the "balance" of the account to reflect:

- additional costs generated by new participants or changes in pay;
- savings generated by investment performance in excess of estimates; and
- distribution to retirees.

¶703   **HOW TIME AND INTEREST AFFECT THE DESIGN OF DEFINED-BENEFIT PLANS**

It's important to consider how different variables affect defined-benefit plans' funding. Keep in mind, however, that funding of defined-benefit plans is based on a purely hypothetical set of assumptions. Experience will never duplicate plan assumptions. Therefore, to the extent your client develops plan parameters because they generate a more favorable allocation of deposits, he will create future problems—when your actuary compares actual plan experience to unrealistic assumptions.

Example: Because of the powerful long-term effect of interest, it is very easy to reduce defined-benefit contributions for younger employees simply by predicting a high rate of interest. You might be tempted to use an eight percent assumption, since that rate is readily available in today's interest market. However, there has never been a 20- or 30-year period in our economic history in which an eight percent interest rate was sustained. Therefore, using an eight percent rate, we might build a future liability for younger employees. And sooner or later, your client will have to increase his deposits to make up for earnings that never materialized.

A Close Look At Interest: The most important variable affecting defined-benefit pension plans is interest. Consider the annual deposit required to generate a lump-sum of $10,000 using the following time and interest variables:

Interest Rate	Annual Deposit To Accumulate $10,000 If Time Period Is:		
	10 Years	20 Years	30 Years
4%	$801	$323	$171
5%	757	288	143
8%	639	202	82

Observation of the 10-year column reveals that doubling the interest rate from four percent to eight percent reduces the contribution required by 20%, from $801 to $639. That is not a substantial difference because the *effect of compound interest is felt most strongly over long periods of time.*

For example, consider the 30 year column. Here, doubling the interest rate from four to eight percent reduces the contribution required by 52% from $171 to $82! This simple exercise demonstrates a major advantage at least in *contribution* terms for defined-benefit plans. Whereas the key man of most small business organizations is older than the average age of his employees, the older an employee the less interest will do the job of funding his promised retirement benefit. However, recall that *unreasonable* interest assumptions, as discussed earlier, may reduce or increase contributions at the expense of creating future liabilities in the form of amortizable experience gains or losses.

As a final point, however, it is clear that the higher the interest rate assumed, the more younger participants' benefits will derive from interest, rather than employer deposits. Since, in most small businesses the prime determinant for choice of one qualified plan over another is relative contribution schedule for key versus regular employees, this is often an important fact.

¶704   HOW TO CHOOSE THE RIGHT ACTUARIAL METHOD FOR YOUR CLIENT

Actuarial assumptions and methods affect plan contributions quite significantly. Actuarial assumptions include many factors (mortality, turnover, interest, settlement factors, and so on). However, a prime consideration for small businesses is the actuarial method you choose. A thorough discussion of actuarial methodology is beyond the scope of this book, however, see the Appendix for an excellent review reprinted with the kind permission of Datair, Inc.

Two philosophically different approaches provide the extremes of actuarial choices for small plans, Attained Age Level and Entry Age Normal With Frozen Past Service Liability. Many variations lie in the middle. Your client's choice will generate dramatic variations in deposit structure. Let's consider the two divergent alternatives, not to preclude any particular actuarial methodology, but simply to avoid lengthy digression.

¶704.1   Choose Attained Age Level Funding If Your Client
                      Wants To Keep Things Simple

Attained Age Level Funding is the actuarial method traditionally favored by many insurance companies and therefore a large segment of the small business pension market. That's because:

— it generates a specific "cost" for each employee and hence lends itself to individual funding products like annuities; and

— it is quite "robust"—it can absorb the problems caused by the historical instability of small business payrolls.

The major concept of attained age level funding is that your client deposits the *exact* amount required to fund a participant's retirement benefit over the years of service remaining in his employment *assuming* level compensation from the date of computation to date of retirement. For instance, if the employee is 55, then we fund his benefit over the 10 remaining years of employment; if he is 45, over 20 years, etc. Whenever salary increases (or decreases) *actually occur*, they are recognized and funded as incremental "blocks" of funding. Finally investment experience gains (or losses) are amortized over 15 years.

The concept of attained age level funding can easily be demonstrated by the following bar graph, which assumes a participant has annual salary increases.

**CUMULATIVE
RETIREMENT
INCOME**

			4th Year Benefit
		3rd Year Benefit	3rd Year Benefit
	2nd Year Benefit	2nd Year Benefit	2nd Year Benefit
1st Year Benefit	1st Year Benefit	1st Year Benefit	1st Year Benefit
Year One	**Year Two**	**Year Three**	**Year Four**

Example: B. Block becomes a participant in his company's pension plan at age 45, when he is earning $30,000. The plan promises a 50% of pay retirement benefit and assumes a 5½ percent rate of return. In his second year of participation, B. Block earns $40,000 and the plan actually earns 12% interest.

A. Computing B. Block's Benefits

Compensation, Year One	$30,000	
Times Benefit Rate	× 50%	
Equals Estimated Retirement Benefit		$15,000
Compensation, Year Two	$40,000	
Minus Original Compensation	(30,000)	
Equals Incremental Compensation	$10,000	
Times Benefit Rate	× 50%	
Equals Incremental Retirement Benefit		$ 5,000
Cumulative Incremental Benefits, End of Year Two		$20,000

B. Computing B. Block's Funding Costs

Initial Benefit (Age 45)	$15,000	
Annual Funding Deposit (5½% interest, *20* yrs. remaining)		$4,248/yr.
Incremental Benefit, Year Two	$ 5,000	
Unadjusted Funding Deposit (5½ interest, *19* yrs. remaining)		$1,538/yr.
Total Unadjusted Funding Costs, End of Year Two		$5,786/yr.

C. Adjustment For Experience Gain

Actual Investment Return on $4,248 Deposit (12%)	$ 510	
Assumed Investment Return (5½%)	(234)	
Net Experience Gain	276	
Annual Amortization for 15 Years		($10/yr.)
ANNUAL FUNDING DEPOSIT		$ 5,776/yr.

The $5,776 annual deposit will continue until either:

1. additional investment differentials; or
2. compensation changes require further adjustment.

Note that each time a change is recognized, B. Block will have fewer years of service remaining. Therefore, the funding cost for an identical incremental benefit change will become progressively larger.

Planning Tip: Plans using the Attained Age Level Funding Method should consider *not* recognizing benefit changes occuring within five years of retirement, since the cost of amortizing even a small benefit increase over five years could disrupt your client's budget. For example, if B. Block had had his $5,000 benefit increase at age 60, your client would have had to pay an *additional* $8,846 for the next five years.

¶704.2   How Attained Age Level Funding Works In Real-Life Situations

The Attained Age Level method of funding can be illustrated utilizing a typical small business employee census. Assume a 25% of pay retirement benefit and a 10% pay increase from year one to year two.

FIRST YEAR PLAN					**SECOND YEAR INCREASES**				
Employee	Age	Annual Pay	25% Benefit @ 65	Annual Deposit	Employee	Age	Annual Pay Increase	Additional Benefit @ 65	Additional Annual Deposit
A	50	$ 75,000	$18,750	$13,979	A	50	$ 7,500	$1,875	$1,603/yr.
B	30	75,000	18,750	1,654	B	30	7,500	1,875	177
C	40	12,000	3,000	537	C	40	1,200	300	54
D	40	12,000	3,000	537	D	40	1,200	300	54
E	25	7,500	1,875	119	E	25	750	188	13
TOTAL		$181,150	N/A	$16,826	TOTAL		$18,150	N/A	$1,901

CUMULATIVE BENEFITS AFTER 2 YEARS

Employee	Age	Annual Pay	Benefit @ 65	Annual Deposit
A	50	$ 82,500	$20,625	$15,582
B	30	82,500	20,625	1,831
C	40	13,200	3,300	591
D	40	13,200	3,300	591
E	25	8,250	2,063	132
TOTAL		$199,650	N/A	$18,727

Observation: Employee A receives 83% of the first year deposit. In year two, despite uniform pay increases, he receives 84% of the incremental change. The closer he gets to retirement, the higher his share of the funding. That's because there's less time to accumulate the specific sum necessary to pay the incremental retirement income.

Additional Observation: Decreases in compensation (and therefore benefits) result in a "negative block" of retirement benefit and cost.

Planning Tip: The closer a participant is to retirement, the more sensitive his funding costs are to changes in benefits. Many plans using the Attained Age Level Funding Actuarial Method exclude from computations changes in compensation (and benefits) which occur within five years of normal retirement date.

Note how Attained Age Level Funding (and in general all defined benefit funding) orients deposits heavily in favor of an older employee. When compared to a nonintegrated defined-contribution plan, defined-benefit plans are clearly superior for older employees in *terms of contributions*.

Example: Compare, Inc. is considering a defined-contribution or a defined-benefit plan, and has $18,727 to spend. Without introducing integration to the picture, here are the choices offered by the two alternatives:

Employee	Age	Pay	Defined-Contribution Deposit		Defined-Benefit Deposit	
			Amount	% of Total	Amount	% of Total
A	55	$ 75,000	$ 7,738	41%	$15,582	83%
B	30	75,000	7,738	41	1,831	10
C	40	12,000	1,238	7	591	3
D	40	12,000	1,238	7	591	3
E	25	7,500	775	4	132	1
TOTAL		$181,500	$18,727	100%	$18,727	$100%

Observation: Doubling Employee A's allocation creates quite an opportunity! But it can create problems, too. Consider Employee B's reaction to the two alternative plans.

¶704.3   Choose Entry Age Normal With "FIPSL" If Your Client
                                    Wants More Flexibility

Entry Age Normal with Frozen Initial Past Service Liability is a second common actuarial method which allows your client to choose from a "range" of contributions. Rather than a fixed deposit, there is a "maximum" and "minimum" contribution. While sooner or later your client must provide an identical "pot" to provide identical benefits, this actuarial method provides the flexibility that small business need so badly.

¶704.4   How Entry Age Normal With "FIPSL" Works In Real-Life
                                         Situations

In effect, Entry Age Normal assumes that your client has always had a pension plan. The actuary asks "If the plan had always been in effect, how much money would already have been accumulated?" The answer to that question is an "unfunded past service liability." Therein lies the key to flexibility. This "unfunded past service liability" represents nothing more than a hypothetical "pool" of money which would be available if the pension plan had always been in effect. Your client funds future benefits currently, as with the Attained Age Level. He may *selectively amortize* the initial unfunded past service liability over a more extended period. In general, he can "pay off" the amount over anywhere from 10 to 30 years, *at his discretion.*
Thus, he could aggressively pay off the unfunded past service liability in "good" years, and limit bad years' funding to current and minimal past service costs only. The "range" generated can be quite substantial. Assuming your client's actuary determines a $150,000 Frozen Initial Past Service Liability, the annual amortization could be as little as $10,281 or as much as $19,227. Your client has complete discretion, *on an annual basis*, to decide whether to deposit the maximum, minimum, or somewhere in between. Such broad flexibility may give your client exactly what he wants:

1. contributions heavily oriented toward older key employees; and

2. a "safety valve" for years when the business needs to retain its cash to weather economic storms or expand.

Example: Up and Down Corporation is in the building trades and has seen successive boom and bust times. The firm's owner wants a plan that will give him a big deduction, but worries about the possibility of a recession. He likes what Entry Age Normal with FIPSL can do for him.

Employee	Age	Yrs Past Service	Pay	% of Total	Minimum Contribution	Maximum Contribution	% of Total
A	50	10	$ 75,000	41%	$14,861	$21,028	71%
B	30	10	75,000	41	3,553	5,027	17
C	40	01	12,000	7	1,398	1,479	5
D	40	20	12,000	7	1,335	2,150	7
E	25	01	7,500	4	296	313	1
TOTAL		N/A	$181,500	100%	$21,443	$29,997	100%

Observation: Entry Age Normal Plans combine the best of all worlds. On the one hand, they allow the favorable skewing of contributions toward older key men. On the other hand, they retain some flexibility for your client to fit his pension plan contribution to his cash flow.

¶704.5   Watch Out For These Problems

If all this seems too good to be true, you might be right. Your client must understand that more flexibility requires more self-discipline. The fact that there is a range of acceptable deposits does not reduce the amount of money ultimately necessary to pay retirement benefits. Two problems frequently trap small businesses that use Entry Age Normal With FIPSL:

1. *underfunding* when key participant's benefits will mature soon; or
2. *overfunding* when the real plan objective was a big tax deduction.

¶704.6   How Underfunding Can Undo Your Client's Plans

Most small business' key men are closer to retirement age than regular employees. If your client promises big benefits to these key men and then makes minimum contributions to his plan (amortizing the Past Service Liability over 30 years) he will be in trouble. If a key man asks for a lump-sum settlement, 15 years down the road it may not be there.

Example: Up and Down Corporation's president's worst fears come true: high interest rates, slow construction, and he needs cash. He makes minimum contributions to his pension plan. Just as he's about to retire, the business "turns around" and the future looks bright. He asks for a lump-sum distribution from the plan to obtain the favorable 10-year income averaging. Annual plan contributions of $21,443 plus interest have generated a trust fund balance of $529,053. His lump-sum will cost $458,355 leaving a balance of $70,698. Up and Down's president can take a lump-sum. However, if he had been 55 rather than 50 when the plan was set up, there would have been nowhere near enough plan assets to pay him a lump-sum. He would have had to forego the favorable tax treatment of 10-year averaging, and lost a lot of taxes.

Solution: The best solution is not to need a solution. Exercise extreme caution with Entry Age Normal. However, if you have to use it in a marginal situation, consider these options:

1. plan to amortize the past service liability over no more than the remaining years of service of the older key men. For example, if key men are 45-years old, use no more than a 20-year amortization period. Save the slower, 30-year amortization for dire emergencies; and

2. restrict the availability of lump-sum distributions, or eliminate them altogether. Your tax loss may be more than offset by enhanced flexibility.

Planning Tip: Make sure your actuary provides an *Emerging Liability Report,* which will compare the projected fund assets with projected payouts on a year-by-year basis. The Emerging Liability Report will tell you when and where to expect trouble.

¶705   HOW ACTUARIAL ASSUMPTIONS CAN ALSO AFFECT COSTS

Your choice of actuarial method clearly has significant impact. However, certain actuarial assumptions cut across all actuarial methods in a powerful manner. These are:

1. interest,
2. turnover
3. salary scales; and
4. benefit costs.

The influence of interest has been thoroughly detailed at ¶703. The other three deserve brief attention.

¶705.1   How Turnover Assumptions Can Lower Your Client's
Costs

Certain types of businesses—construction or restaurants are good
examples—historically show exceptionally high levels of turnover. Employees
in those industries tend to be transient, staying at most for several years and
departing. Why should your client make contributions for a group of
employees who, though eligible to participate, will in all probability never
become fully vested? That's the question which "Turnover Tables" can help
answer.

"Turnover Tables" are nothing more than statistical compilations of
the *probability* of termination of different categories of employees. Usually the
primary factor reviewed by these tables is participant *age*, since that most
closely correlates to termination rate. However, some tables incorporate
morbidity and mortality estimates, since some participants may not receive
estimated pension benefits due to sickness or death.

This application of Turnover Tables to your client's plan will result in
a "discount" to his costs, the size of his discount depending on the age
distribution of participants. Since, in many tables, the probability of a
participant between age 25 and 30 receiving retirement benefits is assumed to
be practically zero, your clients with a young employee pool may benefit from
this discount. The money saved, as with any other plan, can be used either to:

1. increase benefits for selected key man; or
2. reduce costs.

A typical table of withdrawal probabilities assigns a percentage to
various age categories. Usually the younger a participant, the higher the
probability of withdrawal. Here's a sample of withdrawal rates combining
termination, mortality and morbidity factors:

Age	Withdrawal Probability	Age	Withdrawal Probability
25	.0843	45	.0335
30	.0640	50	.0289
35	.0492	55	.0288
40	.0400	60	.0364

Example: Eat Company is a large restaurant chain with average employment duration of less than five years. The key men of Eat Company are in their mid-50s and want to receive the maximum benefit out of a $25,000 deposit. Use of an aggressive turnover table, they find, "unlocks" about 20% of their budget for higher key man benefits.

Warning: Like all assumptions, turnover will never equal the predicted amount. Sooner or later actual experience will receive some modification of assumptions. Don't use too aggressive a turnover table unless:

1. there's a large enough population of employees to allow "nature to take it's course," or
2. there's history to back up the reasonableness of your assumption.

¶705.2   Salary Scales Are Important Too

The inflation of the last five to ten years has left many defined-benefit plans underfunded. That's because when the plans were implemented, the actuary didn't feel compelled to use assumptions about wage increases. Thus, he might have felt benefit increases occurring because of salary changes would be small enough either:

1. to ignore until they actually occurred; or
2. to be covered by excess investment performance

However, the doubling of salary levels that has occurred during the last decade has countered that assumption.

"Salary Scales" are assumptions about ultimate salaries. For example, a young participant's salary might be expected to climb by an average of eight percent during his working life. An older participant may show less dramatic change. Alternatively, an actuary might simply apply an "inflation rate" to the entire payroll. Whatever the method, it has become increasingly important to avoid the funding cost disruptions that will occur without adequate inflation planning.

Example: Look what happens to benefits and plan costs if we project a four percent salary increase.

Employee	Age	Pay	PLAN I: NO SALARY PROJECTION		PLAN II: 4% SALARY PROJECTION	
			Retirement Benefit	Annual Contribution	Retirement Benefit	Annual Contribution
A	50	$ 75,000	$43,908	$18,260	$50,088	$16,338
B	30	75,000	43,908	3,560	98,100	4,821
C	40	12,000	7,020	1,439	11,856	1,656
D	40	12,000	7,020	1,439	11,856	1,656
E	25	7,500	4,392	302	11,356	529
TOTAL		$181,500	N/A	$25,000	N/A	$25,000

*Maximum benefit is currently $110,625 per year.

Observation: Note how benefits and contributions shift with the introduction of the four percent assumption. The effects depend on relative age. Observe that Employee A's retirement benefit increases only marginally. Four percent over 15 years doesn't make a tremendous difference. Twenty-five-year old Employee E, however, has almost *three times* the estimated retirement income. On the other hand, Employee A's contriubtion decreases by about 10%, which Employee E's almost doubles. Assuming a common $2,500 budget, the Salary-Scaled Plan must spend more of its funds to prepay the inflation and boost benefits of younger participants.

In the long run, salary scale assumptions will reduce plan costs for younger employees. That is because by initially boosting contributions for a young participant because of projected increases in salary allows compound interest to work for a longer period and to provide a greater ultimate percentage of the future value needed to pay the promised benefit. Salary scales theoretically avoid the problem of incrementally increasing salaries and decreasing remaining years of service inherent in the Attained Age Level Funding actuarial method.

However, if salaries don't increase at the assumed inflation or projection rate, or if a participant terminates employment early in his career, a salary-scale plan will probably have overfunded benefits and when that occurs, your client must either:

1. reduce his tax deductible contribution, in the case of terminated employees, or
2. amortize the experience gain, in the case of lower-than-estimated payroll increases.

However, many actuaries prefer that potential risk to the alternative of unfunded benefit increases close to retirement age.

¶705.3   What Will These Benefits Ultimately Cost?

Defined-contribution plans make no specific promise of retirement benefits. However, the "definitely determinable benefits" requirement in defined-benefit plans creates a specific, easily computed future liability for each plan participant. If an employee earning $10,000/year participates in a 50% of pay pension plan, he *must* receive $5,000/year when he retires. But how much money will the plan need to meet that liability? The answer can affect plan costs by as much as 25%.

Some insurance companies prefer to use their minimum guaranteed settlement option rates to compute the lump-sum's required to pay benefits. (A "settlement option rate" is nothing more than a commitment to distribute funds at some future date over a participant's estimated remaining lifetime.) These minimum guaranteed rates reflect the company's "worst case" scenario and are usually far less attractive than the company's current rates.

For example, one major insurance company currently guarantees that its future payout won't be less than $6.25 per month for each $1,000 of principal. However, for the same $1,000 received *today*, the company will pay $8.10 per month. (Based on 10 Year Certain and Continuous Option.)

Alternatively, many actuaries favor using the 1971 Group Annuity Table for estimating the cost of future pension liabilities. The 1971 Group Annuity Table predicts that the plan will be able to pay out approximately $7.80 for each $1,000 of plan assets. That makes compound benefits far less expensive. A "middle-of-the-road" approach finds many actuaries utilizing a *graded* settlement cost table, which assumes employees retiring in the near future will benefit from high current settlement option rates, but that more remote retirements will cost progressively more.

Example: Option, Ltd. wants to know the funding costs associated with conservative and more aggressive settlement cost assumptions.

FUNDING COSTS TO PRODUCE $5,000/YEAR OF RETIREMENT INCOME

Employee Age	With Conservative Assumption		With Aggressive Assumption	
	Lump-Sum	Annual Deposit	Lump-Sum	Annual Deposit
25	$67,313	$ 410/yr.	$52,083	$ 317
35	67,313	803	52,083	622
45	67,313	1,726	52,083	1,336
55	67,313	4,818	42,083	3,728
TOTAL	N/A	$7,757	N/A	$6,003

That's quite a difference! The conservative plan assumes that for every dollar per month of retirement increase, the plan will need to have accumulated $161.55. The aggressive plan assumes that only $125 will be necessary to provide $1 of retirement income.

But remember: In the long run, only actual experience will determine plan costs. Using artificial conservative or aggressive settlement cost assumptions will, like unreasonable interest projections, ultimately require some adjustment.

¶706   **HOW COMMON REDUCTIONS TO**
AND LIMITATIONS ON BENEFITS WILL IMPACT
YOUR DESIGN

Defined-contribution plans are limited primarily by one factor—the Maximum Annual Addition. A participant's account cannot be increased in any year by the lesser of $36,875 or 25% of pay, including:

1. employer contributions;
2. forfeitures; and
3. a portion of voluntary employee contributions.

Defined-benefit plans, on the other hand, are subject to several restraints primarily designed to prevent your client from establishing a qualified plan for a short period of time (for instance, within two years of normal retirement) and thereby artificially increasing contributions for one or two key participants. It's important to consider these limitations during the design process.

¶706.1   How Maximum Retirement Benefits Are Computed

The maximum annual pension benefit which may be provided by a defined-benefit plan is the lesser of (a) $110,625 or (b) 100% of a participant's average pay over his three highest years. For example, an employee earning $150,000 at retirement date would be limited to a retirement benefit of $110,625 per year. A participant with final pay of $25,000 could have a retirement benefit of $25,000 per year. Usually these maximum benefits require further reduction.

¶706.2   What Is The Normal Form Of Retirement Benefit?

ERISA's maximum retirement benefits assume payment in the form of life only or joint and full survivor annuities. If payment is made under any other settlement form, for instance 10-year certain and continuous, then plan benefits must be actuarially reduced. That's because the life contingencies involved with alternative settlement options make them actuarially "more valuable" than the basic form assumed by ERISA.

Example: Here's how some of the more common settlement option forms will affect your client's benefits. Assume a $1,000 retirement income under the life only option:

Benefit Form	Reduction Required	Net Annual Benefit
Life Only Annuity	None	$10,000
10 Yrs Certain and Continuous	91%	9,100
20 Yrs Certain and Continuous	75%	7,500
Annuity Certain for 15 Years	92.5%	9,250

¶706.3   A Joint And Full Survivor Annuity Provides The Biggest
                      Deduction For Older Key Men

ERISA doesn't require any reduction in maximum benefits for joint and full survivor annuities, which are about the most expensive form of retirement benefit. If your client is a professional corporation or a business with lots of disposable cash, the Joint and Survivor option can provide tremendous tax deductions.

Example: Consider the annual funding cost of providing a $98,100 Joint and Survivor Annuity Benefit for the following participants ($98,100 was 1979's maximum benefit):

Employee	Age	Annual Deposit To Fund $98,100/Yr At Age 65
A	55	$106,384
B	45	38,119
C	35	17,737

A joint and full survivor benefit can cost as much as 20% more than a life annuity benefit. For example, one major insurance company's Settlement Option Rate Table assumes that for every dollar of retirement income, the plan will need to have accumulated $182. That compares to about $125 for an average life only annuity.

Caveat: integrated defined-benefit plans must reduce, by approximately 21%, any *integrated* benefits based on Joint and 100% Annuity forms, to insure comparability with Social Security.

¶706.4   Using Earlier Normal Retirement Ages Can Further
                              Enhance Your Client's Deduction

Your client can use a retirement age as early as 55 without any reduction to plan benefits. Earlier Normal Retirement boosts plan contributions because

- it shortens the funding period; and
- the earlier in life an annuity is purchased, the more expensive it is.

That means your younger clients can benefit from big deductions, too.

Example: Here's the annual deposit to buy a $98,100/year annuity at age 55:

Employee	Age	Annual Deposit To Fund $98,100/Yr At Age 65
A	45	$142,363
B	35	51,011
C	25	23,735

Observation: Recall from our discussion at ¶706.3 that the annual cost to fund a $98,100 benefit at 65 for a 45-year-old participant was $38,119. By shortening the fund period to 10 years (normal retirement age of 55), we increase funding costs by 273% to $142,000. Note that the $142,000 deposit is 33% more than the funding required (¶706.3) for a 55-year old in an age 65 retirement plan. That's because comparable benefits cost more when provided at an earlier age. A 55-year old presumably has an additional 10 years' life expectancy over a 65-year old. Early normal retirement dates can dramatically increase plan costs.

Warning: If your plan is integrated, see ¶707.1 and ¶707.3 for additional reductions that apply.

¶706.5   Special Reduction For Participants With Less Than 10 Years Of Service

IRS requirements mandate that benefits must be reduced by one-tenth for each year of service less than 10 years. Therefore, an employee hired at age 59 by an employer whose plan specifies a normal retirement age of 65 will be entitled to only six-tenths of the otherwise normal retirement benefit. As a practical matter, this restriction seldom applies, since many defined-benefit plans set retirement age as the later of 65 or completion of 10 years plan participation. However, then the pension plan designer must always review employer census data to pinpoint any prospective participants who would be affected by this mandatory reduction.

¶707   SPECIAL REDUCTIONS APPLY TO INTEGRATED PLANS

For benefits that are integrated with Social Security, special reductions apply. Note that the reductions are required only for that portion of a participant's benefits that are integrated. However, as a practical matter, they are frequently applied to total benefits, to avoid the additional administrative burdens resulting from an attempt to apply different sets of assumptions to different portions of a participant's compensation. The most significant reductions applicable to many small plans are for:

1. retirement earlier than age 65;
2. service less than 15 years;
3. joint and survivor annuities;
4. compensation averaging period; and
5. ancillary death benefits.

¶707.1   How Liberal Retirement Ages Affect Benefits In Integrated Plans

The integrated portion of the benefit (that portion based on compensation in excess of the integration level) must be reduced for each year prior to age 65 that an employee retires. Although Revenue Ruling 71446 (the "Bible" of Plan Integration) provides three alternative reduction methods, by far the most commonly used formula requires that an affected employee's benefits be reduced one-fifteenth for each of the first five years prior to age 65 and one-thirtieth for each of the next five years prior to age 65 that the employee retires. Unlike many of the other reductions, this one is commonly applied separately, meaning only to "pure excess" benefits.

> *Example:* Early Bird Company's retirement plan calls for a normal retirement age of 55. The plan provides *excess benefits only.* The plan provides income of 30% of excess pay. C. Worm computes his excess pay as $20,000, and expects a $6,000/year benefit. *Not so,* says the IRS requirement. Mr. Worm's benefits must be reduced one-fifteenth for each of the first five years and one-thirtieth for the next five years that his age 55 retirement precedes the IRS's standard. Thus, C. Worm's retirement income is limited to $3,000 per year.

¶707.2   How Short Service Employees Fare In Flat-Benefit Excess Integrated Plans

Another reduction applicable to integrated benefits in Flat-Benefit Excess Plans (the most common variety in small businesses) applies to participants who retire with less than 15 years of service. This reduction is comparable to the basic reduction to *all* defined-benefit plan participants retiring with less than 10 years of service, and is designed to preclude an employer from setting up a corporation shortly before the key men reach age 65, implementing a heavily-integrated plan, and thereby boosting key man contributions artificially. Reduction is simply pro rata—that is, one-fifteenth for each year of service less than 15. (See Chapter 8 for a complete discussion of flat-benefit plans.)

¶707.3   Why Joint And Survivor Annuity Reduction Restricts Your Deduction For Integrated Benefits

Paragraph 706.3 and paragraph 706.4 illustrated the enormous tax deduction potential inherent in the use of the very expensive Joint and 100% Survivor Annuity as your client's normal form of distribution. That won't work in an integrated plan. If you use a J & S, you must reduce benefits for actuarial equivalency. The adjustment factor is approximately 80%—exactly the amount of cost increase occasioned by use of a J & S Annuity. Thus, there isn't much incentive for this retirement form in integrated plans.

¶707.4 A Different Compensation Averaging Period Applies For Integrated Plans

Nonintegrated defined-benefit plans can use the average of a participant's three highest years of compensation to determine plan benefits. Integrated plans must use a five-highest-consecutive-years averaging period, obviously limiting the potential for artificially boosting plan benefits for key participants by raising their salaries abruptly just prior to retirement.

¶707.5 Providing A Current Death Benefit Reduces Future Retirement Income

If your client wants his plan participants (i.e. himself) to receive their accrued benefit in the event of death prior to retirement age, then integrated benefits must be reduced to eight ninths of their otherwise applicable level.

> *Example:* After learning how the early normal retirement date cut his integrated plan benefits, C. Worm receives further bad news— the plan includes a death benefit. Benefits must be reduced by one ninth, to $2,667. This reduction applies *whether or not* he actually dies prior to retirement, since he *theoretically* had a death benefit all along.

¶708 DON'T BE DISCOURAGED—THE OPPORTUNITIES FAR OUTWEIGH THE COMPLICATIONS

Clearly, defined-benefit pension plans are more complex and sophisticated than defined-contribution plans. Unquestionably, they are less flexible and more expensive to operate. That probably accounts for small business' traditional orientation toward defined-contribution plans (particularly profit-sharing). However, if your client has a cash flow to meet the ongoing commitment, a good actuary to keep the plan's funding "on track," and a good administrator to control the complex reporting and disclosure obligations, then the flexibility inherent in defined-benefit plans is worth pursuing.

Most important, defined-benefit plans, by their very nature, favor older employees in terms of relative contributions. Defined-contributions plans benefit younger participants. Often a small business' key employees form an older group than their average regular employee counterparts. If that's the case with your client, and if there's a limited budget to be oriented toward the key group, try a defined-benefit plan. The opportunity for real design capacity will reward the practitioner who diligently pursues his defined-benefit education.

8

How To Use
Flat-Benefit Plans For
Obtaining Minimal Complication
And Maximum Flexibility

Perhaps the simplest form of defined-benefit plan is the "flat-benefit" variety. These plans simply provide a flat-benefit, expressed as a percentage of pay, to all participants when they reach retirement age. Starting with this basic concept, various levels of sophistication can be added:

- reductions for service less than a stated number of years;
- integration; and
- actuarial assumptions and parameters.

Each of these factors involves its own separate "subgroup" of subordinate rules and regulations, adding up to the potential for a very complicated and specifically designed retirement plan.

In this chapter we will discuss these specific rules and regulations and how you can use them to your advantage to design a plan that fits your client's objectives. This chapter also provides a transition from the conceptual discussions of Chapter 7 to the more sophisticated defined-benefit plans discussed in Chapters 9 and 10.

¶800   HOW FLAT-BENEFIT PLANS WORK

Flat-benefit plans are conceptually the simplest of the defined-benefit family. They simply promise a specific future retirement benefit, expressed as a flat percentage of final pay. Having computed and specified the retirement benefit, your client's obligation is to make deposits which, assuming reasonable actuarial assumptions, will develop a sufficient fund, at retirement age, to pay the promised benefit.

Observation: Note the discrepency between a flat-benefit and a defined-contibution (namely, money-purchase) plan. A money-purchase plan might promise annual *deposits* equal to 25% of pay with no guarantee of ultimate benefits, whereas a flat-benefit plan might promise a retirement *benefit* equal to 25% of pay and whatever it costs to fund that benefit becomes a variable.

¶800.1   How To Determine Future Benefits

It's easy to compute retirement benefits under flat-benefit plans. Simply apply the guaranteed benefit rate to participant's compensation (current or projected.) For example, suppose your client's plan provides that at normal retirement date a participant will receive 50% of his final five year average compensation as a pension benefit for the rest of his life.

Example: Certain Company establishes a 50% of pay flat-benefit pension plan. Here's what would happen:

Participant	Age	Pay	Retirement Benefit Payable @ Age 65
A	50	$ 50,000	$25,000/yr.
B	30	50,000	25,000
C	40	20,000	10,000
D	45	20,000	10,000
E	25	10,000	5,000
TOTAL	N/A	$150,000	N/A

Observation: Participants earning the same compensation earn the same retirement income, *regardless* of their respective ages. That highlights the major difference between defined-contribution and defined-benefit plans. The "definitely determinable" benefits requriement for qualified plans is met by the benefit payable at normal retirement date. Recall that defined-contribution plans use their contribution rate to meet this "definitely determinable" test.

¶800.2   How To Determine Annual Contributions

Having computed benefits, the next step is to calculate annual contributions. Those depend on a variety of factors, primarily, assumed interest and participation age. The younger the participant, the longer the funding period. The longer the funding period, the smaller the contributions because:

1. with a fixed future funding objective, more years of participation don't mean an increased benefit; and
2. compound interest will provide the bulk of the benefits.

The actual computation is complicated unless you have a Present Value-Future Value calculator. To perform the calculation, you will need to assemble the following data:

1. assumed interest rate of plan;
2. years of future participation;
3. sex of participant; and
4. settlement option factor

Assume a 45-year-old male participant whose benefit at 65 (20 years' future participation) is predicted to be $500 per month, based on receipt of a life only annuity which requries $120 of principal for every one dollar of monthly retirement income.

Monthly Benefit	$500
Multiplied by Settlement Option	× 120
Equals Future Value Necessary @ 65	$60,000

Given this funding objective, we can consult a compound interest table to find that the annual payment necessary to accumulate one dollar after 20 years at six percent interest is .025649. Therefore, the annual deposit for our sample participant is

Accumulation Required in 20 Years	$60,000
Multiplied by Annual Payment Per $1	× .025649
Equals Annual Deposit To Fund Benefit	$1,539

The calculation process can be onerous for plans with lots of participants. Also, the simple demonstration above does not apply to more complex actuarial methods. The concept, however, is the same.

Planning Tip: The complexity of deposit calculations has, more than any other single factor, probably discouraged practitioners from using defined-benefit plans. However, many firms such as insurance companies, pension consultants, and banks have the capacity to generate defined-benefit proposals quickly and accurately. Consider using them before you reject these plans as overly sophisticated.

Example: Certain Company asks you the cost of the 50% of pay flat-benefit plan it proposes. Your answer:

Participant	Age	Pay	Retirement Benefit @ 65	Annual Deposit	% of Total
A	50	$ 50,000	$25,000/yr.	$10,555	50%
B	30	50,000	25,000	2,205	13
C	40	20,000	10,000	1,791	10
D	45	20,000	10,000	2,671	15
E	25	10,000	5,000	317	2
TOTAL	N/A	$150,000	N/A	$17,359	100%

Observation: Participants A and B earn identical salaries, but have vastly disproportionate contributions. That results from their different ages. Even Participants C and D have widely divergent deposits and their ages differ by only five years. This illustration emphasizes the inherent nature of flat-benefit plans and defined-benefit plans in general—they will always skew contributions toward older participants.

That frequently meshes nicely with the typical small business. It also demonstrates the fact that a company with a limited budget should carefully consider whether the flat benefit type of plan offers a sufficiently weighted contribution allocation to offset its on-going fixed commitment. Even the most aggressive defined contribution plan cannot come close to this skewing of employer funds toward older key individuals. Many small buisnesses are run by one or two key individuals who started their company years ago and have now reached their late 40s or early 50s. Flat-benefit plans become a viable alternative.

¶800.3   How To Develop A Formula On Your Client's Budget

In the "real world" small businessmen are more concerned with their budget than with plan formulas. Therefore, our discussion at ¶800.1 and ¶800.2 puts the cart ahead of the horse. Most of your clients will want to compare alternative pension plans—such as profit-sharing, money-purchase or defined-benefit plans—not on the basis of future benefits but rather according to the distribution of current plan deposits.

For example, you are likely to be asked how a $25,000 deposit would be distributed in a defined benefit as opposed to a profit-sharing plan. That's very easy for a defined-contribution plan, but not for a defined-benefit program. For the practitioner without sophisticated equipment, such a calculation is almost impossibly time-consuming except in the smallest cases.

Planning Tip: Use the facility of insurance companies, pension consulting firms or banks to obtain the budget-determined plan illustrations you need. That will conserve your time and, if you review the proposals *vis á vis* planning tips discussed in this and subsequent chapters, serve the best interests of your client.

¶800.4   How To Maximize Contributions For Older Key Men

Without capitalizing on various forms of flat-benefit plans, you can orient the program toward older key participants. The two most obvious methods for achieving that result are:

1. choice of interest assumption; or
2. service reductions

How Interest Assumptions Can Help

Defined-benefit plans operate within the constraints of a hypothetical actuarial model. An integral part of that model is the assumed interest rate for the plan assets. While ultimately actual experience will replace the actuarial model, choice of assumed interest rates can have a dramatic effect on plan funding. Low interest assumptions will raise initial contributions for all plan participants, but particularly younger ones—older participants are too close to retirement for compound interest to have a significant role. High interest assumptions will lower overall contributions, but most specifically for younger participants. High interest tends to create a much bigger funding "gap" between younger and older employees.

> *Example:* Up and Down Company wants, within reason, to skew their $25,000 budget towards the company's president who started the company at age 25. You illustrate the effect of using a 5 or 6½% interest assumption:

ANNUAL CONTRIBUTIONS REQUIRED

Participant	Age	Service @ 65	Pay	5% Interest As A $	5% Interest As A %	6½% Interest As A $	6½% Interest As A %	% Change From 5 to 6½
A	55	40 yrs.	$ 50,000	$19,230	77%	$19,786	80%	+3%
B	45	20	15,000	2,194	9	2,063	8	–6
C	40	30	15,000	1,520	6	1,360	5	–10
D	40	25	15,000	1,520	6	1,360	5	–10
E	30	35	10,000	536	2	431	2	–20
TOTAL			$105,000	$25,000	100%	$25,000	100%	N/A

The illustration clearly shows how time and interest combine to cut costs for younger participants. Fifty-five-year-old Employee A, with only 10 years until retirement, simply doesn't allow much time for interest to go to work. Hence his contribution remains practially constant. At the other end of the spectrum, 30-year-old Employee E gives interest 35 years to show its effect, and the result is dramatic—a 20% reduction in annual deposits. The moral of the story is that higher interest rate assumptions will allow your client to focus their budgets to a greater extent on older participants.

Observation: This illustration held the $25,000 *budget* constant, and allowed plan *benefits* to "float." An alternative approach might hold *benefits* constant with resultant changes to the budget. Costs for younger participants will be substantially reduced.

How Service Reductions Can Provide Further Efficiency

You can achieve an even more powerful effect than interest by including benefit reductions in your flat-benefit plan. The logic is simple. If the key man will have "x" years of service at retirement, why not reduce benefits for all participants with less than "x" years of service? The results can be spectacular for an organization with key men who started young.

Example: Up and Down Company's president will have 40 years of service when he reaches 65. No other current employee will have that much service. Therefore, Up and Down's attorney reduces plan benefits by one-fortieth for each year of service less than 40.

Participant	Unadjusted Contribution $	%	×	Service @ 65 40		=	Adjusted Contribution $	%
A	$19,786	(80%)		40/40	(1.00)		$19,786	85%
B	2,063	(8)		20/40	(.50)		1,532	6
C	1,360	(5)		30/40	(.75)		1,020	4
D	1,360	(5)		25/40	(.63)		760	3
E	431	(2)		35/40	(.88)		377	2
TOTAL	$25,000	(100%)		N/A	N/A		$23,455	100%

With the service reduction, plan costs are reduced by seven percent without reducing either benefits or contributions for key employee A. Alternatively, your client could spend the saving generated by the service reduction for higher benefits, approximately 85% of which will inure to his benefit.

Observation: Many fact situations don't start out with contributions so heavily skewed in favor of a key man as in the above illustration. In those more typical cases, benefit reductions for service can make the difference between successful plan design and a waste of time.

¶801   HOW TO INTEGRATE FLAT-BENEFIT PLANS FOR MAXIMUM RETURN

Defined-contribution plans have relatively simple integration rules which allocate an extra percentage (usually seven percent) to compensation above a specified integration level. Thus, a defined-contribution plan could provide a contribution equal to 10% of the first $25,900 and 17% of the balance of any participant's compensation. A "floating seven percent rule" was the key to correct integration under the plan. Further, defined-contribution plans can use any flat dollar amount integration level up to and including the taxable wage base in force at the time your client's plan year ends.

Flat-benefit/defined-benefit plans promise specific future *benefits,* rather than a *rate* of current contribuiton. It seems reasonable, therefore, that the integration of such plans should also be tied to ultimate benefit levels. In fact, that's how integration of flat-benefit plans is achieved.

The basic theory is that since Social Security provides benefits for the "covered compensation" (roughly the equivalent of the average of all taxable wage bases in effect during his years of employment) of each empoyee at his normal retirement date, then your client should be able to provide "catch-up" benefits for pay in excess of covered compensation.

> *Example:* If the estimated Social Security benefit for one of your client's participants amounts to $500 per month, which benefit your client funded through payroll taxes, shouldn't it be reflected somehow in the formula for plan retirement income established by your client? Flat-benefit plans recognize Social Security benefits by allowing an "extra" benefit for participant compensation not covered by the Social Security system. The theory is that under a properly integrated plan, the sum of benefits provided by Social Security and your client's plan ought to provide uniform retirement for all participants, regardless of their compensation.

¶801.1   How To Determine The Integration Level

The integration level of a defined-benefit plan must be equal to one of the following three alternatives, each of which is directly related to covered compensation.

Covered compensation, you will recall, is approximately the average of taxable wage bases to which an employee has or will have been subject during his working life.

Table I simply reflects an average maximum covered compensation for any employee retiring (e.g., turning age 65) in a certain calendar year. Since the taxable wage base has progressively been rising through the history of the Social Security system, employees reaching age 65 some years from now have relatively high covered compensation levels. A flat-benefit plan may specify an integration level which is each participant's covered compensation according to Table I.

Alternative One

The first choice for integration level is the IRS' "Table I" reproduced below for 1979:

Year Age 65	Amount	Year Age 65	Amount
1979	$ 9,000	1998	$16,800
1980	9,600	1999	17,400
1981	10,200	2000	18,000
1982 - 1983	10,800	2001 - 2002	18,600
1984	11,400	2003	19,200
1985	12,000	2004	19,800
1986 - 1987	12,600	2005 - 2006	20,400
1988 - 1989	13,200	2007	21,000
1990 - 1991	13,800	2008 - 2009	21,600
1992 - 1993	14,400	2010 - 2011	22,200
1994	15,000	2012 - 2013	22,800
1995 - 1996	15,600	2014 or later	22,900
1997	16,200		

Example: Integral Company's flat-benefit/defined-benefit plan's integrated according to 1979 covered compensation. Your job is to determine each participant's excess pay:

TABLE I INTEGRATION

Participant	Age	Pay	Calendar Yr of 65th Birthday	Covered Compensation	Excess Pay
A	55	$ 50,000	1989	$13,200	$36,800
B	48	40,000	1996	15,600	24,400
C	43	15,000	2001	18,600	0
D	38	15,000	2006	20,400	0
E	32	15,000	2012	22,800	0
TOTAL	N/A	$135,000	N/A	N/A	$64,800

The older the participant, the lower his covered compensation, and the higher his excess pay. Since integrated plan benefits are a derivative of excess pay, and will inure primarily to the benefit of higher-paid key men, use of this integration level will obviously fit well into the situation of a typical defined-benefit plan candidate.

Alternative Two

The second alternative for flat-benefit plan integration level is the IRS' Table II, which is nothing more than individualized covered compensation. Table II provides a more exact method for the determining excess compensation, and can be worth the effort if your client's facts are right. Table II is reproduced below:

1979 TABLE II

Year Age 65	Amount	Year Age 65	Amount	Year Age 65	Amount
1979	$ 8,724	1991	$14,040	2003	$19,344
1980	9,396	1992	14,304	2004	19,776
1981	10,008	1993	14,556	2005	20,208
1982	10,572	1994	14,796	2006	20,640
1983	11,088	1995	15,312	2007	21,072
1984	11,556	1996	15,828	2008	21,468
1985	12,000	1997	16,344	2009	21,816
1986	12,396	1998	16,860	2010	22,092
1987	12,768	1999	17,388	2011	22,344
1988	13,116	2000	17,904	2012	22,560
1989	13,452	2001	18,420	2013	22,740
1990	13,752	2002	18,888	2014 or later	22,900

Example: Integral Company decides that an individual determination of covered compensation is not too complicated and asks how Table II would work:

TABLE II

Participant	Age	Pay	Calendar Yr of 65th Birthday	Covered Compensation	Excess Pay
A	55	$ 50,000	1989	$13,452	$36,548
B	48	40,000	1996	15,828	24,172
C	43	15,000	2001	18,420	0
D	38	15,000	2006	20,640	0
E	32	15,000	2012	22,560	0
TOTAL	N/A	$135,000	N/A	N/A	$64,980

The difference in excess compensation resulting from the use of Table II as opposed to Table I is small. However, to maximize benefits for older key men—for whom funding even relatively small additional benefits is quite expensive—use of Covered Compensation Table II frequently provides the most efficient system.

Alternative Three

The third alternative for integrating flat-benefit plans is a uniformly-applied flat dollar amount. This flat dollar amount can't exceed the lowest covered compensation of any person who is or might become a participant in the plan. Many defined-benefit plans preclude participation of employees hired within five years of normal retirement date. (Because of the staggering cost of funding benefits over such a short period of time, Congress thought the absence of such a provision might discourage employers from establishing defined-benefit plans.)

In such plans adopted during 1979, an employee could not be or become a participant in the plan and retire any earlier than 1984 (1979 plus five-year exclusion period). Covered Compensation Table I indicates that employees turning 65 in 1984 have covered compensation of $11,400. Therefore, defined-benefit plans precluding participation for those hired within five years of normal retirement date could utilize an integration level for all participants of $11,400. Using a flat dollar amount integration level simplifies the task of determining benefits under the plan by streamlining the process.

When Can A Higher Integration Level Be Used? Your client can select a uniformly applied flat dollar amount integration level higher than that described for alternative three (above) if he applies a reduction to excess benefits otherwise available. The reduction is similar to that in defined-contribution plans utilizing integration levels higher than the current taxable wage base. The formula for defined-benefit plan reductions is simply:

$$\frac{\text{maximum flat dollar integration level (Alternative Three)}}{\text{integration level chosen by your employer}} \times \frac{\text{integrated}}{\text{benefits other-}} \text{wise available}$$

Example: Suppose your client wants to use a flat $15,000 integration level. He can, as long as he reduces excess benefits otherwise available by the percentage resulting from the formula:

$$\frac{\$11,400 \text{ (maximum from Alternative Three)}}{\$15,000 \text{ (desired integration level)}} \times 37\frac{1}{2}\% \text{ (maximum "excess" benefit)}$$

Therefore your client's flat-benefit plan can provide "excess" benefits equal to 28.5%.

¶801.2   How To Select An Integration Level For Your Client

The above discussion and illustrations yield several conclusions. Here are some fact situations where one or another integration level ought to be considered:

- key men are relatively old—use Covered Compensation from either Table I or Table II. Covered Compensation Tables will establish lower integration levels (and therefore higher integrated benefits) for older participants;

- key men relatively young—use a flat dollar amount selected to be just above the median compensation level for all plan participants;

- limited budget—consider a flat dollar amount higher than $11,400 so as to isolate key men; and

- calculations must be hand-done—for preliminary purposes, use a flat dollar integration level. Though slightly less efficient, it will greatly simplify the calculation procedure and conserve your time.

¶802   HOW TO DETERMINE MAXIMUM INTEGRATED BENEFITS

What "catch-up" benefits are available for compensation in excess of the integration level? Revenue Ruling 71-446 allows that an employer may provide benefits for excess participant compensation not to exceed 37½%.

Example: Assume John earns $15,000 per year in a plan with a $9,000 flat integration level. His maximum integrated benefit is:

Total Pay	$15,000
Less: Integration Level	(9,000)
Equals: Excess Pay	$ 6,000
Times: Maximum Benefit Rate	× .375
Equals: Maximum "Integrated" Benefit	$ 2,250/yr.

Observation: The 37½% maximum excess benefit assumes a life only annuity and no ancillary benefits. Many reductions apply to excess benefits.

¶802.1   Consider That There May Be Excess Benefit Reductions
For Pre-Retirement Death Benefits

For plans that provide a pre-retirement death benefit, in the majority of cases the reduction will be eight-ninths, thereby lowering the maximum excess benefit to 33.33% of pay. Since virtually all small business plans include death benefits, the eight-ninths reduction is almost universally applicable.

> *Example:* John's plan includes a pre-retirement death benefit. Therefore, his retirement benefit based on excess pay must be recalculated:

Total Pay	$15,000
Less: Integration Level	(9,000)
Equals: Excess Pay	$ 6,000
Times: Maximum Adjusted Benefit Rate	× 33.33%
Equals: Maximum "Integrated" Benefit	$2,000

¶802.2   Consider That There May Be A Reduction For Form Of
Distribution

The maximum integrated retirement benefits assume distribution in the form of a life only annuity. Any other mode of distribution requires a reduction to the 33.33% benefit rate discussed at ¶802.1.

> *Example:* John's plan distributes benefits in the form of 10 year certain and continuous annuity payments. Therefore his benefit will be reduced by 10%.

		Dollar Amount	Percent
Maximum Retirement Benefit From ¶802		$2,250	37.5%
Less: Pre-retirement Death Benefit Reduction	× 8/9		
Adjusted Maximum Benefit		2,000	33.3%
Less: Reduction for 10 Certain and Continuous (cc)* Annuity	× –10%		
Net Adjusted Maximum Excess Benefit		$1,800	30%

---

*A major distribution option from pensions is 10 years certain and continuous, which means that the distributee will receive payments for as long as he lives or, if longer, for 10 years.

Observation: Distribution of Joint and 100% Survivor Annuities requires a reduction (to 79%) of a life only annuity. Recall that nonintegrated defined-benefit plans do not require adjustments for this annuity form, giving an opportunity for substantially increased contributions.

¶802.3   Consider That There May Be A Reduction For
                                    Retirement Prior To Age 65

Nonintegrated defined-benefit plans can specify a normal retirement date as early as 55 without reducing benefits. However, since Social Security benefits are not available (at full rates) until age 65, integrated defined-benefit programs require adjustment for early retirement provisions. The most commonly-used reduction is:

1. 1/15 for each of the first 5 years; and
2. 1/30 for each of the next 5 years by which normal retirement date preceded age 65.

Example: John's plan is amended to specify a normal retirement age of 55. His excess benefit must be reduced as follows:

		Dollar Amount	Percent
Maximum Benefit Adjusted For Pre-Retirement DB		$2,000	33.3%
Reduction for first 5 years	5/15		
Reduction for next 5 years	5/30		
Total Early Retirement Reduction	15/30		(16.67)
Net Excess Benefit		$1,000	16.67

Example: Even with these significant reductions certain key men, particularly those in the 35-40 age range, will profit from an early normal retirement age. Consider two plans, both integrated at $9,000, one providing retirement at 65, the other 55.

				PLAN I: RETIRE AT 65		**PLAN II: RETIRE AT 55**	
Participant	Age	Pay	Excess Pay	33% of Excess Benefit	Annual Contri-bution	16.67% of Excess Benefit	Annual Contri-bution
A	45	$50,000	$41,000	$13,530	$3,033	$6,765	$4,364
B	40	15,000	6,000	1,980	293	990	356
C	35	50,000	41,000	13,530	1,363	6,765	1,517
D	30	15,000	6,000	1,980	139	990	146
E	25	10,000	1,000	330	16	165	17
TOTAL		$140,000	$95,000	N/A	$4,844	N/A	$6,400

Observation: Older participants profit from a shortening of their potential funding period. The 45-year-old key man's contribution increases by over 40%; the 35-year old's by only 10%. This reinforces our earlier observation that the effects of interest are most strongly felt by participants with the longest to go until retirement. In this example, we have, even with a 50% reduction in benefits, increased plan costs by about 30%, but 85% of that increase goes to one participant.

¶803   WHEN TO USE ONE-TIERED FLAT-BENEFIT PLANS

Your client can set up one-tiered flat-benefit plans, the contributions of which inure almost totally to older key men. However, the potential for employee dissatisfaction and the potential for pending legislation to minimize this opportunity may reduce the efficiency of this approach.

The ideal time to use flat-benefit excess-only plans is when your client's key man is substantially older and higher-paid than his regular employees. That's frequently the case in professional corporations. (See paragraphs 803.2 and 803.3 for what to watch out for when using a one-tiered flat-benefit plan.)

¶803.1   How Flat-Benefit Excess-Only Plans Work

Dr. Kelly sets up an excess-only plan integrated at $9,000 and providing a pre-retirement death benefit. The plan promises each participant 33.33% of excess pay at retirement. Because of relative ages and pay, the program works quite well:

Employee	Age	Pay	Excess Pay	Retirement Benefit	Annual Contribution	Percent of Total
A	55	$ 99,000	$ 90,000	$29,997/yr.	$21,096	97%
B	40	14,000	5,000	1,667/yr.	282	1
C	35	14,000	5,000	1,667/yr.	195	1
D	35	12,000	3,000	1,000/yr.	117	1
E	25	9,000	0	0	0	0
TOTAL		$148,000	$103,000	N/A	$21,690	100%

If the facts are right, as they clearly are in this example, excess-only plans can achieve powerful and specific results. This illustration represents an opportunity for a key man to garner a deposit equal to 22% of his pay. To accomplish that with a defined-contribution plan, even an integrated one, would have required contributions for other employees totalling $8,000. With an integrated flat-benefit plan we've cut that to about $600. That's quite an increase in efficiency!

Observation: Recall that with an excess-only defined-contribution plan, Dr. Kelly couldn't have garnered more than seven percent of excess pay—in this case yielding a deposit of $6,300.

¶803.2   Public Relations May Be A Problem

Employees who had previously maintained IRAs may be irritated that because of the meager benefit provided by a plan like Dr. Kelly's, they are barred from continuing those personal savings programs.

> *Example:* Employee B in Dr. Kelly's plan had counted on making $1,500 per year contributions to an IRA for the 25 years. At six percent interest, that means an accumulation of $87,235 and income of $9,411 per year at age 65. Because Employee B is now an active participant in Dr. Kelly's plan, IRA is no longer an option and the trade-off—a $15,452 lump-sum or $1,667 per year—is not very attractive.

¶803.3   Pending Legislation Could Affect Your Clients

For several years, various legislation has been introduced which could eliminate or substantially reduce the utility of excess-only plans.

Congress has been unhappy with plans like Dr. Kelly's, from which highly-paid executives derive substantial tax gains with virtually no benefit for regular employees and for whose primary benefit most pension laws and regulations were originally enacted. If your client sets up an excess only or equivalent plan, make certain you inform him of its potentially transient existence and that amendments or termination can be difficult and costly.

¶804   WHEN TO USE TWO-TIERED FLAT-BENEFIT PLANS

The integration spread discussed at ¶802 can be used in two-tiered flat-benefit plans. Two-tiered plans can dramatically increase budget and benefit options for your client, while retaining all-important contribution-efficiency for older key men.

Your client will want to use a two-tiered flat-benefit plan if:

1. he needs a bigger deduction;
2. he wants to provide more than miniscule benefits for lower-paid employees; or
3. he wants to provide more benefits for himself than can be generated by an excess only program.

¶804.1   How Two-Tiered Flat-Benefit Plans Work

Your plan can provide one level of benefits for compensation up to the integration level and another, higher level of benefits for excess pay. Another way of looking at that is that the plan might provide one level of benefit for total pay with an additional benefit for excess pay. As discussed above, the spread between benefit levels, assuming a pre-retirement death benefit, can't exceed 33.333%. Thus, your plan could provide a benefit equal to, for example, 50% of total pay plus 33.33% of pay above the $9,000.

Example: Dr. Kelly is persuaded to:

1. lower his salary so he can put more away; and
2. provide more substantial benefits for his employees.

He elects to set up a 40% of total pay, 33.33% excess pay plan:

Employee	Age	Pay	Excess Pay	33% Excess Benefit	40% of Pay Benefit	Total Benefit	Annual Contri- bution
A	55	$75,000	$66,000	$21,998	$30,000	$51,998	$33,538
B	40	14,000	5,000	1,667	5,600	7,267	1,074
C	35	14,000	5,000	1,667	5,600	7,267	732
D	35	12,000	3,000	1,000	4,800	5,800	584
E	25	9,000	0	0	3,600	3,600	178
TOTAL		$124,000	$79,000	N/A	N/A	N/A	$36,106

The two-tiered formula increases the plan's contribution substantially, without significantly compromising the plan's efficiency. Dr. Kelly still receives over 90% of the contribution. Furthermore, he's providing meaningful retirement benefits for his employees.

Example: Dr. Kelly asks about the maximum plan deposits possible under a two-tiered flat-benefit plan. The formula works out to be 70.669% of total pay, plus 33.333% of excess pay.

Employee	Age	Pay	Excess Pay	33% Excess Benefit	70.669% Total Benefit	Total Benefit	Annual Contri- bution
A	55	$ 75,000	$66,000	$21,998	$53,002	$75,000	$48,374
B	40	14,000	5,000	1,667	9,864	11,560	1,709
C	35	14,000	5,000	1,667	9,864	11,560	1,165
D	35	12,000	3,000	1,000	8,480	9,480	955
E	25	9,000	0	0	6,360	6,360	315
TOTAL		$124,000	$79,000	N/A	N/A	N/A	$52,518

This illustration highlights the opportunity for dramatic plan deductions available to higher paid, older key men who participate in integrated flat-benefits plans. Dr. Kelly's contribution represents 72% of his salary—not many clients will be able to afford the luxury of putting that much away. Yet, his share of the total deposit is still 92%—so he can't use the cost of covering employees as an excuse for not establishing a plan.

¶805   WHEN AND WHERE TO USE FLAT-BENEFIT PLANS

Flat-benefit plans work well whenever:

1. key men are relatively old;
2. key men are middle-aged, but the plan's budget is somewhat limited (use an earlier normal retirement date);
3. your client believes that retirement income should be equated; or
4. your client can live with a fixed annual commitment (tempered, perhaps, by using the Entry Age Normal with FIPSL Actuarial Method).

However, notwithstanding their potential for large, highly-skewed contributions, there are more potential situations in which flat-benefit plans don't make sense:

1. your client feels length of service should be the prime benefit determinant;
2. your client's profits and cash flow fluctuate dramatically from year to year;
3. key men are young relative to other employees;
4. the plan might have to be terminated within 10 years of its inception;
5. employee ill-will might be a controlling factor.

Flat-benefit plans provide the simplest defined-benefit formula and are frequently utilized. They're easily explained. They work particularly well for small businesses, where principals tend to be older. Make sure your clients are aware of the potential.

9

When and How Unit-Benefit Plans Can Be Effective

Unit-benefit plans present an opportunity to reward long-standing service in the most direct and visible way. Retirement income in unit-benefit plans is a multiple of compensation and years of service or participation. Participants accrue a small "piece" of their retirement income annually, adding another "piece" each year until they retire, at which time the pieces earned cumulatively are totalled. Thus, the longer the period of a participant's service, the higher his retirement benefits.

Frequently, the owner or key man of a small to medium-sized business will have worked for the organization since he was quite young, and therefore will have substantial service accumulated as he approaches retirement. He may value most highly those employees who, like himself, have contributed the better part of their lives to the business. Here, unit-benefit plans can be the answer.

This chapter will show you how unit-benefit plans work, how they compare to their flat-benefit cousins, and how to use them effectively. It will explain the peculiar integration rules that apply and highlight the situations most amenable to unit-benefit plans. The information will add measurably to your "bag of tricks" and enhance your ability to match your client's objectives with the right plan.

¶900   **HOW A UNIT-BENEFIT PLAN WORKS**

Conceptually, unit-benefit plans are as simple as their flat-benefit cousins. Flat-benefit plans promise future benefits equal to a percentage of compensation (such as 50% of pay). Unit-benefit plans simply translate these calculations to an annual event. Each year a plan participant accrues another "unit," and at retirement, his pension will be the sum of all units earned during his working life. In other words, a participant "earns" a new benefit each time he completes a year of service.

You can visualize a unit-benefit plan in the same manner we illustrated the Attained Age Level Actuarial Funding Method. You will recall that in that actuarial method, each year's change in compensation was reflected in an incremental and cumulative change in funding. In unit-benefit plans each year's service adds a new incremental benefit to the total. Therefore, employees with substantial amounts of service at retirement age, will have accumulated the greatest number of incremental "blocks." For example, if a plan provided a benefit for each year of service equal to one percent of pay, then a participant retiring after 40 years of service would receive 40% of his pay; a participant retiring after 10 years of service would receive 10% of his pay.

Example: U. Knit Company establishes a simple unit-benefit plan. The plan promises each participant a retirement benefit equal to two percent of his pay for each year of service. The result is a plan offering vastly disproportionate benefits to participants with different service at retirement date.

Participant	Age	Pay	Service @ 65	2% Annual Benefit Increment	Benefit @ 65	Annual Contribution
A	50	$ 50,000	40 yrs.	$1,000/yr.	$40,000	$14,397
B	45	30,000	20 yrs.	600	12,000	2,690
C	45	30,000	40 yrs.	600	24,000	3,547
D	35	15,000	30 yrs.	300	9,000	907
E	30	10,000	35 yrs.	200	7,000	491
TOTAL		$13,500	N/A	N/A	N/A	$22,032

Observation: The illustration clearly shows how unit-benefit plans work. Participant A receives an annual increment of two percent of his $50,000 pay. That works out to $1,000. Assuming 40 years of service at that compensation rate, his retirement benefit will simply be the sum of 40 annual increments or

$40,000. The real key to unit-benefit plans is shown by the relationship between participants B and C. Each earns $30,000 and each is 45-years old. Their annual increments are $600. But Participant B will only have 20 years of service at age 65; Participant C will have 40 years. Therefore, Participant C will retire with twice as much income as his counterpart. Unit-benefit plans, more than any other discussed in this book, specifically reward long-standing service. That can be a plus or a minus depending upon the facts of your client's situation.

¶900.1   Why Incremental Benefits Can Add Up Big For Long-Standing Participants

The illustration at ¶900 for U. Knit Company generated a whopping benefit for Participant C because of that employee's having 40 years of service at retirement. The beneficiaries of the unit approach are typically young employees, who are assumed, for purposes of the plan, to be employed for the duration of their working lives. Therefore, a 25-year-old participant will generally receive the maximum possible benefit under the unit approach.

¶900.2   How Unit-Benefit Plans Can Work Against Older Key Men

Frequently, your client's older key men will have either:

- joined the company during middle age; or
- purchased the business (and, therefore, commenced employment) during middle age.

Either of those two fact situations can disrupt the efficacy of a unit-benefit plan. That's because an employee hired at, for example, age 45 would—except for adjustments discussed below—find, at best, he receives a smaller benefit than average employees of the firm who are probably much younger (and, therefore, have more future service).

Example: Joe had worked as general manager for a paint store for 20 years before he managed to save enough money to start his own business. When he finally started his own store, he hired one of his competitor's key men—a 50-year-old buyer. Business boomed and the company soon employed 10 sales, clerical and stock personnel with an average age of 30. Joe considered setting up a unit-benefit plan—but only for a moment. He and his key man were 45 and 50 respectively and, therefore, couldn't receive more than 15 or 20 incremental units. The younger employees could receive up to 40 units thus yielding twice the retirement income.

¶901   HOW TO MAKE THE PLAN WORK BEST FOR KEY MEN

Your client can improve the performance of his unit-benefit plan in several ways. One is to make the threshold decision of whether or not a unit-benefit plan is likely to work given the client's basic census information. Another is to restrict eligible service.

¶901.1   What Are The Critical Factors For Evaluating Census Information

A cursory review of your client's basic census data may reveal hidden basic opportunities or pitfalls inherent in the selection of a unit-benefit plan. You will generally reject unit-benefit plans if any of the following factors are present:

1. the key man has less than 20 years service at normal retirement date;
2. the average service potential of regular employees is significantly (e.g., more than five years) greater than that of the key man or men; and
3. the key man plans to retire early, thereby further shortening his relative service span.

On the other hand, certain census or subjective factors may favor adopting a unit-benefit plan:

1. Is the business your client's life-long work? Frequently, small businesses will have been started and operated by one individual years ago. In those cases, the key man may have as many as 40 or 45 years of service when he reaches retirement age.
2. Does your client want to reward service above all else? If your client's motivation is to reward long-standing service, no plan can do it better than a unit-benefit program.

3. Does your client's business tend to hire older employees? Certain industries have traditionally hired older, more mature employees. If that's the case with your client, and if he started the business when fairly young, his employee pool is likely to have a shorter average working life than his own. That would be a good situation for a unit-benefit plan.

¶901.2   How To Use The Key Man's Past Service For Optimal Efficiency

To insure that none of your client's employees will receive benefits greater than those of the key man, consider a limitation on credited years of service under the plan's formula. For example, if the key man will have 30 years of service at age 65, the plan's annual increment should be limited to 30. That way, employees who will have more service upon retirement than the key man will not receive larger pension benefits.

Example: Limit, Ltd.'s key man will have been employed for 25 years when he reaches age 65. He purchases the business at age 40. While he is oriented toward rewarding service, he doesn't want to provide benefits for any employee that are greater than his own. He considers two alternative unit-benefit plans. The first provides 2½% of pay for each year of service. The second provides 2½% for each year of service not to exceed 25. Since Limit, Ltd., when purchased by the key man, retained some of its existing employees who had substantial service, the results are dramatic.

| | | | | PLAN I | | | PLAN II | |
| | | | Service @ 65 | 2½%/yr Benefit | Annual Deposit | 2½% to 25 yrs Benefit | Annual Deposit |
Participant	Age	Pay					
A	40	$50,000	25 yrs	$31,250	$ 4,619	$31,250	$ 4,619
B	50	30,000	40 yrs	30,000	10,798	18,750	6,749
C	50	20,000	15 yrs	7,500	2,699	7,500	2,699
D	45	20,000	20 yrs	10,000	2,242	10,000	2,242
E	30	15,000	40 yrs	15,000	1,053	13,124	921
TOTAL		$135,000	N/A	N/A	$21,411	N/A	$17,230

Observation: Limit Ltd.'s president has saved $4,181 without reducing his own benefits! By limiting eligible service to 25 years, he has excluded from benefit computations 15 years of service for Employees B and E, who—except for the limitation—would have received retirement income equal to 100% of their pay (2½% × 40 years = 100%).

Planning Tip: Always review your client's census information to see how many years of service the key man will have when he reaches age 65. If it is more than 30, then a unit-benefit plan is worth considering. And if a unit-benefit plan is worth considering, make sure you include a limitation on credited service that corresponds to the amount of service your key man will have when he retires.

¶902   HOW TO OBTAIN MAXIMUM BENEFITS USING UNIT-BENEFIT PLANS

Maximum benefits under unit-benefit plans are the same as those for flat-benefit plans (e.g., the ultimate retirement benefit can't exceed the lesser of 100% of an employee's average compensation of $110,625 with the exception of the $10,000 minimum retirement benefit option). Also, benefits paid in a form other than a life annuity must be reduced to actuarial equivalencies.

Planning Tip: The best way to attain maximum benefits for your key man is to divide his pay (not in excess of $110,625) by his years of service. This will be the exact annual increment necessary to achieve the highest benefit level.

Example: Jim earns $150,000 and will have 30 years of service at normal retirement age. If Jim wants maximum benefits, the plan's formula should be 2.458% for each year of service not in excess of 30. ($110,625 ÷ 30 years ÷ $150,000.)

¶903   HOW TO INCREASE MAXIMUM BENEFITS USING INTEGRATED UNIT-BENEFIT PLANS

If the facts of your client's situation warrant consideration of a unit-benefit plan, then proper integration can only make things better. Integration of unit-benefit plans is quite similar to that of their flat-benefit cousins except that the integration "system" is applied to the annual incremental benefit rather than aggregate retirement income. In addition, unit-benefit plans offer added flexibility for choosing an integration level. Finally, two alternative approaches to unit-benefit plans are available.

1. career average; and
2. final average plans (see paragraphs 903.4 through 903.7.)

All these options make unit-benefit plans a potentially sophisticated tool for solving your client's problems.

¶903.1   How Integration Works In Unit-Benefit Plans

Like integrated flat-benefit plans, integrated unit-benefit programs establish separate benefit levels for compensation above and below integration levels. Ultimate retirement benefits are therefore a combination of years of service times compensation up to the integration level and years of service times compensation in excess of the integration level.

> *Example:* Integral Corporation's president participates in a unit-benefit plan which recognizes all his 30 years of service with a benefit formula providing one percent of pay up to the $10,000 integration level for each year of service and 1.5% of pay in excess of $10,000 for each year of service. Based on his $50,000 salary, benefits are easy to compute.

Excess Pay	$40,000	
Excess Pay Benefit Rate	× 1.5%	
Annual Increment, Excess Pay		$ 600
Pay Below Integration Level	$10,000	
Benefit Rate	× 1%	
Annual Increment, Basic Pay		$ 100
Total Annual Increment		$ 700
Times Years of Service		× 30
Total Retirement Benefit		$21,000

Clearly the integration of unit-benefit plans is not complex. However, there are more alternatives and variations with unit-benefit plans than with their flat-benefit cousins. Let's consider some of those now.

¶903.2   How To Choose The Right Integration Level

Unit-benefit plans offer the same choices as their flat-benefit counterparts. (See Covered Compensation Table I, Covered Compensation Table II, and flat dollar amounts.) Finally, higher flat dollar amounts can be used assuming you make certain benefit reductions. The application of integration levels to employee compensation in unit-benefit plans is virtually identical to flat benefit programs.

Alternative One

Table I: Covered Compensation Table I (reproduced at ¶801.1 Alternative One) is your first alternative for calculating participant's "excess pay." Table I applies an averaged covered compensation amount to each participating employee. Here's how it would apply to a typical situation.

TABLE I: COVERED COMPENSATION

Participant	Age	Calendar Year of 65th Birthday	Pay	Covered Compensation	Excess Pay
A	55	1989	$50,000	$13,200	$36,800
B	48	1996	45,000	15,600	29,400
C	43	2001	20,000	18,600	1,400
D	38	2006	20,000	20,400	0
E	32	2012	20,000	22,800	0

Alternative Two

Table II: Covered Compensation Table II presents a comparable alternative based on individual participant ages. While Table II offers more specificity, it also complicates calculation of a participant's covered compensation. Table II is reproduced at ¶801.1 (Alternative Two) and can apply as follows:

TABLE II: COVERED COMPENSATION

Participant	Age	Calendar Year of 65th Birthday	Pay	Covered Compensation	Excess Pay
A	55	1989	$50,000	$13,452	$36,548
B	48	1996	45,000	15,828	29,172
C	43	2001	20,000	8,420	1,580
D	38	2006	20,000	20,640	0
E	32	2012	20,000	22,560	0

Alternative Three

Taxable Wage Base: Flat-benefit plans can use a uniform flat dollar integration level not to exceed the covered compensation of the oldest employee who is or might be a participant of the plan. As discussed at ¶801.1 (Alternative Three) that effectively limits flat dollar integration levels to $11,400. Unit-benefit plans can utilize flat dollar integration levels up to and including the taxable wage base in effect during a particular plan year. Since the taxable wage base for 1980 is $25,900, that's a substantial increase that allows for the exclusion of substantially more lower-paid employees. Continuing with the examples given above, let's consider how a $20,000 uniform dollar amount integration level can maximize excess pay for key plan participants.

FLAT DOLLAR AMOUNT INTEGRATION LEVELS

Participant	Age	Calendar Year of 65th Birthday	Pay	Covered Compensation	Excess Pay
A	55	N/A	$50,000	$20,000	$30,000
B	48	N/A	45,000	20,000	25,000
C	43	N/A	20,000	20,000	0
D	38	N/A	20,000	20,000	0
E	32	N/A	20,000	20,000	0

When Can A Higher Flat Dollar Amount Integration Level Be Used: It's possible to use a uniformly applied flat dollar integration level *higher* than the taxable wage base if integrated benefits otherwise allowable are properly reduced. The reduction is accomplished by applying the following formula:

$$\frac{\text{Taxable Wage Base in force}}{\text{Other Integration Level Desired}} \times \frac{\text{Benefits Other-}}{\text{Wise Allowable}} = \frac{\text{Net Reduced}}{\text{Benefits Available}}$$

> ***Example:*** XYZ, Incorporated wishes to exclude from coverage all employees earning less than $30,900. Let's assume maximum integrated benefits were otherwise one percent of pay. Given those facts, XYZ Incorporated's plan can't provide an "excess benefit" in excess of:

$$\frac{\$25,900}{\$30,900} \times 1\% = .86\%$$

Observation: The exclusion of participants earning $30,900 or less is accomplished only at the expense of reducing otherwise available benefits for higher-paid key participants.

¶903.3   Which Integration Level To Use

As we discussed with respect to integration level choices for flat-benefit plans, the choice of which integration level to use should not be taken lightly. Certain situations lend themselves to the use of one integration system versus another. Here are some tips:

1. Use Table I Covered Compensation when your key men are relatively old and in situations where there will be so many participants that the individual calculations of Table II might become burdensome.

2. Table II will be most productive in situations where key men are relatively old and the plan's budget is limited enough to warrant getting "every dollar's worth" of excess benefit. Particularly, in plans with relatively few participants, the extra effort for an individual calculation is not so burdensome that it needs to be avoided.

¶903.4   How A Career Average Unit-Benefit Plan Works

If ultimate retirement benefits are the sum of annual increments based on *actual* compensation earned in each year of participation, then the

Year	Compensation	Integration Level	Excess Pay	1.24% Annual Increment	Cumulative Annual Increment
1	$12,000	$9,000	$ 3,000	$ 37.33	$ 37.33
2	14,000	9,000	5,000	62.00	99.33
3	16,000	9,000	7,000	86.80	186.13
4	18,000	9,000	9,000	111.60	297.73
5	20,000	9,000	11,000	136.40	434.13
6	22,000	9,000	13,000	161.20	595.33
7	24,000	9,000	15,000	186.00	781.33
8	26,000	9,000	17,000	210.80	992.13
9	28,000	9,000	19,000	235.60	1227.73
10	30,000	9,000	21,000	260.40	1488.13
11	32,000	9,000	23,000	285.20	1773.33
12	34,000	9,000	25,000	310.00	2083.83
13	36,000	9,000	27,000	334.80	2418.13
14	38,000	9,000	29,000	359.60	2777.73
15	40,000	9,000	31,000	384.40	3162.13
TOTAL	N/A	N/A	N/A	N/A	$3162.13

annual increment for pay in excess of the integration level can be as much as 1.4%. Assuming the plan has a pre-retirement death benefit, that percentage must be reduced by eight-ninths giving a net excess increment of 1.24%

> *Example:* Fred participates in an "excess only" unit-benefit plan, which is integrated at $9,000. The plan provides an annual incremental benefit of 1.24% for excess pay. Fred's pay and benefits are shown over his 15 hypothetical years of participation as shown in the table at top of page 189.

Observation: Fred's retirement benefits are simply the sum of actual increments earned each plan year. Keep in mind, however, the burdensome requirements inherent in an "actual earnings" unit-benefit plan for keeping records of increments earned during each year of plan participation. That can be quite burdensome for plan participants that have 40 years service.

¶903.5   How A Two-Tiered Career Average Plan Works

The integration "spread" discussed in ¶903.2 can be used in two-tiered unit-benefit plans. That's true, as long as total benefits don't exceed the familiar 100%/$110,625 limitation.

> *Example:* U. Fural Company establishes a career average unit-benefit plan which provides one percent of total pay per year of service and 1.24% for each year of service above $22,900. Maximum years of service are 30—the number that will have been worked at age 65 by the president (Employee A).

Participant	Age	Pay	Service @ 65	1%/yr Total Pay Benefit	+	1.24%/yr Excess Benefit	=	Total Benefit	Annual Deposit
A	50	$ 50,000	30 yrs.	$15,000		$10,081		$25,081	$ 9,027
B	40	30,000	40	9,000		2,641		11,641	1,721
C	40	30,000	20	6,000		1,761		7,761	1,147
D	35	15,000	30	4,500		0		4,500	453
E	30	12,000	35	3,600		0		3,600	253
TOTAL		$137,000		N/A		N/A		N/A	$12,601

Observation: The actual calculation of career average pay, although not sophisticated, involves the retention of a potentially extraordinary amount of information. In the illustration above, the five participants have, between them, 155 years of service at age 65. A career average plan would require that all of those 155 years' payroll records be available. In a medium-sized company without the computer capacity to retain these records, the averaging process can be more effort than it is worth. The effect of averaging, particularly in a period of high inflation, is primarily to lower benefit rates for plan participants. However that reduction could also be accomplished by simply using a lower benefit formula in the first place, and preclude the requirement of retention of reams of historical data. However, career average plans do allow for the use of a slightly higher excess benefit rate (1.24% after consideration of the pre-retirement death benefit) than their final average cousins. Frequently the decision will be based on the simplest choice—which means a final average plan, even at the loss of some design efficiency.

¶903.6   How Final Average Pay Plans Can Ease Your
                                    Administrative Burdens

Unit-benefit plans can provide retirement income based on a five-year average (assuming the plan is integrated—three-years if it isn't). In these cases, benefits are a multiple of the plan's accrual rate, years of service, and final average compensation. The big difference is in the compensation averaged. Typically, an employee's five final years' compensation will be substantially higher than pay averaged over his entire working life. Therefore, this approach will generate higher retirement income.

For that reason, the incremental benefit that can be earned for pay in excess of the integration level is limited to one percent. Reduced for pre-retirement death benefits, that means an effective annual accrual of .89%. Thus, a final average pay plan provides lower incremental benefits for higher compensation.

Example: Fred wants to know what his benefits would be under a final average pay plan. For that we need only consider his compensation averaged over the last five years.

Average compensation, last 5 years	$36,000
Less: Integration level	9,000
Times: Years of service	15
Times: Annual increment for excess pay	.89%
Equals: Excess pay retirement benefit	$3,338

Observation: Fred's benefit under the final average pay approach is 5½% higher than under the career average formula. The potential effects of inflation make final average pay plans much more attractive to younger participants.

¶903.7   How A Two-Tiered Final Average Pay Plan Works

The "spread" discussed at ¶903.3 applies to two-tiered unit-benefit plans as well. Therefore, subject to the constraints of the $110,625/100% rule, your client could establish a unit-benefit plan, providing, for example, one percent for each year of service up to $25,900 and .89% for each year of service for compensation for each year in excess of $25,900.

Example: U. Fural Company considers a final average pay plan providing just such a formula. Because final average pay will tend to be higher than career average, compensation is assumed to be 25% higher than under the alternative approach discussed at ¶903.5.

Participant	Age	Pay	Service @ 65	1%/yr Total Pay Benefit	+	.89%/yr Excess Benefit	=	Total Benefit	Annual Deposit
A	50	$ 62,500	30 yrs.	$18,750		$ 9,772		$28,522	$11,334
B	40	37,500	40	11,250		4,130		15,380	2,593
C	40	37,500	20	7,500		2,065		9,565	1,612
D	35	18,750	30	5,625		0		5,025	567
E	30	15,000	35	4,500		0		4,500	316
TOTAL		$171,250		N/A		N/A		N/A	$15,339

Observation: The above illustration assumed a 25% increase in participant payroll over the comparable example at ¶903.5. As a practical matter, any assumption about inflation as it relates to payroll will mean that younger participants will derive the greatest additional advantage from final average pay unit-benefit plans. That's because the effect of compound interest on their salaries will be far more strongly felt than it will for their older counterparts.

¶904   A CHECKLIST OF KEY QUESTIONS WHEN USING
                    UNIT-BENEFIT PLANS

Most of what can be done with a unit-benefit plan can also be done with a flat-benefit program, and vice versa. Therefore, the choice will often boil down to which approach you and your client feel most comfortable with. The key, under either approach, is to maximize your client's key man's share of benefits and contributions. In situations where the use of a unit-benefit plan is dictated, use the following checklist to "cover your bases":

☐ Have you limited maximum credited service to years your key man will have accumulated at normal retirement date?

☐ Does the sum of excess pay increments for the key man equal 33.33%?

☐ Does the sum of excess and regular pay increments fall within the 100%/$110,625 limitations?

☐ Does an average or final pay plan make more sense?

☐ If a career average plan is selected who will be responsible for the potentially onerous recordkeeping responsibilities?

☐ Will your client's level of sophistication make a unit-benefit approach more or less attractive?

¶905   PRINCIPAL ADVANTAGES AND DISADVANTAGES OF UNIT-BENEFIT PLANS

Because of their inherent orientation toward relative service, unit-benefit plans can present challenging limitations or opportunities. While completing the checklist at ¶904 you should be constantly aware of these obstacles and challenges. Most can be overcome or avoided by diligent review of your client's census information.

¶905.1   Situations Where Unit-Benefit Plans Can Work

Unit-benefit plans can be a powerful tool where one or more of the following factors are present:

1. The key man will have substantially more service than the average employee.

2. Your client is philosophically attuned to a plan where he recognizes service above all else.

3. Your client finds the annual benefit increment approach to ultimate pensions conceptually simpler than the flat-benefit approach.

¶905.2   Situations Where Unit-Benefit Plans Can Work Against You

The converse of the above positive statements can be equally true. The presence of some or all of the following factors might mitigate against using the unit-benefit approach:

1. Potential service of regular employees exceeds that of key men.

2. The business was acquired relatively recently by the key man, thereby limiting his potential for eligible service under the plan.

3. Your client finds the flat-benefit approach conceptually simpler.

4. Your client doesn't feel relative service should be a controlling factor for determining plan benefits.

The brevity of this chapter underscores the similarity of unit and flat-benefit plans. Flat-benefit plans which provide a pro rata reduction for service less than the number of years that key men will have at retirement achieve virtually the identical result as unit-benefit plans. More often than not, the ultimate decision about which approach to use will be based on a particular practitioner or client's comfort with an aggregate versus annual approach to pension benefits. The only defined-benefit plan to offer significant, substantive differences from unit and flat-benefit plans is discussed in the following chapter dealing with offset plans.

10

Offset Plans Provide A Simple Integration Alternative

Unit-benefit and flat-benefit pension plans recognize Social Security benefits directly by providing separate benefits for compensation above and below the integration level. Very often it is difficult to explain to plan participants how these two-tiered computations affect them. Offset plans provide a simple alternative. Offset plans provide all participants with a unified pension benefit without regard to Social Security. However, the benefit is provided by two sources: first, from the government-sponsored Social Security, and second, from employer contributions. Theoretically, an offset plan provides uniform retirement income for all participants which is the sum of these two components.

Chapter 10 will explain in detail what offset plans are, various alternative formats you can choose, and how or when to use offset plans. In addition, Chapter 10 will discuss various "tricks" to improve the efficiency of your offset plan.

¶1000 **WHAT IS AN OFFSET PLAN?**

Offset plans provide a unique and easily explained alternative to their more sophisticated unit and flat-benefit cousins. While unit and flat-benefit plan integration is governed by complex rules about the relationship of plan benefits above and below the integration level, offset plans utilize a much more basic approach.

Offset plans theoretically provide benefits for *all* plan participants, under a traditional nonintegrated unit or flat-benefit formula. There is no annual computation of "spread" or "excess-benefit" rates. Whenever a participant reaches retirement age, however, his benefits are simply *reduced* by a portion of his Social Security payments. The maximum reduction, or "offset," is 83.33% of the Primary Social Security Amount (PIA). Because of the rapid escalation of Social Security benefits—bound to continue with the advent of cost-of-living and coupling adjustments—this offset can provide a more effectively integrated plan than traditional flat or unit-benefit plans. That's because Social Security benefits replace a high percentage of lower-paid employees' salaries and that percentage is often higher than the retirement benefits provided by the employer's underlying plan. In other words, the offset amount can frequently exceed your client's commitment—meaning he may have no funding commitment.

¶1000.1   How Offset Plans Qualify

Virtually any defined-benefit plan can utilize an offset format. Either a flat or unit-benefit plan can establish a benefit level from which a social security offset may be deducted.

Example: Offshore Ltd. establishes a 50% of pay flat-benefit plan with an offset equal to 60% of primary social security. John has worked for Offshore for 20 years, always earning more than the taxable wage base. His final average pay is $28,000. Here's his plan benefit computation:

Compensation		$28,000
Times Benefit Rate		× 50%
Plan Benefit		$14,000
Social Security Benefit	$7,935	
Times Percentage of Offset	60%	
Net Offset	($4,761)	
John's Benefit From Offshore Ltd.		$ 9,239

Example: John's brother Jim has worked for Exit Company for 30 years and earned $30,000. Exit Company gives exiting employees a retirement benefit of three percent of pay for each year of service offset by 70% of primary social security. Jim can look forward to:

Compensation		$30,000
Times Annual Benefit Accrual Rate	× 3%	
Annual Benefit Increment	$900	
Times Years of Service	× 30	
Gross Retirement Benefit		$27,000
Social Security Benefit	7,935	
Times Offset Percentage	70%	
Net Offset	(5,553)	
Jim's Benefit		$21,447

Observation: Many lower paid employees have such a high percentage of their income replaced by Social Security that a high level of offset may provide their entire retirement income. The effect can be as efficient as traditional excess-only plans.

Example: Savit Incorporated provides employees with 40% of their pay, less 70% of Social Security. Mark's average pay is $9,000/yr. Therefore, his employer-sponsored benefit is:

Compensation		$9,000
Benefit Rate	× 40%	
Plan Benefit		$3,600
Social Security Benefit	$5,747	
Offset Percentage	× 70%	
Offset Amount	(4,026)	
Net Employer Benefit		0

¶1000.2   How Is The Amount Of Offset Determined

Assuming your client elects to use the Social Security Table in effect for the retirement year of a particular participant to determine that participant's offset, the maximum offset is 83.33%. Thus, a flat-benefit plan whose normal form of benefit is a life only annuity could provide participants with retirement income of, for example, 90% of pay minus 83.33% of Social Security. The maximum offset is usually reduced to 8/9 to allow pre-retirement death benefits. That means most of your clients will use a maximum offset of 74.07%

Example: XYZ Company's plan, which provides a pre-retirement death benefit, uses a benefit formula of 60% of pay, less 74.07% of Social Security. The plan qualifies.

¶1000.3   Choosing The Best Combination For Your Client— Critical Choices

The best combination of benefits and offset depends on your client's objectives. Assuming his objectives center around maximization of contributions for older key men, he will naturally choose the full 74.07% offset. However, many clients have an ethical, or public relations problem setting up a pension plan which, because of heavy offsetting, effectively eliminates most lower-paid employees. If that's the case, consider a reduced offset amount.

Example: In the interests of simplicity and good public relations, Fair Play Company decides to compare a maximum offset plan with a 50% offset program. Basic plan benefits are held constant at 75% of pay. The results illustrate the dramatic shift of benefits in favor of lower-paid participants as shown on page 199.
    The illustrations clearly show how significant effective integration can be, particularly for lower-paid employees. Make sure that your client understands that any reduction in the maximum integration rate or offset rate will skew benefits towards the lower-paid people. That may be a high price to pay for a simpler or "more equitable" plan. Remember that, assuming integration rules that have been worked out over the last several decades accurately reflect the proper relationship between private plan benefits and Social Security, that the only discriminatory plan is one that *doesn't* maximize integration.

¶1001   **HOW TO USE FLAT-BENEFIT OFFSET PLANS EFFICIENTLY**

Flat-benefit plans are most amenable to an offset format. This is because basic benefits under the plan are computed in a parallel fashion to the offset amount. Flat-benefit offset plans will work best in the same situations where traditional flat-benefit or flat-benefit excess plans will be effective. The differences will be in slight contribution discrepancies.

COMPARISON OF NET FAIR PLAY COMPANY BENEFITS

	Participant		74.074% Offset Plan			50% Offset Plan		
#	Comp.	S.S. Benefit	75% Basic Benefit -	less:74.074% Offset =	Net Fair Play Benefit	75% Basic Benefit -	less: 50% Offset =	Net Fair Play Benefit
A	50,000	6,000	37,500	4,444	33,056	37,500	3,000	34,500
B	30,000	6,000	22,500	4,444	18,056	22,500	3,000	19,500
C	30,000	6,000	22,500	4,444	18,056	22,500	3,000	19,500
D	20,000	6,000	15,000	4,444	10,556	15,000	3,000	12,000
E	10,000	6,000	7,500	4,444	3,056	7,500	3,000	4,500

COMPARISON OF TOTAL RETIREMENT INCOME

	74.074% Offset Plan			50% Offset Plan			
Participant	Net Fair Play Benefit +	Social Security =	Total Benefit	Net Fair Play Benefit +	Social Security =	Total Benefit	% Increase
A	33,056	6,000	39,056	34,500	6,000	40,500	+4%
B	18,056	6,000	24,056	19,500	6,000	25,500	+6%
C	18,056	6,000	24,056	19,500	6,000	25,500	+6%
D	10,556	6,000	16,556	12,000	6,000	18,000	+9%
E	3,056	6,000	9,056	4,500	6,000	10,500	+16%

¶1001.1   When Flat-Benefit Offset Plans Will Work Best For
Your Clients

Chapter 8 described in considerable detail fact situations warranting consideration of flat-benefit plans. Those situations include:

1. Key men older than average employees;
2. Key men higher paid than average employees; or
3. Client wants all retiring employees to receive a comparable retirement income.

Virtually any time a flat-benefit excess plan makes sense, so does an offset program.

> *Example:* Reduction Company considers establishing a 60% of pay flat-benefit plan offset by 74.07% of a participant's social security (based on the Table in effect in 1978), but asks how that plan would compare with a traditional flat-benefit (excess) plan spending the same budget. Here's your answer:

Partici-pant	Age	Pay	Offset Plan				Flat-Benefit Excess Plan	
			Gross Benefits	S.S. Offset	Net Benefit	Annual Deposit	Benefits*	Contri-butions
A	50	$50,000	$30,000/yr	$5,803	$24,197	$8,709	$24,467/yr	$8,755
B	45	15,000	9,000	5,387	3,613	810	4,000	890
C	40	25,000	15,000	5,803	9,197	1,359	9,133	1,339
D	35	50,000	30,000	5,803	24,197	2,438	22,866	2,290
E	25	10,000	6,000	4,462	1,538	76	2,400	118
TOTAL		$150,000	N/A	N/A	N/A	$13,392	N/A	$13,392

*The formula is 24% of total pay plus 33.33% of pay above Covered Compensation, Table I for 1978.

Observation: It's interesting to note how similar the results are under either approach. The similarity adds power to the arguments that choosing between the alternatives is more a matter of style than substance. The offset and flat-benefit excess plans provide benefits and contributions that are almost identical. Note that Participant A's benefit increases by only one percent. The various integration alternatives set forth in Revenue Ruling 71-446 have been carefully prepared to insure this comparability among the alternatives.

¶1001.2   How Service Reductions Can Improve Your Results

Adding another element to your benefit formula—a pro rata reduction in benefits for service less than a specified number of years—will enhance the performance of your offset plan.

> *Example:* Reduction Company (¶1001.1) implements the offset plan, but adds a requirement of 40 years service for full benefits. That has a significant impact on plan benefits and costs, since Employee A started working for the firm at age 25:

Partici-pant	Age	Pay	Assumed Service	Gross Benefit	Service Reduction	Net Benefit	Deposit
A	50	$50,000	40 yrs	$24,197	N/A	$24,197	$ 8,709
B	45	15,000	20	3,613	20/40	1,806	405
C	40	25,000	30	9,197	30/40	6,989	1,019
D	35	50,000	30	24,197	30/40	18,148	1,829
E	25	10,000	40	1,538	N/A	1,538	76
TOTAL		$150,000	N/A	N/A	N/A	N/A	$12,038

Observation: The participants with less than 40 years of service at retirement receive a substantial reduction in their benefits and therefore, contributions.

> *Example:* Participant B, except for the service reduction, receives a retirement benefit of $3,613. But since Participant B is assumed to have only 20 years service at retirement, his plan benefits can be reduced by twenty fortieths and his contribution cut in half. The effect of these service reductions can be quite dramatic, particularly with relatively old employees who, under a flat-benefit alternative, require a much larger deposit. This illustration reinforces the fact that flat-benefit plans, used in conjuction with the right modifications and reductions, can be a powerful planning tool for your client.

¶1002   HOW UNIT-BENEFIT OFFSET PLANS PROVIDE FURTHER DESIGN OPPORTUNITY

If your client's key men will have substantially more service at retirement than most employees, or if your client believes retirement benefits should be directly tied to years of service, then a unit-benefit offset plan can be effective. The arguments in favor of unit-benefit offset plans are obviously the same as those for regular unit-benefit programs.

¶1002.1   How Unit-Benefit Offset Plans Work

Unit-benefit offset plans are simple to operate. There are two basic approaches:

1. Compute the gross retirement benefit and subtract a *flat* percentage of social security; and

2. Compute the gross retirement benefit and subtract an incremental percentage of social security.

Under the first approach, your client would compute total retirement benefits in the conventional unit-benefit manner, such as:

*   Years of service times the benefit rate equals retirement income and then subtract a portion of the total Social Security benefits available at age 65; or

*   Retirement income minus X% of social security equals net plan benefits.

This first approach, therefore, uses a flat offset to a unit-benefit format. The second approach uses a unit-benefit offset, as well as a unit-benefit retirement income calculation. The total plan benefit is calculated in an identical manner. But the offset is determined on an incremental approach.

$$\text{Years of Service} \ \times \ \text{Offset Rate} \ = \ \text{Total Offset}$$

With this latter approach, participants with the most service will have the largest offset. In many small to medium-sized businesses, that's contrary to typical objectives.

Planning Tip: The incremental approach to offset amounts is most effectively used in the *unusual* circumstances where your client has key men who *do not* have more service than typical employees, but still insists on a unit-benefit approach.

Example: Reduction Company changes its corporate mind and sets up a two percent-of-pay-per-year-of-service unit-benefit plan offset by 74.07% of Social Security. Here's the result:

Participant	Age	Pay	Service	Basic Benefit 2% × yrs × Pay	Offset Amount	Net Benefit	Annual Deposit
A	50	$ 50,000	40	$40,000	$5,803	$34,197	$12,308
B	45	15,000	20	6,000	5,387	613	137
C	40	25,000	30	15,000	5,803	9,197	1,359
D	35	50,000	30	30,000	5,803	24,197	2,438
E	25	10,000	40	8,000	4,462	3,538	175
TOTAL		$150,000	N/A	N/A	N/A	N/A	$16,417

The above example illustrates a unit-benefit plan with a flat-offset. Basic plan benefits were a multiple of years of service and the incremental benefit rate. For example, Employee C receives a benefit of 60% (30 years of service × 2% per year) of pay. Offset amounts are a flat 74% of estimated Social Security benefits, without regard to years of service at retirement. That results in a larger offset for participants with less service.

Example: Unite, Incorporated has identical census facts as Reduction Company, but elects a two percent-of-pay-per-year-of-service unit-benefit plan offset by 1.85% of Social Security for each year of service. That's a more complicated approach, but adds consistency to the plan:

Participant	Age	Pay	Service	Basic Benefit 2% × Yrs × Pay	Offset - 1.85% × Service × S. Sec.	Net Benefit	Annual Deposit
A	50	$ 50,000	40 yrs.	$40,000	$5,803	$34,197	$12,308
B	45	15,000	20 yrs.	6,000	2,690	3,309	742
C	40	25,000	30 yrs.	15,000	4,348	10,652	1,574
D	35	50,000	30 yrs.	30,000	4,348	25,652	2,584
E	25	10,000	40 yrs.	8,000	4,462	3,538	175
TOTAL		$150,000	N/A	N/A	N/A	N/A	$17,383

Unite, Incorporated's plan generates identical basic retirement benefits. For example, Employee C still receives 60% (30 years of service × 2% per year) of pay. However, the *offset amount* is calculated on an incremental approach. Employee C's offset, rather than being a flat 74% of Social Security, is now 30 years times 1.85% times Social Security. Thus, his offset is $4,348 (55.5% of Social Security). Note that net plan benefits to be provided by Unite, Incorporated, for Employee C, are now $10,652 and the annual deposit is $1,574. Under the flat offset approach, net plan benefits were $9,197 and the deposit was $1,359. This 12% increase in benefits and costs may be in opposition to your client's objectives.

Observation: The latter approach, using an incremental offset technique, dramatically boosts benefits and contributions for participants with *less* service and *lower* pay. That's an unusual goal for most businessmen and may well limit the utility of this type of unit-benefit offset plan.

¶1002.2   When Your Clients Should Use These Plans

Unit-benefit offset plans work best in the same situations where traditionally unit-benefit plans are effective. That means you should consider them in the following situations:

1. when your client is philosophically oriented towards long service as a prime determinant of pension benefit;
2. when key men have substantially more service than the average participant;
3. when key men are relatively young; and
4. when your client finds the incremental approach to benefits conceptually simpler than the flat-benefit alternative.

The opportunity to use either a flat offset amount (i.e., 70% of Social Security) or an incremental offset (i.e., two percent of Social Security for each year of service up to 35) allows you virtually endless capacity to design hybrid plans. Thus, the potential sophistication of unit-benefit offset plans is limited only by your creativity.

¶1003   OTHER IMPORTANT PRACTITIONER
            CONSIDERATIONS WHEN USING OFFSET PLANS

There are some additional factors which might warrant or preclude more detailed analysis of offset plan alternatives. Most of them represent positive opportunities, and include special options to enhance benefits for key participants who were employed late. Simplicity and cost control can be improved dramatically by using these factors. Each has important ramifications and may influence your attitude toward offset plans.

¶1003.1   How Offset Plans Can Help Key Men Who Started Late

Unit-benefit and flat-benefit plans integrated in the traditional manner must contain a provision which reduces excess benefits for each year of service less than 15. For a client whose key men were employed by their corporations late in their careers, offset plans may be uniquely attractive. That's because no such one-fifteenth reduction is applicable to offset plans.

Example: Dr. Remove incorporates his practice at age 55 and wants to maximize his share of contributions to a pension plan. He compares a flat-benefit excess and offset approach:

Flat-Benefit Integrated at $9,000

Participant	Age	Pay	37% Basic Benefit	+	33.3% Excess Benefit	=	Total Benefit	Annual Deposit	Deposit As A %
A	55	$50,000	$18,500		$ 9,110*		$27,610	$17,734	71%
B	45	15,000	5,511		2,000		7,511	1,690	7
C	40	25,000	9,250		5,333		14,583	2,147	8
D	35	50,000	18,500		13,665		32,165	3,229	13
E	25	10,000	3,700		330		4,030	199	1
TOTAL		$150,000	N/A		N/A		N/A	$25,000	100%

Offset Plan Alternative

70% Total Benefit	-	74.07% S.S. Offset	=	Net Plan Benefit	Annual Deposit	Deposit As A %
$35,247		$5,803		$29,444	$19,018	75%
10,500		5,387		5,113	1,149	5
17,500		5,803		11,697	1,736	6
35,247		5,803		29,444	2,971	12
7,000		4,462		2,538	126	1
N/A		N/A		N/A	$25,000	100%

---

*Reduced by 5/15 for service less than 15 years.

Observation: Dr. Remove's alternatives are dramatically different. Under a flat-benefit approach, his excess benefits are substantially reduced. Since he will have less than 15 years of service at age 65, he must reduce the otherwise maximum benefit by one-fifteenth for each year of service less than 15. However, no such reduction is necessary with an offset plan. Therefore, the effect of integration is greater with the offset plan. Under the offset plan, Dr. Remove increases his estimated retirement income from $27,610 to $29,444—an increase of about 18%. His annual deposit increases from $17,734 to $19,018, a comparable increase. However, assuming a common budget ($25,000) Dr. Remove actually increases his share of the total deposit at the expense of all other plan participants. Note that under the flat-benefit plan he received 71% of the total deposit. Under the offset alternative he receives 76%.

¶1003.2   The Inherent Value Of Simplicity

Many employers feel that offset plans are the simplest defined-benefit plan to explain. If you agree, don't underestimate the importance of that fact. Defined-contribution plans like money-purchase and profit-sharing often are chosen by "default." Many clients prefer something they can understand and explain as opposed to an alternative that is cumbersome or overly complicated, no matter how attractive it appears. Saying to a key man or other participant, "Your benefit is X% of pay minus Y% of your Social Security Benefit" is much easier than explaining the complicated relationship between integration level and excess benefits under other defined-benefit approaches. If your client has decided on a defined-benefit plan, he might as well—given approximately comparable contributions—use one that everyone understands.

¶1003.3   Effective Control Of Future Costs

Because Social Security benefits are inflation-indexed and coupled, they have been rising dramatically over the last several years. So have Social Security taxes, as any of your clients will testify. The higher the Social Security benefits climb, the higher the offset they will provide to an offset defined-benefit plan. Therefore, your client may, if he sets up that sort of plan, have a built-in "cost control" mechanism for his pension plan—one that will probably keep pace with, or even exceed, his payroll costs. Furthermore, a Social Security offset plan is self-adjusting, that is, it does not require annual amendment of the plan's integration level to keep benefits in perspective. That helps simplify the administration of the plan and adds to the simplicity that makes offset plans an attractive option for your clients.

Alternative integrated plans—flat benefit or unit benefit—typically require periodic amendments to the integration level (with the exception of unit-benefit plans that use the taxable wage base as their integration level). The amendments can be irritating from several points of view:

1. Someone needs to keep track of the required amendments.
2. Someone needs to prepare the amendments.
3. After three amendments, pensions typically need to be resubmitted to the Internal Revenue Service for approval.

Therefore, any type of plan can decrease the need for future administration and qualification functions can be a long range advantage to your client.

11

Target Benefit Plans:
The Best Choice For
Many Small Business Employers

Target benefit plans represent a hybrid between defined-contribution and defined-benefit plans. If the facts of your client's situation are right, this hybrid may provide the best of both worlds.

Target plans are infrequently used. That's primarily because they are little known or understood. This chapter will explain the intricacies of target benefit plans so that you can use these effective tools. Target benefit plans come in all forms—flat-benefit, unit-benefit and offset. In general, they work similarly to defined-benefit programs. Chapter 11 will explain the differences and help you use them to your advantage.

¶1100   HOW TO EXPLAIN TARGET BENEFIT PLANS TO YOUR CLIENTS

Target benefit pension plans share attributes of both defined-benefit and defined-contribution plans. They are hybrid creatures operating within a unique sphere in the pension industry. Unfortunately, the uniqueness implies some additional complexity. In fact, target benefit plans are more sophisticated than some of their "cousins," but the opportunity they present for additional flexibility shouldn't be overlooked.

The best way to understand target benefit plans is to consider them in contradistinction to defined-contribution and defined-benefit plans. By understanding which aspects of target plans fit in the defined-contribution realm and which in the defined-benefit, you will enhance your effectiveness at explaining target plans to your clients.

¶1100.1   A Checklist Of Similarities To Defined-Contribution Plans

In many respects target plans closely resemble defined-contribution plans, particularly the money-purchase variety. Both in terms of the "maximum annual addition" and the "account balance" system of measuring benefits, they fit the mold quite well.

In one other important respect, too, target benefit plans share a relationship with their defined-contribution cousins: they don't require annual actuarial certification. That will obviously help your small clients to keep costs down to a minimum.

☐ *A. Maximum Annual Addition.* No participant in a target benefit plan can have his account increased during a limitation year by more than the lesser of:

- $36,875; or
- 25% of compensation.

You will recall from Chapters 4 through 6 that the maximum annual addition includes the following components:

- employer contributions;
- forfeitures; and
- a portion of employee voluntary contributions.

> *Example:* Mr. Bullit participates in his employer's target benefit plan. He earns $20,000 per year. His employer's contribution is $4,000. In addition, he receives $1,000 in forfeitures. Finally Mr.

Bullit makes a $2,000 contribution to his voluntary account. He has exceeded his maximum annual addition because:

Employer Additions To Account			$4,000
Forfeitures			1,000
			$5,000
Voluntary Contribution		2,000	
a. One-half voluntary contribution	$1,000		
b. Excess voluntary contribution (above 6% of pay)	800		
Lesser of a. or b.			800
TOTAL ANNUAL ADDITION			$5,800
MAXIMUM ANNUAL ADDITION, LESSER OF—			
a. 25% of pay	5,000		
b. Dollar limitation	$36,875		
MAXIMUM ANNUAL ADDITION			$5,000
EXCESS ANNUAL ADDITION			$800

☐ **B. Account Balances:** The most striking similarity between target plans and other defined-contribution plans is that they utilize account balances to record participant benefits. As with regular defined-contribution plans, a target benefit account balance is composed of the following:

- employer contribution;
- forfeitures;
- earnings (or losses).

When a participant retires, his benefit is simply the account balance that has been accumulated. If investment results have been good, benefits might be quite substantial. If investment experience has been disappointing, then his benefits may be less than attractive.

☐ **C. No Actuarial Certification:** Since benefits are not *guaranteed*, there is no reason for a plan's funding to be certified by an actuary. Therefore, target benefit plans share with their defined-contribution cousins, a less expensive administrative process. Since actuarial certification can represent a significant expense component of small plans, programs that avoid it will be well received by your client.

¶1100.2   A Checklist Of Similarities To Defined-Benefit Plans

Target benefit plans are also quite similar to defined-benefit programs. Contributions are computed in virtually the same fashion—through actuarial determinations—and maximum limitations apply.

☐ *A. Maximum Benefit Limitations Applicable to Target Benefit Plans:* Your client's target benefit plan can't call for estimated retirement benefits greater than the lesser of:

- $110,625 (for 1980); or
- 100% of pay.

What is ultimately paid out of the plan is irrelevant as long as the assumptions used for generating deposits were reasonable.

Example: XYZ Company establishes a target benefit plan providing estimated retirement income of 100% of pay for plan participants. Contributions are determined with an implicit assumption that fund earnings will average two percent. Fund earnings actually average eight percent. The plan will not qualify because the targeted benefits were computed by reference to unreasonable assumptions.

Observation: Target benefit plans will generally be considered reasonable if they utilize an assumed interest rate of 5½% to 6½%.

☐ *B. Actuarial Computations:* Target plans set up estimated retirement benefits for plan participants and then fund toward those estimated benefits. Actual investment experience (which would affect the funding standard account of a traditional defined-benefit plan) is ignored during the accumulation period. However, contributions *are* based on the estimated retirement income. Therefore actuarial computations are necessary to determine annual contributions.

> *Example:* Mr. Ring is 45 years old and earns $50,000 per year. He participates in a target benefit plan which provides an estimated retirement income of 70% of pay. Assuming 6½% interest, his annual plan contribution will be

Compensation	$50,000	
Benefit Percentage	× 70%	
Estimated Target Benefit		$35,000/yr.
Funding Period	20 years	
Assumed Interest	6½%	
Annual Contribution		$ 7,846

If Mr. Ring's contributions actually earn nine percent interest the excess earnings will simply be *added to* his account. The contribution won't change. Therefore, when he reaches age 65, he will have a retirement income of $47,200. On the other hand, if the $7,846 contribution only earned one percent interest, his retirement income would be $18,824 per year. *Participants* bear the risk of investment loss. Contributions, once actuarially determined, remain level except for incremental benefit changes.

¶1100.3   The Biggest Advantage—The Allocation Of Excess
                                    Interest

The allocation of excess interest to participant accounts can benefit everyone.

- It can benefit the employee because actual retirement benefits can exceed targeted estimates;
- It can benefit the employer because his annual cash flow requirement for the plan is not disturbed by a Funding Standard Account amortization of excess interest.

If conservative assumptions are used and actual investment performance exceeds expectations the results can be pretty spectacular.

Example: Consider five employees of varying age who participate in a target benefit plan whose benefit formula calls for 50% of pay. Each of the participants earns the same income. Depending upon investment performance, results can vary widely.

Partici-pant	Age	Pay	Target Benefit	Deposit @ 65	Pot @ 65 Assuming 6% Return	Pot @ 65 Assuming 2% Return	Pot @ 65 Assuming 10% Return
A	50	$20,000	$10,000	$3,757	$92,695	$66,271	$131,306
B	45	20,000	10,000	2,377	92,686	58,910	149,757
C	40	20,000	10,000	1,594	92,701	52,077	172,422
D	35	20,000	10,000	1,106	92,701	45,766	200,123
E	25	20,000	10,000	565	92,687	34,810	275,071

Observation: Since deposits, once computed, remain fixed, target benefit participants are directly affected by interest higher or lower than the assumed rate. For example, Participant E, who is youngest and therefore has the greatest to gain or lose from interest, could receive as much as $272,071 or as little as $34,810, depending on whether the average rate of return is two percent or ten percent. Unlike a defined-benefit plan, which would require amortization or "spreading" gains or losses above or below the assumed plan interest rate, target benefit plans, like defined-contribution plans in general, simply add surplus gains or losses to participant accounts.

Note that the contribution initially fixed for each participant assumes level compensation for that participant from the time of entry to the plan to retirement. Each time a participant's pay changes, a new deposit "increment" is added to the previous total and funded on a level basis to retirement. You'll recall that this sort of computation is comparable to the attained age level funding method used by many defined-benefit plans. The only difference is the absence of a provision to handle interest differentials between the hypothetical plan model and actual experience.

¶1101   HOW FLAT-BENEFIT TARGET PLANS CAN FULFILL MOST SMALL BUSINESS EMPLOYER'S NEEDS

Flat-benefit target plans are substantially similar to their flat-benefit cousins. Benefits are simply a percentage of compensation. The only difference is that excess (or shortfall) earnings do not increase or decrease plan contributions. They are simply added to accounts.

Example: Center Company implements a 40% of pay flat-benefit plan using a 6½% interest assumption. Here are the results:

Participant	Age	Pay	40% Target Benefit	Lump-Sum Necessary	Annual Contribution	Contribution As A %
A	54	$50,000	$20,000	$185,391	$11,325	80%
B	40	15,000	6,000	55,617	887	6
C	30	50,000	20,000	185,391	1,403	10
D	30	12,000	4,800	44,494	337	3
E	25	10,000	4,000	37,078	198	1
TOTAL		$137,000	N/A	N/A	$14,150	100%

Since target benefit plan contributions are calculated similarly to defined-benefit ones, you might have anticipated that contributions would be skewed heavily toward older participants. This, in fact, occurs as illustrated above. Participants A and C each earn comparable salaries and are entitled to the same estimated retirement benefit. Yet Participant A's contribution is eight times that of his counterpart. Target benefit plans can, therefore, often provide the orientation toward older key men. Your clients will want the convenience and simplicity of account balances as opposed to the more cumbersome actuarial model and funding standard account with which defined-benefit plans must constantly be reconciled.

Observation: The allocation of the $14,150 deposit is so favorably inclined toward the key man A, that your client may ask why he should bother with a traditional defined-benefit plan when he can accomplish the same funding objectives through the target benefit alternative. For many small clients that is a good question but keep two facts in mind:

1. No participant's contributions can exceed 25% of pay—and employee A is quite close to that ceiling;

2. Target benefit plans cannot use the entry age normal actuarial method which means the contribution is an annual fixed amount with no flexibility for troublesome economic times.

¶1101.1   What Are The Special Problems With Integration And How To Avoid Them

Integration of target benefit plans is traditionally troublesome. That's because IRS requires excess benefits to be limited to "properly" integrated levels. Since target benefit plans do not provide a *guarantee* of either integrated or basic plan benefits, it is impossible to predict in advance whether benefits ultimately paid at retirement will be properly integrated.

Example: Guess Company establishes a flat-benefit excess target plan with an assumed interest rate of 5½%. Based on the assumed interest rate, benefits in excess of the integration level will not exceed the 33% limitation associated with this plan form. However, the plan earns an average rate of return of 12%. That means ultimate benefits will be far in excess of those assumed, and will exceed what IRS deems properly integrated.

There are two possible solutions to these issues:

1. Distribute excess earnings attributable to benefits above the integration level *evenly* to all employee-participants (i.e., according to relative total payroll); or

2. Use the "safe harbor" provision which allows unit-benefit target plans using an assumed interest rate not less than 5½% to let the actual investment return of each participant's account "stay where it is" without artificial reallocation.

Because of the cumbersome nature of flat-benefit excess plan integration, most of your clients will opt for the second solution discussed at ¶1102.2.

¶1101.2   When Flat-Benefit Plans Will Be Most Effective

Flat-benefit target plans are effective any time their defined-benefit cousins would be, with some additions:

1. When key men are older and higher paid than the average employees;

2. When the plan's budget is limited enough so that the 25% maximum annual addition requirements are not troublesome;

3. When the business includes few enough employee-participants to preclude using the entry age normal method that might, in some circumstances, make defined-benefit plans more attractive; or

4. When your client wishes to stabilize his budget and avoid the funding disruptions that would occur in defined-benefit plans as a result of earnings above or below the assumed rate.

¶1101.3   Don't Forget Service Reductions In Your Flat-Benefit Target Plans

Like traditional defined-benefit plans, target programs can include benefit reductions based on service less than a certain number of years. If the key men in your client's organization will have more service at retirement than an average participant, you'll want to include a provision requiring a certain number of years' participation for full benefits.

Example: Center Company (¶1101) adds a provision to its plan requiring that participants have 40 years service at retirement for full benefits. Here's the impact on plan funding:

Partici-pant	Age	Pay	Assumed Yrs Service	40% Target Benefit	×	Target Benefit Yrs 40	Annual Contri-bution	Contri-bution As A %
A	50	50,000	40 yrs	20,000		$20,000	$11,325	83%
B	45	15,000	25 yrs	6,000		3,750	554	4
C	40	5,000	35 yrs	20,000		17,500	1,228	9
D	35	12,000	35 yrs	4,800		4,200	295	2
E	25	10,000	40 yrs	4,000		4,000	198	2
							$13,600	100%

The illustration for Center Company reinforces the utility of one of the simplest and most overlooked design tools. Recalling the illustration at ¶1101 and comparing it to the above, note that without reducing the contribution or benefit for Participant A we have increased his share of the total contribution dramatically. Alternatively, we have cut down substantially on costs for other employees, which reduction we used to increase the benefit level of participants—and Participant A would receive substantially all increased funding to pay for those additional benefits.

The illustration at ¶1101 uses the same compensation level for all plan participants to drive home a point about the interrelated age, interest, and service. In the real world of your clients' situations, key men will not only tend to be older, but also higher paid than the typical employee. Any such differential in compensation will further enhance efficiency of a target plan, particularly when the plan will be integrated.

¶1102   HOW UNIT-BENEFIT TARGET PLANS PROVIDE MORE FLEXIBILITY

Unit-benefit target plans are considerably more useful than their defined-benefit counterparts. That is because they provide the one specific "safe harbor" for integration. (See ¶1102.2.) These plans will give you and your client traditional planning flexibility and lessen the risk for problems if you choose an integrated format. Your goal in designing a unit-benefit target plan will be the same as for any other plan—maximize benefits (and therefore, contributions) for key men.

¶1102.1   How to Use Unit-Benefit Target Plans

Generally you will want the sum of annual benefit increments for your client's key man to provide the highest percentage of pay above any plan participant. Typically that will mean your annual benefit increment will be equal to retirement income desired divided by years of service of the key man at normal retirement date.

> *Example:* Mr. Bullseye will have 40 years service when he retires. He wants to replace 40% of his pre-retirement income. Therefore, his target plan should call for annual benefit increments of one percent of pay. Furthermore, the plan should limit credited service to 40 years. That way, no participant can receive a higher benefit than Mr. Bullseye. Here's how the plan would work out.

Partici- pant	Age	Pay	Assumed Service @ 65	Annual Increment	Target Benefit	Annual Contri- bution	Contri- bution As A %
A	50	$ 60,000	40 yrs	1%	$24,000	$8,638	74%
B	45	40,000	20	1	8,000	1,793	15
C	40	15,000	25	1	3,750	554	5
D	35	15,000	30	1	4,500	453	4
E	30	10,000	35	1	3,500	246	2
TOTAL	N/A	$140,000	N/A	N/A	N/A	$11,684	100%

Observation: A nonintegrated unit-benefit plan provides no particular advantage, unless your client finds it easier to understand, to a flat-benefit alternative. In the example above, Participant A receives 40% of pay at retirement. All other participants receive less, based on their relative service. A flat-benefit plan could have achieved *exactly* the same result by using a formula calling for 40% of pay at retirement reduced pro rata for each year of service less than 40. Therefore, whether you use a flat or unit-benefit target plan in *nonintegrated* situations is primarily a matter of personal preference or the philosophical approach of your client. However, if you wish to integrate a target benefit plan, the story is different. Here, unit-benefit plans offer a substantial advantage.

¶1102.2   "Safe Harbor" From Integration Problems

Revenue Ruling 71-446, Section 18.01 provides that unit-benefit excess plans can allocate earnings in excess of the assumed rate and can be allocated according to relative benefits. That's true, *as long as*, the assumed interest rate under the plan is at least 5½%. Therefore, your client could set up a unit-benefit target plan which provided the following annual benefits for pay in excess of the integration level assuming appropriate reductions for pre-retirement death benefit.

- If you use *actual* compensation 1.24%
- If you use *average* compensation .... .89%

As we discussed in Chapter 9, you are most likely to use *average* compensation because of the burdensome recordkeeping requirements associated with actual compensation plans. Furthermore, keep in mind that the integration level of a unit-benefit plan can be:

- covered compensation; or
- a uniform dollar amount up to and including the taxable wage base in effect for a particular plan year.

> *Example:* Aim, Incorporated establishes a target benefit plan integrated with Social Security. The plan uses average compensation and provides a retirement benefit equal to 1% of total pay plus .89% of pay in excess of $15,000 to plan participants.

Participant	Age	Pay	Service @ NRD	1%/Yr Basic Benefit	.89%/Yr Excess Benefit	Total Benefit	Annual Deposit
A	50	$50,000	40 yrs	$20,000	$12,460	$32,460	$11,683
B	45	20,000	20 yrs	4,000	890	4,890	1,096
C	40	15,000	30 yrs	4,500	0	4,500	665
D	35	40,000	35 yrs	14,000	7,788	21,788	2,195
E	30	15,000	35 yrs	5,250	0	5,250	368
TOTAL		$14,000	N/A	N/A	N/A	N/A	$16,007

The efficiency of Aim Incorporated's plan is equal to that of a conventional defined-benefit program. Yet, this exceptional efficiency is achieved:

- without cumbersome and expensive actuarial certification; and
- while maintaining the conceptually simple account balance method of record keeping.

The disadvantages are the same as for any target plan:

- participants can't be *certain* of the benefits they will ultimately receive;
- maximum contributions are 25% of pay, which may be a limiting factor; and

- the flexibility of entry age normal with its attendant "range" of contributions isn't available.

Observation: Aim Incorporated's plan is very efficient for employee A. He receives 36% of total payroll but 73% of the plan contribution. If you're going to use a target plan as your primary retirement accumulation vehicle, the unit-benefit variety can be used safely and effectively.

¶1102.3   How To Maximize Plan Efficiency For Key Men

Most of the methods for increasing the efficiency of defined-benefit unit programs are applicable to target hybrids as well. Make sure your plan does the following:

1. Places a "cap" on the number of years key men will have when they reach retirement age;

2. Uses a relatively high interest assumption in order to keep contributions lower for younger participants; and

3. Provides annual benefit increments that generate exactly the right benefit or contribution for the key man. Once the plan is designed for him, you may let the other "chips fall where they may."

¶1103   **HOW OFFSET TARGET BENEFIT PLANS WORK**

Offset target benefit plans offer substantially similar opportunities to those of more traditional defined-benefit programs. First, compute a participant's *gross* retirement benefit under the plan. Then, subtract the amount of offset to determine the net plan benefit for which the employer must fund. The resultant benefit is an estimate only. Each year changes in compensation are reflected in incremental benefit/contribution increases or decreases.

> *Example:* Mr. Bumble participates in a target benefit offset plan promising 50% of pay less 50% of Social Security benefits as an assumed benefit at normal retirement age. Mr. Bumble is 45-years old earning $50,000 per year and will receive estimated Social Security benefits of $8,000 per year at 65. His target benefit under the plan would be calculated as follows:

Gross benefit (50% of pay)		$25,000
Less: Estimated Social Security at 65	$8,000	
Times Offset percentage	50%	
Net Social Security Offset		($ 4,000)
Net Plan benefit		$21,000

The annual deposit for Mr. Bumble based on this preliminary calculation will be $5,809. If, in his second year of participation, Mr. Bumble receives a $5,000 pay increase but his estimated Social Security benefits do not change, then the plan administrator must begin funding for an additional retirement benefit of $2,500, the cost of which is $753.48. Thus, after two years, Mr. Bumble's contribution is "pegged" at $6,562.48. Regardless of whether investment performance yields a larger or smaller benefit, these funding amounts will be continued and future amounts added or subtracted depending on changes in pay.

¶1103.1   What Types Of Offset Target Benefit Plans Will Qualify

All the traditional defined-benefit formula approaches are available in the target offset domain. The major alternatives—flat and unit-benefit—are the major alternatives here as well. Flat-benefit alternatives are illustrated above with the example of Mr. Bumble. Unit-benefit plans offer a second important alternative. Under a unit plan, benefits are calculated on an incremental annual basis.

Example: Suppose Mr. Bumble will have 40 years of service when he retires, and that he participates in a *unit-benefit* offset plan rather than the flat-benefit program indicated above. The plan's formula calls for 1.666% for each year of service less 1.666% of estimated Social Security benefits for each year of service. Mr. Bumble's retirement benefit would be calculated as follows:

Gross benefit (1.666% × $50,000 × 40)		$25,000
Offset amount (1.666% × $8,000 × 40)	($4,000)	
Net retirement benefit		$21,000

Keep in mind as well that unit-benefit programs have traditionally been a safe harbor as long as they use an assumed interest rate of not less than 5½%.

¶1103.2   When Will Target Benefit Offset Plans Work Best

Many people find the "offset approach" to integration the simplest of their alternatives. Offset plans are fairly easy to describe to employees. Therefore in cases where a defined-benefit or target benefit approach is wanted because of key man parameters, the offset approach may have some advantage because of its relative simplicity.

Furthermore, offset plans have a significant advantage. They do not require a 1/15th reduction to integrated benefits for service less than 15 years. You will recall that this is a problem associated with standard unit-benefit plans.

Caveat: In a case where your key man is within 15 years of retirement, this advantage may be wiped out because restrictions on annual limitations or additions apply to target benefit contributions. That limitation is likely to come into play in many circumstances which have key men within 15 years of retirement.

¶1104   WHY TARGET PLANS SHOULD BE USED MORE OFTEN BY SMALL BUSINESS EMPLOYERS

Target plans are quite sophisticated and difficult to explain. That's because they contain attributes of both the defined-contribution and defined-benefit family of retirement plans. However, in many situations the effort will be well rewarded. Target plans provide some unique opportunities that many clients can utilize with great efficiency.

¶1104.1   Stability of Cash Flow Preserves Tax Budgeting

Traditional defined-benefit plan contributions are affected by a variety of factors. Two significant factors are forfeitures, which reduce contributions directly, and investment gains and losses, which reduce contributions indirectly through the amortization or "spreading" process. Since each of these factors is largely uncontrollable, they reduce your client's ability to budget the cash flow and tax aspects of this plan. Target benefit plans enhance this management ability by eliminating one source of volatility—investment experience. The fact that in target plans excess earnings (or losses) are simply added to account balances means that annual plan funding will be subject to less fluctuation.

¶1104.2   Simplicity Means Reduced Costs For Your Clients

The absence of actuarial certification requirements means that your client who adopts a target plan can eliminate a substantial annual expense. For many small employers, that's a significant factor. Furthermore, the requirement for actuarial certification attendant with traditional defined-benefit plans creates an aura of complexity and inflexibility that scares many potential clients. Finally, a simpler plan will obviously, in the long run, minimize the amount of *your* time spent explaining and re-explaining how a particular retirement program works. For the same reason, employees should be more highly motivated by a plan they understand.

¶1104.3   Interest Earnings Have A Major Effect

Today's inflationary environment has created a unique opportunity to "lock in" high rates of return. High rates of return in a defined-benefit plan are often counterproductive because they will eventually reduce plan costs. Most small businessmen implement defined-benefit plans in order *to create* tax deductions of a certain magnitude and will be irritated by a constant decrease occasioned by superior investment performance.

Target plans, on the other hand, can utilize excess earnings very effectively. They are simply added to participant accounts. The effect of these high rates of return over a long period of time can be staggering. Paragraph 1100.3 illustrated this dramatic opportunity. Therefore, assuming your client can afford to "live with" a *fixed* annual commitment concommitant with a target benefit plan, today's investment environment may provide additional incentive for target plans.

¶1104.4   Few Employers Can Spare 25% Of Payroll

As a practical matter, the 25% of payroll limitation on annual additions affects only a very few potential clients. Twenty-five percent of payroll is a very large amount of money for most individuals to save. For all but the highest paid professionals, it will probably create a sufficient tax deduction and retirement benefit.

¶1104.5   Summing Up Target Plans

Target plans provide some very unique opportunities. Their only drawbacks appear to be:

1. They lack contribution flexibility which may be obtained through use of the entry age normal actuarial method with a defined-benefit plan; and

2. They limit an employee's contribution to 25% of pay which, for some older participants, may not build up a retirement benefit quickly enough.

However, these drawbacks, plus the complexity of the target plans, should not serve to diminish their utility. Particularly in the current inflationary environment, the target benefit plans provide, for many small businessmen, the best of all possible worlds.

12

Multiple Qualified Plans
For Maximum Tax Deductions

A few of your clients, particularly those in noncapital intensive industries or professional occupations, will find that even after maximization of their deductions to a particular pension plan, they still have disposable cash. For these clients, multiple qualified plans may be the answer. Given the fact that qualified plans represent one of the most efficient capital accumulation and transfer vehicles, it makes sense to maximize their use.

The government, however, has sought to curtail the overutilization of qualified plans, believing that too much revenue might be lost if the unfettered use of qualified plans were allowed. This curtailment has taken the shape of restrictions on aggregate benefits and contributions that may be received by an individual. The rules surrounding these restrictions, such as the familiar "1.4" rule, are extremely complex. This chapter will explore these rules in considerable detail so that you can help your clients to achieve maximum effectiveness with their plans. The proper use of aggregate plans can generate tax deductible contributions far in excess of most businesses' ability to pay for them. However, for those with the disposable cash, multiple plans are remarkable opportunities.

¶1200   **WHEN SHOULD YOUR CLIENT CONSIDER
MULTIPLE PLANS**

The tax deductions associated with the traditional defined-benefit plans discussed in Chapters 7 through 10 are far in excess of most small and medium-size business budgets. Particularly, as businesses get larger, the cost of providing a 100% of pay defined-benefit retirement income for employees is prohibitive. However, many smaller businesses—particularly, professional organizations in which one principal is significantly older and higher paid— can not only afford to exceed the tax deduction limitations of single pension plans but actually should. When these specific situations arise, you should be aware of the extensive planning potential offered by the effective use of multiple qualified plans.

¶1200.1   Significant Estate Planning Considerations

Many small businessmen can be typecast in one of two categories:

1. Business-owners whose business represents a large illiquid estate tax obligation; or
2. Professionals whose lifestyle has precluded the accumulation of substantial savings.

Either type of individual should consider the significant estate planning opportunities inherent in aggressive use of qualified plans. Death benefits paid by qualified plans to named beneficiaries over two or more taxable years of the beneficiary are exempt from federal and state estate taxes. Since the named beneficiary can include a trust authorized (but not required) to:

- *buy* assets from the estate;
- *loan* money to the estate (followed by a merger of the estate and trust with concommitant elimination of the debt); or
- *pay* estate taxes subject to the discretion of the executor or Trustees.

A qualified plan may represent the most efficient estate accumulation and transfer vehicle available. Keep in mind that your client will build his estate faster with a qualified plan because:

- contributions are tax deductible; and
- interest earnings are tax-exempt and the opportunity to include life insurance in the plan can further enhance the estate creation potential.

Example: Jim has turned his small business into a gold mine. Several potential buyers have offered as much as $300,000, but Jim feels the business is worth far more than that. Besides, he wants to keep it in the family. Jim's attorney reminds him that the business represents an estate tax liability of almost $75,000, and since he is only insurable at highly substandard rates, life insurance does not appear to be a solution. The solution is to establish multiple qualified plans, even though it requires reducing Jim's salary, to accumulate $75,000 within the shortest possible period.

Warning: The indirect use of qualified plan death benefits for estate tax payments is a highly technical area fraught with pitfalls. A full discussion of the issue is far beyond the scope of this book. Estate planning which anticipates the use of qualified plan proceeds should only be implemented after thorough review of the applicable law and regulations.

¶1200.2   Efficient Capital Transfer Vehicle

Qualified plans, particularly multiple plans with their attendant large tax deductions, offer an exceptional interbusiness capital transfer vehicle. Not only can they help effect a tax deductible change in management, but they can also do so more quickly than most other alternatives because of the tax-free nature of accumulation with plans. Many small businesses have one or two key men who are likely successors to each others' interests should one or the other retire, become disabled or die. Typically, an older key man will have a younger counterpart who is "heir apparent" a couple of years down the road. That's an ideal situation for multiple qualified plans.

A. Tax Deductible Change Of Management

Frequently the older/younger key man succession is threatened by one major problem—cash. The younger key man will generally not have capital accumulated to buy out his "mentor." Taking a larger salary won't help because of the burden of income taxes. One or more qualified plans may represent the most efficient method for "buying out" the older partner.

Example: Bail-Out Company's president, Mr. Bilge, is 55. Several years ago he attended a business seminar and was impressed by the importance of creating successor-management. He hired a 30-year-old business school graduate, Tom Tuck. Mr. Bilge currently earns $50,000 per year. Tom Tuck earns $25,000. Mr. Bilge agrees to sell Tom the business in 10 years for the book value—the lowest possible sale price for an organization of that type. In return, Tom agrees to forego a $20,000 salary increase he had anticipated. The $20,000 will instead be used to fund one or more qualified plans designed to maximize contributions to Mr. Bilge's account.

Caveat: You should be aware of two potential problems with the above scheme:

- any business transfer must be justifiable as an arms-length transaction; and
- pension plans must be for the exclusive benefit of the employees. It would not be wise to specifically tie together the buy-out and pension agreements.

B. Making Up For Lost Time With Tax-Free Dollars

Many small business owners enjoy the fruits of their labors currently, that is, they spend virtually all of the income created by their business. That's historically true, especially for professionals. Professionals, however, usually don't create a valuable asset through their labors. For example, a medical practice has little inherent value. Your clients who fit this mold may suddenly realize that they can't work forever and yet be trapped on one side by prohibitive income taxes and on the other by a demanding lifestyle. That combination may ostensibly preclude "making up for lost time" with an accumulation plan. However, the tax-favored environment afforded by qualified plans may offer a palatable solution.

> *Example:* Dr. Spendit is 50. After-expense distributable earnings of his practice are $150,000. He has accumulated virtually nothing with the exception of several beautiful homes. He feels he needs a $50,000 after-tax income to live on and, therefore, requires an $80,000 salary. That leaves $70,000 of disposable cash. If he takes the $70,000 as income, half will be chewed up in additional income taxes. The solution is to establish multiple qualified plans for a $70,000 deductible contribution. Dr. Spendit's retirement fund will grow twice as fast with twice as many dollars.

¶1200.3   The Limitations Imposed On Your Clients By Individual
Plans

It's hard to generate a deductible contribution for any one participant in excess of $60,000. Situations such as Dr. Spendit's are not particularly unusual. Multiple qualified plans will boost deductible opportunities by as much as 20%. For your clients who are seriously trying to "make up for lost time," these plans may provide the only kind of realistic option.

¶1201   STRATEGIES FOR USING THE "1.4" RULE—KEY TO MULTIPLE PLANS

ERISA imposes limitations when multiple qualified plans are implemented. The limitations are imposed by the application of the "1.4" rule. The "1.4" rule effectively states that the sum of the percentages of their maximums that each of the multiple qualified plans "uses up" cannot exceed 140.

For example, since defined-benefit plans can provide a retirement benefit of up to 100% of pay, a plan that called for a benefit of 80% of pay would "use up" 80% of the 140% of the multiple plan maximum. Thus, if a second, money-purchase plan were implemented by the same employer, it couldn't call for a contribution of more than 15% of pay. That's because 15% would be 60% of 25%—the maximum contribution of a money-purchase plan standing on its own.

The "1.4" rule is conceptually simple and its application is not difficult. Assuming your client desires to maximize contributions to his multiple plans, you will most likely fulfill the 140% rule with a 100% of pay defined-benefit plan supplemented by a defined-contribution program limiting the annual addition for any plan participant to 10% of pay (10% equals 40% of 25%). Let's consider the application of the "1.4" rule to defined-benefit and defined-contribution plans.

¶1201.1   How To Compute The Defined-Benefit Fraction

The defined-benefit portion of the "1.4" rule is readily ascertainable. It is simply:

$$\frac{\text{Benefit Provided Under The Plan}}{\text{Maximum Benefit (100\%/\$110,625)}}$$

In other words, what percent of the maximum legal defined-benefit (the lesser of $110,625 or 100% of pay) does your plan provide? The resultant percentage should then be subtracted from 140% to determine the portion of the maximum available for the second plan. For example, a 50% of pay plan obviously uses 50% of the maximum benefit and therefore would leave 90% available for the defined-contribution fraction.

The fraction is somewhat more difficult to apply in an integrated defined-benefit plan. For those plans, you will need to compute the benefit for the participants receiving the highest retirement income and apply that to the "1.4" rule.

Example: Tom participates in a defined-benefit plan which provides 65% of total pay plus 33.33% of pay in excess of the $9,000 integration level. Tom earns $75,000 per year and will, by far, be the biggest beneficiary of the plan. Therefore, the plan's defined-benefit fraction is computed as follows:

Tom's Pay		$75,000
less: Integration Level	($9,000)	
Tom's Excess Pay		$66,000
Tom's 65% of Pay Basic Benefit	$48,750	
Tom's 33% Excess Benefit	+21,780	
TOTAL BENEFIT		$70,530
TOTAL BENEFIT AS A % OF SALARY		94%

Therefore, Tom could participate in a defined-contribution plan providing as much as 46% of the normal contributions (94 + 46 = 140%).

¶1201.2   How To Compute The Defined-Contribution Fraction

Computing the defined-contribution fraction in the "1.4" rule is somewhat more complicated:

$$\frac{\text{Cumulative Contributions Actually Made, If Any}}{\text{Cumulative Additions Which Could Have Been Made}}$$

In effect, the defined-contribution fraction creates an opportunity for a "catch-up" since the "Cumulative Additions Which Could Have Been Made" include additions for those years in which your client didn't have a plan.

Example: Tom has participated in his company's 15% of pay money-purchase plan for each of the five years of his employment. His fraction is computed as follows:

Year	Pay	Actual (15%) Contribution	Maximum (25%) Contribution
1	$ 15,000	$ 2,250	$ 3,750
2	20,000	3,000	5,000
3	25,000	3,740	6,250
4	27,000	4,050	6,750
5	75,000	11,250	18,750
TOTAL	$162,000	$24,300	$40,500

$$\frac{\text{Actual Additions Made (\$24,300)}}{\text{Additions Which Could Have Been Made (\$40,500)}} = 60\%$$

Therefore, Tom could participate in a defined-benefit plan which provided 80% of pay.

However, based on the illustrative facts presented at Paragraph 1201.1, Tom is using 94% of the maximum defined-benefit. Therefore, his participation in the defined-benefit and 15% of pay money-purchase plan, means he is exceeding the 140% rule (60% + 94% = 154%). His participation in one or the other plan would have to be cut back. Assuming the cutback is made in the money-purchase plan, his contribution to that plan could not exceed 11.5% (11.5 ÷ 25 = 46%. 46% + the 94% defined-benefit fraction = 140%).

¶1202   HOW TO CHOOSE THE RIGHT COMBINATION OF PLANS FOR YOUR CLIENT

The object of multiple qualified plans is almost invariably maximization of tax-deductible contributions. In virtually all cases, that means a defined-benefit program will be the primary accumulation vehicle—usually providing 100% of pay—and some form of defined-contribution or target plan will be the "backup" program, typically providing a 10% of pay contribution (40% of 25%). That's because defined-benefit plans provide substantially higher tax deductible contributions for higher paid key men, the vast majority of whom are relatively older than their average participants.

¶1202.1   Age Considerations Are Paramount

The above will be particularly true if your client's key men are age 40 or older. For those key men, a defined-benefit plan will provide a significantly larger tax deduction than a defined-contribution plan. However, at younger ages (35 and below) the reverse will probably be true. The younger your key participants, the more likely they are to have older rank and file employees, which would require relatively higher contributions.

¶1202.2   Which Plan To Integrate

Only one qualified plan can be fully integrated with Social Security. You should make sure that you integrate the plan which will provide the biggest boost for your client's key man. The following illustration compares integrated contributed contributions for participants of varying age who earn $100,000. For simplicity, the integration level is presumed to be $9,000.

Age	Pay	Excess Pay	7% Excess Money-Purchase Contribution	Contribution For 33% of Excess Pay Benefit
25	$100,000	$91,000	$6,370	$1,488
30	100,000	91,000	6,370	2,107
35	100,000	91,000	6,370	3,026
40	100,000	91,000	6,370	4,439
45	100,000	91,000	6,370	6,732
50	100,000	91,000	6,370	10,809
55	100,000	91,000	6,370	19,369

The above illustration shows maximum *integrated* contributions under defined-benefit or defined-contribution approaches to integration. For example, defined-contribution integration can't exceed seven percent of pay in excess of the integration level. Assuming a $9,000 integration level, any one of the participants above would have $91,000 excess pay. Seven percent of $91,000 is $6,370. On the other hand, each participant could receive, under an integrated defined-benefit plan, 33% of their excess pay at retirement age. Thirty-three percent of $91,000 is $30,000+. Therefore, the contributions shown are those required to fund a $30,000 benefit at age 65.

At ages under 45, defined-contribution integration appears to be superior. At ages above 45, defined-benefit integration is much more powerful. While the individual facts and circumstances of each case will ultimately determine which of your multiple plans ought to be integrated with Social Security, the above should serve as a rule of thumb regarding the potential opportunities.

Planning Tip: The relative age of your key men and their rank and file employees together with the various defined-benefit plan reductions for early retirement and participation less than 15 years can affect the above calculations. Make sure you are careful to calculate the relative contributions for maximum integrated contributions under defined-benefit and defined-contribution plans for your client's unique facts and circumstances.

¶1202.3   When To Use A Target Benefit Plan As A "Backup"

Since the vast majority of multiple plans will be used by businesses with key men substantially older than their average employee, defined-benefit plans will be the primary plan in almost all cases. You should then consider a target benefit plan as your backup. That is because a target benefit plan will have the added advantage of skewing the plan contributions in favor of older participants.

Planning Tip: Determine your target benefit plan formula "backwards," by computing what 10% of pay will provide as an assumed benefit for your key man. Then apply the results to the balance of participants. That way you will be sure to maximize benefits for your client's most important participants.

Example: Stone Company's defined-benefit plan provides 100% of pay for its key man, 50-year-old Mr. Stone. Mr. Stone earns $75,000. Therefore, his defined-contribution fraction deposit can't exceed $7,500 (10% of $75,000). Determine the target benefit plan formula as follows:

Annual Deposit	$7,500
Years of Deposits	15
Assumed Interest	6%
Estimated Accumulation @ 65	$185,044
Estimated Retirement Income From Accumulations	19,963/yr.
Estimated Retirement Income As A % of Pay	27%

Therefore, Stone Company should establish a 27% of pay target benefit plan. Consider how much money that would save as compared to a 10% of pay money-purchase plan given the following facts:

Participant	Age	Pay	10% Money Purchase Deposit	Target Benefit Deposit
Mr. Stone	50	$ 75,000	$ 7,500	$ 7,500
B	40	15,000	1,500	646
C	40	12,000	1,200	516
D	35	30,000	3,000	896
E	30	10,000	1,000	212
TOTAL		$142,000	$14,200	$ 9,760

Mr. Stone has saved $4,440 without sacrificing one dollar of contribution for himself.

The illustration emphasizes the need to select each of your multiple plans with care. If your key men are relatively old, then a target benefit plan may well be the best bet for a secondary program. That's because target plans, like defined-benefit plans, tend to skew plan contributions toward older participants.

¶1203   WATCH OUT FOR PROFIT-SHARING PLANS

If a profit-sharing plan is one of your multiple plans, you have a special problem. I.R.C. 404(a)(7) provides that an *overall* tax deduction limitation of 25% of payroll applies to multiple plans, one of which is a profit-sharing program. Except for your clients with the largest payroll, who would probably not use multiple plans anyway, this limitation will probably rule out your clients' being able to take advantage of the flexibility offered by a profit-sharing plan. Note that the 25% limitation overrides otherwise applicable limitations of the 140% rule. Frequently, that may mean that your client may have to terminate or amend and restate a pre-existing profit-sharing plan when he has made a decision to maximize plan contributions under the 140% rule.

Conclusion

Your client should consider adopting multiple plans as a result of either:

- severe estate planning needs; or
- severe income tax problems.

Multiple qualified plans can provide far more tax deductions than most businesses can afford. Also, because of the constraints of I.R.C. 404(a)(7) multiple plans will probably limit your client's flexibility and create a massive ongoing commitment. For the right client—usually an older professional with very few common-law employees—qualified plans provide a tremendous bonanza. For the vast majority of businesses, however, a single, well-designed qualified plan can fulfill all estate and income tax planning needs without the additional costs and inflexibility imposed by multiple plans.

SECTION C
How To Design Plans
For The Self-Employed

13

Keogh Plans Provide More Flexibility Than You Thought

Keogh plans, also known as HR-10 plans, represent a group of retirement plans available to nonincorporated businesses. Keogh plans first appeared in the 1960s, offering limited opportunities for deductions. With the advent of ERISA, however, Keogh plans became a viable alternative for this group of employers. Prior to ERISA, particularly in the professional community (e.g., doctors, lawyers, and accountants), there had been a great rush to incorporate practices and escape the stringent limitations on Keogh deductions.

While ERISA did not erase all the advantages of corporate plans, it certainly was a major step in the right direction. Apart from increasing the deductible limits for defined-contribution Keogh plans from $2,500 to $7,500, ERISA opened up an entire new area of Keogh plans—defined-benefit Keogh plans. Furthermore, a little used variety of Keogh, target-benefit, received new attention as a result of the larger deductible limits.

In this chapter we will explore the new range of options created by ERISA so that you can provide your unincorporated clients with a meaningful alternative to incorporation. While you won't be able to obtain the large deductions associated with corporate plans, with a little creativity you can satisfy the needs of many small businesses, particularly professionals.

**¶1300   HOW KEOGH CAN HELP YOUR SMALL BUSINESS
PROFESSIONAL CLIENTS WHILE AVOIDING
INCORPORATION**

Most Keogh plans follow the money-purchase or profit-sharing format. Since they can't be integrated with Social Security except in very unusual circumstances, the key man in an unincorporated business must deposit the same percentage of pay for common law employees that he does for himself.

For example, if your physician-client earns $100,000 and wants a $7,500 deduction, he'll need to put 7½% of each common law employee's pay into the "pot" as well. That's true even though he must contribute the same percentage of their pay to Social Security as do his incorporated peers. For that reason, the cost of covering common law employees often makes adoption of a traditional money-purchase or profit-sharing Keogh plan a marginal decision other than in unincorporated businesses with very few common law employees.

However, you should be aware of significant options that exist within the Keogh domain. For instance, some plans will allow a tax deductible contribution of $15,000 or more for self-employed individuals earning $50,000 or more. An opportunity for a deduction that large may preclude your small business owner's feeling that he has to incorporate.

Furthermore, target benefit Keogh plans often fit nicely into small professional practices. While they limit the owner-employee to a $7,500 deduction, they usually restrict to a much greater degree the cost of covering common law participants. That's because target benefit plans allow for recognition of relative age and service, the bulk of which usually rests squarely with the key self-employed individual. However, before considering the opportunities inherent in Keogh plans, you must be aware of their pitfalls.

**¶1301   KEOGH'S SPECIAL REQUIREMENTS REQUIRE
CAREFUL PLANNING**

Many unusual restrictions apply uniquely to Keogh plans. You should apply them to your client at the census review level since they can have significant effects. While, in general, the limitations underscore the discrimination against Keogh plans relative to their corporate counterparts, there are occasions on which you can use them to your advantage.

¶1301.1   One-Hundred-Percent Vesting Can Be Costly

One of the more unique aspects of Keogh plans is the requirement that they provide 100% immediate vesting on any employer deposits/accrued benefits. Thus, the opportunity for using the "carrot and stick" approach to give employees an incentive to stay with your unincorporated business is absent. In effect, Keogh deposits for common law participants are mandatory pay increases. Once your client contributes to an employee's account there is nothing he can do, regardless of the employee's work habits, employment longevity or relative value of skills to recover those contributions. There are only two ways to offset this restriction.

¶1301.2   How Stretching The Eligibility Requirements Can Ease
                                    The Burden

Keogh plans generally ought to require three years of service as a condition of plan participation. However, keep in mind that an employee must participate in the plan for the year in which he completes the eligibility requirements. And since contributions must be 100% vested, it's more difficult to squeeze any "additional mileage" from your eligibility requirements. The following language presents a good combination of administrative simplicity and use of the eligibility rule to benefit your client:

> Employees will participate in the plan effective on the January 1st of the Plan Year during which they complete three years of service. Thereafter participants will accrue benefits during any plan year in which they complete a year of service.

Caution: Note that plans using the three year eligibility requirement *may not* impose an age 25 participation restriction.

Further Caution: Note that participants must share in benefit accruals for any plan year in which they complete a year of service. A year of service usually means a plan year during which 1,000 or more hours of service are completed. That means some employees who have terminated service by the end of the plan year may have to receive an allocation.

> *Example:* Mary J. starts working for Dr. X February 1, 1976. She completes three years of service on January 31, 1979, and therefore must be in the plan January 1, 1979. She quits on August 31, 1979 after working 1,001 hours. Dr. X must include Mary J. in his Keogh plan for 1979, at least to the extent of her compensation earned during that year.

¶1301.3   How High Turnover Can Help

Good business as well as intelligent pension planning dictates that your unincorporated clients should frequently cull their employee group to minimize Keogh participation. Real responsibility and knowledge should be imparted only to the employees most likely to remain employed for a long period of time. Skills of recently employed persons should be minimized for as long as possible to preclude their becoming a "necessary liability" to the business.

The most successfully run small unincorporated businesses centralize the few internal management functions required in the hands of one or two key employees. These employees effectively become "office manager" or "right hand man" type individuals who "ride herd" over less skilled, easily replaceable, and "high turnover" clerical employees. If you can help structure your client's unincorporated business in that manner, you'll save him a lot of time and money, even apart from his Keogh plan.

> *Example:* Dr. Disperse and Dr. Central each have medical practices requiring five common law employees. Dr. Disperse teaches important skills to each. Dr. Central makes two of the five employees "key people" in his professional business, teaching them all the essential skills and insisting that the other three be substantially restricted in their opportunities for advanced skills. Three years later, Dr. Disperse finds himself in a predicament: None of his five employees is particularly exceptional but each has one skill so central to the business that replacement would be more costly than continuing to pay the inefficient employee. Dr. Disperse must bring all five of his employees into the Keogh plan. Dr. Central, on the other hand, has two key individuals with overlapping skills. His other three employees turn over frequently and, since they have no irreplaceable skills, that turnover doesn't adversely affect his business. Dr. Central has only two employees to cover in his plan.

¶1302   WHAT ARE THE SPECIAL CONSIDERATIONS WHEN COMPUTING DEPOSITS TO KEOGH PLANS

In addition to restrictions on vesting and eligibility, certain factors come into play when you help your client determine his Keogh contribution. The limitations put a ceiling on considered compensation for owner-employees as well as affecting the manner in which the clients deduct their deposits. Here's how they work.

¶1302.1   How The $100,000 Limitation On Compensation Works

Keogh contributions can be based only on the first $100,000 of owner-employee net income. In corporate plans no such compensation limit applies. That means your unincorporated client will have to deposit relatively more for his common law employees than will his incorporated counterpart.

Example: Dr. Healthy and Dr. Sickly each generates $150,000 from his medical practice after deducting expenses. Each wishes to contribution $7,500 to a retirement program. Dr. Healthy incorporates. Since Dr. Sickly can only consider the first $100,000 of his income, he must contribute 7½% of pay for himself and all his employees. Dr. Healthy contributes only five percent, since he can consider *all* of his compensation. If both doctors have a substantial non-professional payroll to cover, the difference can be dramatic.

Nonprofessional Participant	Pay	Five Percent Contribution Required Under Dr. Healthy's Plan	7½% Contribution Required Under Dr. Sickly's Plan
A	$20,000	$1,000	$1,500
B	15,000	750	1,125
C	10,000	500	750
D	10,000	500	750
E	7,500	375	563
TOTAL	$62,500	$3,125	$4,688

As noted above, Dr. Healthy can consider all his corporate compensation (150,000) to determine contributions to his corporate pension plan. Assuming his objective is to contribute $7,500, he simply needs to deposit five percent of his pay. Therefore he needs to contribute five percent of employee pay. As shown, employee deposits amount to only $3,125.

Dr. Sickly, on the other hand, must ignore all his compensation in excess of $100,000. To contribute the same $7,500, therefore, he must deposit 7½% of his eligible compensation and therefore 7½% of his employee compensation. Thus, he must spend $4,688 for employees to get the same $7,500 contribution for himself. That increases employee deposits by 50% over the corporate counterpart.

Note that this comparison does not include the additional effect of integration which would be available to Dr. Healthy.

¶1302.2   Deposits Come From Net Income

In corporate retirement plans, all benefits and contributions are based on employee salaries and bonuses, with no distinction between common law and shareholder-employee participants. All funding costs are derived from the corporation. Keogh plans operate differently.

Owner-employees must deduct nonowner-employee contributions as expenses (usually from Schedule C of the income tax return) to arrive at their own net income eligible for Keogh contributions. Then the plan formula is applied to their own net income. Self-employed participant contributions come from net income, as if from personal funds.

Planning Tip: Make certain you consider the effects of common-law employee contributions on your owner-employee client's net income *before* you set a plan formula. Otherwise you'll end up undercontributing for your client.

Example: Dr. X has $100,000 of net income before implementing a Keogh plan. Eligible employees have a total payroll of $60,000. Dr. X establishes a 7½% of pay money-purchase Keogh plan, hoping to get a $7,500 contribution for himself. His plans are foiled because:

- he must contribute 7½% for employees .... $ 4,500
- that reduces his own eligible income to $95,000
- and his allowable contribution to .... $ 7,163

Possible solution: Trial and error will ultimately yield the most efficient plan. Dr. X should set up a 7.875% of pay Keogh plan because then:

- 7.875% of employee payroll .... $ 4,725
- will reduce his net income to $95,275
- and 7.875% of this adjusted net income yields ..... $ 7,500

¶1303   HOW THE UNAVAILABILITY OF INTEGRATION LIMITS PLAN EFFECTIVENESS

The most significant discrimination against self-employed individuals comes from their inability to integrate Keogh plan benefits with Social Security deposits/benefits. Earlier chapters discussed remarkable opportunities inherent in proper integration of qualified corporate plans. However, even though self-employed individuals must contribute to the Social Security system for themselves and their employees, they are not allowed, except in *very* unusual circumstances to consider Social Security contributions when they determine Keogh plan deposits. That means lower paid employees will receive proportionately higher contributions:

ILLUSTRATION 1

Participant	Pay	Total Social Security Deposit	Keogh Deposit	Total Deposit	Total Deposit As A % of Pay
A	$ 75,000	$2,098	$ 7,500	$ 9,598	13%
B	75,000	2,098	7,500	9,598	13%
C	12,000	1,471	1,200	2,671	22%
D	12,000	1,471	1,200	2,671	22%
E	7,500	920	750	1,670	22%
TOTAL	$181,500	$8,058	$18,150	$26,208	N/A

Or benefits (assuming all participants are 45):

ILLUSTRATION 2

Employee	Pay	Social Security Benefit	Keogh Benefit	Total Benefit At 65	Total Benefit As % of Compensation
A	$ 75,000	7,836/yr	$26,486/yr	34,322/yr	46%
B	75,000	7,836/yr	26,486/yr	34,322/yr	44%
C	12,000	6,193/yr	4,211/yr	10,404/yr	87%
D	12,000	6,193/yr	4,211/yr	10,404/yr	87%
E	7,500	4,906/yr	2,632/yr	7,538/yr	101%
TOTAL	$181,500	N/A	N/A	N/A	N/A

Illustration 1 above shows that the sum of Social Security deposits and Keogh deposits differ dramatically as a percentage of current compensation for high versus low paid participants. For example, Employee A (of whose compensation only the first $25,900 is taxed) deposits $2,098 (8.1%) to Social Security and $7,500 to his Keogh plan. The sum of those two deposits, $9,598, represents only 13% of his $75,000 compensation. On the other hand, Participant E receives Social Security deposits on all of her pay and a full Keogh contribution. The resulting total deposit, $1,670, represents 22% of her current level of pay. That's 83% more than Participant A.

Illustration 2 translates these differing annual deposits into future benefits, assuming each of the five participants is 45 years old (to eliminate the effect of compound interest). Participant A can look forward to a Social Security benefit of $7,836 per year, and a Keogh benefit of $26,846 per year for a total annual income at 65 of $34,322. This annual sum represents 46% of his current pay. On the other hand, Participant E can look forward to a Social Security benefit of $4,960 per year, and a Keogh benefit of $2,632 yielding a total annual income at 65 of $7,538—101% of her current pay.

The unavailability of integration in Keogh plans combine with very restrictive limits on contributions or benefits accounts for the increasing number of professional corporations. Ultimately, perhaps, there will be a uniform integration rule applicable to either Keogh or corporate plans. At the present time the Keogh options you can present your client are pretty restrictive.

¶1304   WHAT ARE THE OTHER SPECIAL LIMITS ON CONTRIBUTIONS OR BENEFITS

Apart from the restrictions discussed above, your unincorporated client faces additional limitations on benefits or contributions available with Keogh plans. These limits will provide further impetus for incorporation.

¶1304.1   The Limits On Defined-Contribution Plans

The familiar "lesser of $36,875 or 25% of pay" limitation on annual additions discussed in Chapters 4 through 6 doesn't apply with Keogh plans. Defined-contribution (money-purchase, profit-sharing or target benefit) Keogh plans cannot provide an annual deposit in excess of the lesser of:

1. 15% of pay; or
2. $7,500.

These limits are not subject to annual cost of living adjutments like their 25%/$36,875 corporate counterparts. Thus, any of your unincorporated clients who want to put more away will be out of luck.

Observation: Furthermore, the "1.4" rule for aggregation of multiple plans is replaced, in the Keogh domain, by a "1.0" rule. Even with multiple Keogh plans your client will not be able to exceed the $7,500/15% limitations, or the very restrictive defined-benefit Keogh guidelines discussed below.

¶1304.2   The $7,500/15% Limitation In Defined-Benefit Keogh
           Plans Is Replaced By A Very Complicated Maximum
           Benefit Computation

While in theory the full 100%/$110,625 maximum annual benefit available with corporate plans applies equally to Keogh plans, most of your Keogh clients will be subject to internal limitations peculiarly applicable to HR-10 plans.

Caveat: The following discussion as it relates to defined-benefit Keogh plans is based on the author's best interpretation of proposed regulations. Many commentators feel that the proposed regulations, which provide only guidance for defined-benefit Keogh plans, are arbitrarily onerous and restrictive. Before implementing a defined-benefit Keogh plan for one of your clients, check any updates to regulations issued under I.R.C. Section 401(j).

A. Maximum Benefits Under Defined-Benefit Keogh Programs:

Maximum benefits for defined-benefit Keogh plans are determined under a "unit benefit" format. For each year of participation an owner-employee can accrue a benefit not greater than $50,000 times the percentage rate applicable to his age as determined by reference to the following chart:

Age When Participant Began	Maximum Accrual Percentage	Age When Participant Began	Maximum Accrual Percentage
30 or less	6.5	45	3.6
31	6.3	46	3.5
32	6.0	47	3.4
33	5.8	48	3.2
34	5.6	49	3.1
35	5.4	50	3.0
36	5.1	51	2.9
37	4.9	52	2.8
38	4.8	53	2.7
39	4.6	54	2.6
40	4.4	55	2.5
41	4.2	56	2.4
42	4.1	57	2.3
43	3.9	58	2.2
44	3.8	59	2.1
		60 or older	2.0

Example: Dr. J. participated in a Keogh plan when he was 45 years old and earning $50,000. His maximum annual retirement benefit is therefore:

- considered compensation $50,000
- times maximum annual accrual percentage .... × 3.6%
- equals annual benefit increment $1,800
- times years of participation .... × 20
- maximum benefit at age 65 .... $36,000

That doesn't sound like such a bad deal. But other limitations apply.

B. Disability Reductions

If your defined-benefit Keogh plan provides a disability benefit (and virtually all Keogh plans will) then you must reduce the benefits otherwise payable under A above by the "disability benefit reduction factor" of 90%. That's not all.

C. Death Benefit Adjustment Further Reduces Your Funding Goals

Depending on the participation age of a self-employed individual, he must further reduce maximum benefits determined in accordance with A and B above by the "death benefit reduction factor" determined according to the following quinquennial age bracket chart:

Age When Participation Began	Death Benefit Reduction Factor
Under 35	83
35–39	.85
40–44	.87
45–49	.89
50–54	.91
55–59	.93
60 and above	.95

It's clear that the various "adjustment factors" will substantially hamper your self-employed client's efforts.

D. Settlement Option Adjustments

Corporate plans can use a joint and full survivor benefit as the "normal form of retirement benefit." Joint and full survivor benefits are quite expensive and can help boost the funding costs of corporate plans. However, if a joint and full survivor annuity is the normal benefit form in a defined-benefit Keogh plan, then the benefits determined under paragraphs A, B, C and D must be further reduced to 79%. Other reductions for distribution options to insure actuarial equivalency are the same as with corporate plans.

E. The Effect Of Commonly Used "Adjustment Factors"

Almost all Keogh plans include disability and death benefits. Assuming your client establishes a plan providing death and ancillary features, the following chart summarizes the *maximum* retirement benefits and approximate funding costs for all ages, assuming a $50,000 compensation, six percent interest, 1971 GA settlement option rates and age 65 retirement:

Participation Age	Adjusted Maximum Benefit Increment	Maximum Annual Retirement Benefit	Annual Funding Costs
30	4.86	$50,000*	$3,919
31	4.71	50,000	4,192
32	4.48	50,000	4,487
33	4.33	50,000	4,805
34	4.18	50,000	5,150
35	4.13	50,000	5,525
36	3.90	50,000	5,931
37	3.75	50,000	6,373
38	3.67	49,572	6,797
39	3.52	45,747	6,755
40	3.45	43,065	6,857
41	3.29	39,463	6,784
42	3.21	36,918	6,862
43	3.05	33,591	6,762
44	2.98	31,244	6,824
45	2.88	28,836	6,847
46	2.80	26,633	6,891
47	2.72	24,511	6,928
48	2.56	21,787	6,746

(continued)

Participation Age	ˆAdjusted Maximum Benefit Increment	Maximum Annual Retirement Benefit	Annual Funding Costs
49	2.48	19,865	6,759
50	2.46	18,428	6,916
51	2.38	16,626	6,912
52	2.29	14,906	6,896
53	2.21	13,268	6,870
54	2.13	11,712	6,833
55	2.09	10,463	6,934
56	2.01	9,040	6,871
57	1.93	7,700	6,796
58	1.84	6,445	7,109
59	1.76	5,273	7,000
60	1.71	4,275	7,022

*Maximum Retirement Benefit is lesser of $110,625 or 100% of pay.

Observation: The annual funding costs (deposits) for these defined-benefit Keogh plans are not, using the assumptions stated above, any more attractive than defined-contribution plan deposits. In fact, it was IRS's intent when computing the 401-J benefit rates, to effectively translate the $7,500 contribution limits of defined-contribution Keogh plans to a comparable defined-benefit which could be purchased for the same price.

¶1305   **WHAT ARE THE CHOICES AMONG DEFINED-CONTRIBUTION PLANS**

All of the traditional defined-contribution approaches can be used, subject to various restrictions within the Keogh domain. Since your client can't integrate, most of the opportunity for creativity is gone. However, with some effort you can improve the efficiency of your client's plan.

¶1305.1   When Using Profit-Sharing And Money-Purchase Keogh Plans Can Be Effective

Money-purchase and profit-sharing Keogh plans are virtually indistinguishable. Each must specify the percentage of payroll to be deposited. Profit-sharing plans may further provide that no contribution need be made in a year when business profits don't exceed a certain minimal level. Lacking is the total employer contribution-discretion *on an annual basis* which so enhances corporate profit-sharing plans. Thus, except in the case of dire business reversals, your client won't gain much by using profit-sharing as opposed to money-purchase Keogh plans.

Using money-purchase and profit-sharing Keogh plans effectively requires choosing the "right" contribution percentage. That means the percentage most likely to maximize the self-employed participant's share of the contribution. Choosing that percentage requires consideration of the additional business expense of common-law Keogh contributions as discussed at ¶1302.1 and ¶1302.2. Your job is to find the contribution percentage which, after deducting common-law employee costs, will result in your client's receiving maximum allowable deductions.

Example: S. Squire, prior to implementing a Keogh plan, has a net proprietor's income of $60,000 after subtracting the payroll of three common-law employees earning $10,000, $15,000 and $20,000 respectively. If S. Squire wants to put $7,500 into his Keogh plan then the plan should specify a 14% deposit. That's because

- his net proprietor's income $60,000
- less 14% of his $45,000 payroll .... (6,300)
- leaves a net proprietor's income of $53,700
- 14% of this net income equals .... $ 7,500

Any contribution rate other than 14% will result in either:

- overfunding for common-law employees; or
- underfunding for S. Squire.

¶1305.2   You Should Make Sure Expenses Are Paid Outside The Plan

Many small Keogh plans invest their assets in insurance company annuity products, which commonly have a five to ten percent sales charge. Since your client can contribute and deduct $7,500 to his account, any diminution of that sum by expenses is counterproductive and wastes the valuable tax-free compounding available with qualified plans.

Example: Maximize, C.P.A. and Minimize, Attorney-at-Law are sole proprietors desiring to contribute $7,500 to their respective Keogh plans. Maximize, C.P.A. pays plan expenses *apart from* contributions: Minimize, Attorney-at-Law has his expenses deducted from his annuity premiums. Look what happens over a 20-year period assuming an eight percent "load":

Item	Maximize, C.P.A.	Minimize, Attorney-at-Law
Total Deductible Keogh Expenses	$8,100	$7,500
Amount Deductible As Sales Charge	(600)	N/A
Net Deductible Keogh Contribution	$7,500	$7,500
Less Expenses Deducted Inside Plan	N/A	(600)
Net Allocation to Keogh Account	$ 7,500	$ 6,900
Account Balance At End of 10 Years	$103,623	$ 95,333
Account Balance At End of 20 Years	$307,466	$282,869

Plan expenses are deductible *whether or not* they are taken directly from contributions. Therefore, if your client wants to get the full advantage of his $75,000 allocation, he should make an arrangement to pay plan expenses separately.

¶1305.3   How Waiver Authorizations Will Protect Your Client

Owner-employees must consent to participate in Keogh plans. Conversely, they can elect to *waive* part or all of what would otherwise have been their annual accrual. That's a unique opportunity not available in corporate plans and helps to give your client an "out" if funds otherwise earmarked for Keogh contribution are needed elsewhere in a particular year.

Planning Tip: Make certain that your Keogh plan includes a provision allowing self-employed participants to waive their participation or alternatively, requires that they specifically *consent* to participation each year.

¶1306   **TARGET PLANS—AN OVERLOOKED OPPORTUNITY**

Target benefit Keogh, like corporate plans, represent a hybrid combining attributes of defined-contribution and defined-benefit plans. Like a defined-contribution Keogh plan, target benefit plans must limit contributions for self-employed individuals to the lesser of $7,500 or 15% of compensation. Like defined-benefit plans, target Keoghs compute deposits on the basis of funding specific future benefits. Like defined-contribution plans, target Keoghs simply add any surplus or shortfall of investment over projected yield to participant account balances. Like defined-benefit plans, target Keoghs can reduce future benefits (and therefore current deposits) for plan participants who have less than a certain number of years of service when they reach retirement age.

The combination of these factors makes target benefit Keogh plans the ideal program for many small unincorporated businesses. Professional service organizations, such as lawyers, accountants, or doctors, are particularly well-suited for target benefit Keogh plans since traditionally the higher paid key self-employed participants are older and have more service than the rest of the employees.

¶1306.1   How To Compute The Best Formula For The Key Man

Since the maximum contribution for self-employed individuals is $7,500, it's fairly easy to arrive at the plan formula which most efficiently achieves that deduction for your key man. Having computed this "best" formula, simply add it in reverse to the remaining participants. Here's how it's done:

Finding The Best Plan Formula

Assumptions about the key man

- He is 50 years old;
- will have 30 years of service at age 65; and
- earns $50,000.

Calculation of Best Formula

- Annual contribution .... $ 7,500
- Estimated future value @ 65 (assuming 6%) $185,044
- Estimated retirement income from future value .... $ 19,963
- Estimated retirement income as a % of salary 40%

Therefore the plan "formula" should be that every participant will receive a target benefit at age 65 equal to 40% of his pay To increase the plan's efficiency, you should also include a requirement that benefits will be reduced for each year of service less than 30 (the number of years our key man will have when he retires). That way, you know that your client will receive the maximum deduction ($7,500) and that common-law employee contributions will be minimized.

Applying The Formula To Census Information

Let's apply the illustrative plan formula to census information of a typical medical office:

Employee	Age	Service At Retirement	Pay	40% Retirement Benefit	Service at NRD Divided by 30 equals Net Target Benefit	Future Value Required	Annual Deposit Required
A	50	30 yrs	$ 50,000	$20,000/yr.	$20,000/yr	$185,044	$ 7,500
B	40	25 yrs	15,000	6,000	5,000/yr	48,348	797
C	60	5 yrs	20,000	8,000	1,333/yr	12,359	2,068
D	30	35 yrs	30,000	12,000	12,000/yr	111,235	1,327
E	25	40 yrs	10,000	4,000	4,000/yr	37,078	226
TOTAL		N/A	$125,000	N/A	N/A	N/A	$11,918

Since we have computed the plan formula based on what the maximum contribution for the key man will buy, we know in advance that his annual deposit will equal $7,500. Thus computing deposits for other plan participants is simply a matter of reversing that process.

For example, Participant C would be entitled to a retirement income equal to 14% of her pay ($8,000). However, the insertion of a service requirement (30 years) reduces her benefits to 5/30ths of that amount ($1,333). In order to pay a $1,333 per year benefit at age 65, the plan will need to have approximately $12,359 on hand. The annual deposit necessary to provide that lump sum is $2,068 per year.

Obviously, target benefit Keogh plans provide quite an opportunity for contribution selectivity with the right situation. Target plans should be superior in all situations where the self-employed individual is older than the average age of plan participants in general.

¶1306.2   A Comparison Of Target And Defined-Contribution
                          Keogh Plans

Here's an illustration showing relative contribution allocations under a typical and target benefit Keogh arrangement in which the objective is to generate a $7,500 deduction for the key man:

Employee	Age	Service at NRD	Pay	Target-Benefit Keogh		Profit-Sharing Keogh	
				Deposit	%	Deposit	%
A	50	30	$ 50,000	$ 7,500	63%	$ 7,500	40%
B	40	25	15,000	797	7	2,250	12
C	60	5	20,000	2,068	17	3,000	16
D	30	35	30,000	1,327	11	4,500	24
E	25	40	10,000	226	2	1,500	8
TOTAL			$125,000	$11,918	100%	$18,750	100%

Key man A receives a $7,500 deposit under either approach. That's the maximum annual addition he can receive under a defined-contribution or target plan. However, other participants' contributions are dramatically altered when we switch from target benefit to profit-sharing format. Note, for example, that Participant E receives a $226 contribution under the target-benefit approach and a $1,500 contribution under the profit-sharing approach. Stating this another way, the company must contribute 6½ times as much for her under the defined-contribution as opposed to the target benefit Keogh plan.

The table represents an opportunity for the key man to boost his percentage of the total contribution from 40 to 63%. Alternatively, and probably more relevant to most Keogh considerations, he can obtain the same $7,500 deduction for himself and spend $6,832 less for his common-law employees. That's a pretty significant increase in design efficiency.

¶1307   USING DEFINED-BENEFIT KEOGH PLANS FOR MAXIMUM DEDUCTIONS

Like target-benefit plans, defined-benefit Keogh plans fund toward future benefits. However, defined-benefit plans must pay specific retirement income rather than the *estimated* income generated by target plans. Most important, defined-benefit plans are not subject to the $7,500/15% limitation applicable to other Keogh plans. Your client can put enough money in his defined-benefit program to fund the benefits discussed at paragraph 1304.2A. There are two types of defined-benefit Keogh plans.

¶1307.1   Keying Unit-Benefit Plans To The Key People

Unit-benefit plan benefits are the sum of annual accruals, each of which is determined by applying the plan's accrual rate (see ¶1304.2E) to participant compensation (not in excess of $50,000). Thus, participants with the most past service at retirement will reap the highest benefits. Funding of the plan is a matter of determining the deposit necessary to generate the benefits determined by the plan formula.

Example: U. Knit Company sets up a unit-defined-benefit Keogh plan primarily for its sole proprietor-owner, Employee A. The plan uses, as its accrual rate, the maximum (¶1304.2E) for a self-employed individual of his age, net of adjustments for death and disability benefits. Here's what happens:

Employee	Age	Participation at NRD	Pay	Accrual Rate	Retirement Benefit	Annual Deposit Required
A	45	20 yrs	$50,000	2.88	$28,836	$ 6,847 42%
B	50	15 yrs	40,000	2.46*	14,760	5,533 35%
C	35	30 yrs	11,000	2.88	9,504	1,051 7%
D	55	10 yrs	11,000	2.88	3,168	2,102 13%
E	25	40 yrs	8,000	2.88	8,000**	452 3%
TOTAL			$120,000			$15,985 100%

*Assumes Employee B also qualifies as "self-employed" and subject to accrual limitations.
**Limited to 100% of pay

The maximum annual accrual rate, after reductions for death, disability and 10 years certain and continuous benefit distribution is 2.88%. Thus, at age 65, Employee A will have had 20 years of participation in the plan. 20 years times 2.88% times $50,000 equals $28,836 annual retirement benefit. The annual deposit required to fund that benefit is $6,847.

On the other hand, assuming that Participant B is also a self-employed individual and therefore subject to the limitations imposed by 401(J), his maximum annual accrual for each of his 15 years of participation will be 2.46%, yielding a retirement benefit of $14,760 which requires an annual deposit of $5,533.

Assuming other participants accrue benefits at the rate of 2.88% per year, their benefits and deposits are as shown. While the deposits indicated are certainly preferable to the allocation under a defined-contribution plan, they aren't exceptional compared to a target program.

Planning Tip: Unit-benefit plans can limit years of participation credited for purposes of benefit accrual. It makes sense to use the number of years of participation that your key man will have at retirement date as a "cap." That will insure that no plan participant will receive a benefit higher, as a percentage of their pay, than the key man

Example: U. Knit Company's unit-benefit Keogh plan is amended such that participants will not receive credit for more than 30 years of participation. That lowers benefits (and contributions) for Participant E who otherwise would have received more service credit than A.

Employee	Age	Participation @ 65	Pay	Unadjusted Benefit	Adjusted Benefit	Annual Deposit	% of Total
A	45	20	$ 50,000	$28,836/yr	$28,836/yr	$ 6,847	43%
B	50	15	40,000	14,760/yr	14,760/yr	5,533	35%
C	35	30	11,000	9,504/yr	9,504/yr	1,051	7%
D	55	10	11,000	3,168/yr	3,168/yr	2,102	13%
E	25	40	8,000	8,000/yr	6,912/yr	390	2%
TOTAL	N/A	N/A	$120,000	N/A	N/A	$15,923	100%

Note that the "participation cap" of 30 years of service affected Employee E's benefit and contribution. Under U. Knit's amended plan, no participant can receive an accrual for service in excess of 30 years. There will be some occasions where this limitation can be particularly helpful, especially in professional offices where key men (e.g., physicians) may have 25 to 30 years of service at retirement but who continually hire young employees, who, but for a participation cap, could receive incremental benefits covering more years than their key man.

¶1307.2   How To Use Fixed Benefit Alternatives

In addition to unit-benefit plans, your Keogh client can establish fixed-benefit plans. The proposed regulations (Sections 1.401(a)-18; 1.401 (j)-1-1401(j)-6; 1.404(e)-1A; 1.1379-1—Published in Federal Register 5/26/78) discuss an extremely complicated method to insure that fixed-benefit accruals do not exceed those available under a unit-benefit approach. Your key man client won't receive a larger deduction under *either* defined-benefit Keogh alternatives since fixed-benefit plans must pass an "internal test" to insure their comparability to unit-benefit plans.

When To Use Fixed-Benefit Plans When most plan participants are younger than the key self-employed individual, they will obviously have more projected participation at retirement. Those situations might warrant the use of a fixed-benefit plan, since excess participation won't result in larger benefits for these employees.

Planning Tip: For safety's sake, it still makes sense to include a provision in your Fixed Benefit Plan which reduces, on a pro rata basis, benefits for any participant with more years of participation at retirement than those of the key man. That way you will insure maximum efficiency for your client.

¶1307.3   How Costs Can Be Reduced For Common Law
                        Participants By Raising The Compensation Ceiling

The maximum accrual rate specified at ¶1304.2E cannot be applied to compensation in excess of $50,000 unless the accrual rates are reduced. The reduction is easily accomplished by multiplying the normal maximum accrual rate by a fraction, the numerator of which is $50,000, and the denominator of which is the compensation ceiling desired (not in excess of $100,000).

The resulting reduced accrual rate can then be applied to participant compensation. Since the reduced accrual rate will be applied to higher compensation (in the case of those employees earning $50,000 or more) the annual accrual for those participants does not change. However, accruals for employees earning less than $50,000 will be lowered. That will help cut down on your costs.

> *Example:* 45-year-old Dr. Cuttit typically has compensation in excess of $75,000. Therefore, he'd like to use a higher compensation base and compare the results to a flat-benefit Keogh plan which uses a $50,000 base. Here's how its done:

$$\text{Adjusted Accrual Rate} = \frac{\$50,000}{\text{Desired Compensation Ceiling}} \times \text{Normal Accrual Rate}$$

$$\text{Adjusted Accrual Rate} = \frac{\$50,000}{\$75,000} \times 2.88$$
(at original Participation)

$$\text{Adjusted Accrual Rate} = 1.92\%$$

Adjusted Accrual Rate × 20 years of participation = Maximum Retirement Benefit

$$1.92\% \times 20 \times 75,000 = \$28,800$$

Maximum Retirement Benefit as a percentage of Pay 38.4%

Employee	Age	Pay	Assumed Participation at NRD	Plan I—58% of Pay (Not Exceeding $50,000)		Plan II—38% of Pay (Up to $75,000)	
				Benefit at NRD	Annual Contribution	Benefit at NRD	Annual Contribution
A	45	$ 75,000	20	$28,800/yr	$ 6,846	$28,800	$6,846
B	45	15,000	20	8,700/yr	2,192	5,700	1,436
C	35	15,000	30	8,700/yr	1,020	5,700	688
D	35	10,000	30	5,800/yr	680	3,800	445
E	25	7,500	40	4,350/yr	261	2,850	171
TOTAL		$122,500	N/A	N/A	$10,999	N/A	$9,586

Dr. Cuttit has obviously performed surgery on a lot of unnecessary costs. In fact, he has reduced costs for common-law employees by $1,413 (34%). That's a substantial increase in efficiency.

¶1308   COMPARING ALTERNATIVE KEOGH PLANS

It is a useful exercise to compare the alternative Keogh plans for a typical small business situation. Each of the following plans is designed to maximize the amount and relative percentage of the contribution for the key man, Employee A.

ANNUAL CONTRIBUTIONS REQUIRED

Employee	Age	Pay	Plan I Money-Purchase[1]		Plan II Target-Benefit[2]		Plan III Defined-Benefit[3]	
A	50	$80,000	$7,500	(42%)	$7,500	(65%)	$6,916	(53%)
B	35	75,000	7,031	(40%)	2,070	(18%)	3,061	(24%)
C	50	15,000	1,406	(8%)	1,406	(12%)	2,080	(16%)
D	40	12,000	1,125	(6%)	477	(4%)	706	(5%)
E	25	7,500	703	(4%)	106	(1%)	250	(2%)
TOTAL		$189,500	$17,765	(100%)	$11,559	(100%)	$13,013	(100%)

[1] Annual contribution is 9.375% of payroll.
[2] Target retirement benefit of 23.5% of pay, reduced for service less than 25 years.
[3] Flat-benefit of 36.9% of pay reduced for service less than 25 years.

The target benefit plan offers the highest level of efficiency with the facts indicated. This relative efficiency compared to a defined-benefit program is further enhanced by the fact that the target plan will not require actuarial certification and will allow surplus investment gains to inure to the benefit of plan participants instead of reducing contributions.

Planning Tip: Many of your clients will not even know that these alternatives exist. You can enhance your own credibility by taking the small amount of time necessary to prepare an analysis of the choices for your client.

¶1308.1   How To Compare Keogh And Corporate Plan
                           Effectiveness

Notwithstanding the flexibility indicated in this chapter keep in mind that Keogh plans suffer from substantial inherent limitations.

1. They can't be integrated with Social Security.

2. They can't use vesting schedules.

3. They can't consider more than $100,000 of a self-employed individual's compensation.

4. In the case of defined-benefit plans:

   a) use of a normal retirement date earlier than 65 is counter-productive; and

   b) joint and survivor annuities cannot be used as the normal form of benefit to boost funding costs.

5. Death and disability benefit reductions restrict benefits and therefore contributions.

Example: Suppose your 48-year-old client, Dr. Resteasy, needs $100,000 to live on but generates another $75,000 after expenses from his practice. He has been self-employed for 10 years. He asks three questions:

1. "What is the maximum contribution I can make to a defined-benefit Keogh plan?"

2. "If I make the same contribution to an integrated corporate plan, what are the respective common-law employee costs?"

3. "What is the largest tax deductible contribution I can make to a defined-benefit Keogh versus a combination of corporate plans?"

ANNUAL CONTRIBUTIONS POSSIBLE

Employee	Age	Pay	Plan I Defined- Benefit Keogh[1]		Plan II Integrated Corporate[2]		Plan III Combination Corporate[3]	
A	48	$100,000	$6,746	(77%)	$7,496	(86%)	$62,684	(72%)
B	50	15,000	681	(8%)	333	(4%)	9,060	(10%)
C	30	50,000	854	(10%)	855	(10%)	11,144	(13%)
D	40	10,000	347	(4%)	42	(0%)	3,114	(4%)
E	25	8,000	98	(1%)	0	(0%)	1,092	(1%)
TOTAL		$183,000	$8,726	(100%)	$8,726	(100%)	$87,094	(100%)

[1] 21.7% of pay, reduced for participation less than 27 years.

[2] Uses similar contribution for Dr. Resteasy. Formula is 5.017% total pay plus 26.58% of pay in excess of $9,000 reduced for service less than 27 years.

[3] 5.771% of pay per year unit-benefit plan, maximum service of 17 years using joint and survivor annuities plus money purchase plan integrated at $15,000 (4.05% total pay plus 7% excess).

The analysis of Plans I and II reveals that Dr. Resteasy is not particularly worse off under the defined-benefit Keogh plan than he would be under the integrated corporate plan. Therefore, if his saving goals were fairly modest, he might be tempted to install the defined-benefit Keogh plan (or a target benefit Keogh plan) rather than going through the process of incorporation. However, it should be noted that the integrated corporate plan is, in fact, superior. Of the $8,726 contribution assumed in each case, Dr. Resteasy would garner 77% ($6,746) under the Keogh alternative and 86% ($7,496) under the corporate alternative.

Once Dr. Resteasy, however, makes a decision that he wants a larger tax deduction, there really is no choice. The combination corporate plan generates a tax deductible contribution so far in excess of anything available under Keogh—without any appreciable loss of efficiency—that the Doctor's other alternatives pale by comparison.

Clearly Keogh and corporate plans are not comparable. However, for a small business owner with very low common-law employee payroll costs, a target or defined-benefit Keogh plan may provide a big enough tax deduction to preclude the time, expense and hassle of incorporation. There are a lot more alternatives than traditionally thought.

PART THREE
Checklists And Charts
That Expedite Plan Design

14

A Practitioner's Guide To Overseeing Qualification, Administration And Investment Aspects Of The Plan

---

¶1400 **HOW TO CHOOSE THE RIGHT PLAN FOR YOUR CLIENT**

The success of your client's pension or profit-sharing plan won't be determinable for several years. By then it will be difficult or impossible to recover the time, expense, and aggravation that went into the qualification and ongoing administration of the plan if it proves to have been a bad choice. Success will be dependent upon both controllable and uncontrollable events, such as:

1. How accurate will your client's forecasts about wage inflation, profitability and stability prove to have been?
2. Will the plan end up benefiting the group it was designed for?
3. Will timely and complete qualification and administration preclude necessary and disconcerting problems with participants or the government?

Many of these issues, profitability for example, can't always be determined in advance, but most fall at least partially within your domain of control.

Frequently a client will become so enamoured of the tax advantages of *any* qualified plan that he may tend to minimize the balance of the design process. It's easy to opt for a simple profit-sharing plan and, therefore, avoid the more sophisticated and complex discussion that would have to surround implementation of a defined-benefit program. However, it is essential that you *force* your client to thoroughly focus upon his objectives and the entire range of alternatives which could, theoretically, fulfill them. That may, at times, seem an exercise in futility, but it isn't. The extra time you spend during the design process, following through with and illustrating the results of your client's hypothetical questions, will be well worth the effort.

¶1400.1   Checklist Of Key Questions—How To Get The Right Information

Your client won't be aware of the semantic implication of pension jargon. Therefore, it's important to clearly define your terms. Frequently, when you are at the design stage of pension planning, your client may think that *estimates* of dates of birth, dates of employment, and other pertinent employee information will suffice. However, in plans with limited budgets a five year age or service discrepency for an employee close to normal retirement age would be very significant.

One of the least addressed topics during design discussions is the definition of "pay." Yet the plan's ultimate definition of compensation can affect benefits and contributions more directly than virtually any other parameter. Integrated plans must use *total* compensation when determining benefits. And actually, that's generally more favorable for your key men.

Following are some questions whose accurate answers early in the design process will save a significant amount of time:

- ☐ Who is the President of the firm?
- ☐ Who is the Secretary/Clerk of the firm?
- ☐ What is the tax identification number?
- ☐ When does the fiscal year end?
- ☐ Is the business a Subchapter S Corporation?
- ☐ What, if applicable, is the original date of incorporation?
- ☐ What is the name, date of birth, date of employment, Social Security number and projected *total* compensation for the fiscal year for all employees who will complete 1,000 hours of service during that fiscal year?

☐ Of the total compensation how much is base pay and how much bonus or overtime?

☐ Who is the business' attorney?

☐ Who is the business' accountant?

☐ What is the exact legal name, address, and telephone number of the business?

The consistency with which the items above are necessary warrants your concerted effort to obtain them as accurately and early as possible. Forcing your client through the exercise of obtaining this data will have an additional advantage: it will emphasize to him the technically demanding detail-oriented "world" he is entering. Early recognition of those attributes will save your time further down the road.

¶1400.2   Identifying Your Client's Objectives

Having gathered accurate information about your client's employees and business you must force him to commit himself to increasingly narrow goals. Since most small businesses have a limited budget, they can only achieve so much with their plans. Therefore, it is extremely important for your client to focus specifically on *who* should benefit most under his plan and *why*.

Frequently small businessmen may, in the preliminary stages of designing a plan, emphasize altruistic motivation. For instance, they may discuss an ethical obligation to help employees save money. As a practical matter, most common-law employees would be more highly motivated by a cash bonus than a deferred pension benefit. Furthermore, the tax advantages of qualified plans aren't as meaningful to low-paid plan participants. Generally, as the design process unfolds, your client will become more oriented toward a plan which favors him.

To conserve your time, energy and expense you must focus your client on key questions. To the extent he provides sincere and realistic answers, plan design time and expense can be minimized. Here are some of the philosophical questions your client should answer:

☐ What is a reasonable, sustainable budget?

☐ How widely does cash flow vary from year to year?

☐ In the worst of the last three fiscal years, how much cash would have been available to fund a retirement program?

☐ If it were technically possible would your client spend the entire plan budget on the two or three highest paid employees?

☐ Who are the most important non-owner employees?

☐ Who should reap the greater benefit from the plan—employees with past service or employees with high pay?

☐ Which is more important to participating key men—income tax deferrals or estate tax advantages?

☐ Is the company likely to have continuity after the departure of the key man?

☐ Will there be any extraordinary demands on cash flow during the next several years for personnel expansion?

Discussions in previous chapters should have given you an impression of why these questions are important. You'll want to add more and tailor the list to your particular client but you'll find that the above will sharpen your client's focus appreciably.

¶1400.3   Plan Design: How To Match Objectives, Client Data and Plan Alternatives

Paragraphs 1400.1 and 1400.2 discuss the information you need to evaluate alternatives. Now, what do you do when you get it? That's the substance of plan design. The following chart compares various census statistics with client objectives. See how many times a particular type of plan results when you apply your client facts. If one type of plan consistently results when you compare census statistics to your client's objectives, chances are that's a good place for you to start your analysis.

How To Use The Chart

To use the following chart, simply compare your client's answers to the simple "yes or no" questions you ask during the plan design interview. If he answers "yes" to a particular question, then cross out the "no" line. If he answers "no," then cross out the "yes" line. If a particular question is not applicable, cross out both lines. When you are done, simply add up the column totals for each type of plan. Whichever plan results in the highest total is likely to be a good start for you to consider for your client.

Questions		Profit-Sharing, Nonintegrated	Profit-Sharing, Integrated	Profit-Sharing, Unit Format	Money-Purchase, Nonintegrated	Money-Purchase, Integrated	Money-Purchase, with Past Service	Flat-Benefit, Nonintegrated, EAN/FIPSL*	Flat-Benefit, Nonintegrated EAN/FIPSL*	Flat-Benefit, Integrated EAN/FIPSL*	Flat-Benefit, Integrated	Unit-Benefit, Nonintegrated	Unit-Benefit, Nonintegrated EAN/FIPSL*	Unit-Benefit, Integrated EAN/FIPSL*	Offset, Flat-Benefit Format EAN/FIPSL*	Offset, Flat-Benefit Format	Offset, Unit-Benefit Format EAN/FIPSL*	Offset, Unit-Benefit, Format	Target Plan, Nonintegrated	Target Plan, Integrated	Unit-Benefit, Integrated
Is Cash Flow Stable?	N	5	5	5	-1	-1	-1	0	-4	0	-4	0	-4	-4	0	-4	0	-4	-4	-4	-4
	Y	-2	0	-2	3	4	3	2	3	2	4	2	3	4	2	4	2	4	3	4	4
Are Key Men Older?	N	4	5	2	4	5	2	-2	-3	-3	-3	-1	-2	-3	-3	-4	-3	-3	1	0	-3
	Y	-4	-3	-4	-5	-4	-2	4	2	4	3	3	2	4	5	4	5	4	3	4	4
Is A Second Plan Likely?	N	3	4	3	0	1	1	2	0	4	2	1	0	4	5	3	5	3	0	1	2
	Y	2	0	2	4	0	3	2	0	3	2	2	0	4	5	3	5	3	4	1	2
Will Key Men Have Substantial Service at N.R.D.?	N	2	3	-4	0	2	-4	2	0	4	2	0	-4	-3	5	3	0	-3	-2	0	-5
	Y	2	3	4	1	2	3	-1	-2	0	-2	2	0	4	2	0	5	3	0	2	2
Is There High Turnover?	N	-3	-3	-3	2	2	2	2	1	3	2	2	1	3	3	2	3	2	2	2	2
	Y	4	5	4	-2	0	-2	1	-2	1	-2	1	-2	1	1	-2	1	-2	-2	0	-2
Is Flexibility Necessary?	N	0	0	0	2	3	2	0	3	0	3	0	3	0	0	3	0	3	3	3	3
	Y	4	5	4	-3	-2	-3	0	-4	0	-3	0	-4	0	0	-4	0	-4	-3	-3	-3
Will Key Men Have Less Than 15 Yrs Service at N.R.D.?	N	2	4	3	2	3	2	1	0	2	1	2	0	1	1	0	1	0	0	0	0
	Y	-1	0	-1	-2	-1	-2	0	-1	0	-1	-3	-5	-3	5	3	4	3	0	0	-5
Will Key Men Have Less Than 10 Yrs Service at N.R.D.?	N	2	3	2	1	2	1	2	1	3	2	2	1	3	3	2	3	2	0	1	2
	Y	-3	-3	-4	-3	-2	-3	-3	-5	-3	-4	-4	-5	-3	5	4	-3	-5	-2	-2	-5
Is Plan Likely to Be Terminated Within 10 Yrs?	N	0	0	0	0	0	0	0	0	0	0	0	0	0	0	0	0	0	0	0	0
	Y	4	5	4	2	3	2	-2	-4	-3	-5	-2	-4	-3	-3	-5	-3	-5	-1	-2	-5
Early Normal Retirement Age?	N	0	0	0	0	0	0	0	0	0	0	0	0	0	0	0	0	0	0	0	0
	Y	0	1	-1	-2	-1	-3	2	0	4	3	0	-2	2	5	4	3	1	0	2	0
Is Simplicity Important?	N	2	2	2	1	1	1	3	2	3	2	3	2	3	3	2	3	2	2	2	2
	Y	5	3	3	4	2	2	0	2	-2	0	0	2	-2	-1	0	-1	0	2	1	0
Used As a Second Plan?	N	0	0	0	0	0	0	0	0	0	0	0	0	0	0	0	0	0	0	0	0
	Y	3	-3	3	4	-3	4	0	-2	-2	-2	0	-2	-2	-2	-2	-2	-2	5	0	-2
Plan Invests Aggressively?	N	0	0	0	0	0	0	0	0	0	0	0	0	0	0	0	0	0	0	0	0
	Y	5	5	5	4	4	4	-1	-3	-1	-3	-1	-3	-1	-1	-3	-1	-3	4	4	-3

*EAN/FIPSL—Entry age normal with frozen intial past service liability.

¶1400.4   What Are The Penalties Or Problems Of Underfunding

Many of the pension plans which are most attractive for older key men are of the defined-benefit or target benefit variety. Money-purchase plans, too, are often in the background as secondary programs. Your client may have problems with any of these plans if he decides he has "bitten off more than he can chew." Defined-benefit, target benefit and money-purchase plans all require a "Funding Standard Account" which helps measure the exact amount of money which *must* be contributed to the plan each year. Failing to meet the requirements of the Funding Standard Account may result in automatic termination of the plan, which could cause:

    1. retroactive disqualification of the plan and loss of previous tax deductions; or

2. 100% immediate vesting for all plan participants.

The consequences of disqualification of 100% vesting should be explained carefully to your client. There are two possible remedies:

1. Built-in flexibility—always try to design a plan or combination of plans which offers the greatest amount of flexibility. In the case of a defined-benefit plan, try to use the Entry Age Normal with F.I.P.S.L. actuarial method to provide a "range" of contributions. Suggest to your client that he cut back his budget by 20% to allow for unforeseen contingencies. Remember, a plan can almost always be amended to *increase* benefits, but a decrease is difficult to accomplish without some punitive consequences.

2. Obtain a temporary waiver of the Funding Standard Account from IRS. Businesses showing need can usually obtain such a temporary waiver by filing various forms (in advance) with the government. Any portion of the Funding Standard Account requirement waived must be repaid under rigid supervision. This remedy should only be considered in the case of dire, unforseen emergencies.

The message of underfunding is loud and clear—don't. Proper plan design, including an allowance for future downturns in business, will probably preclude the issue of underfunding from arising.

¶1400.5   What Can Your Client Do And Not Do When Dealing
                 With A Pension—Fund-Prohibited Transactions

Because of the potential conflict of interest involved in transactions between the pension plan, its sponsor, the trustee, stockholders, and plan administrators, ERISA sought to create a class of actions which are automatically disallowed. This class is known as "prohibited transactions." ERISA added muscle to its intentions by specifying certain nondeductible excise taxes applicable in ever more punitive steps to prohibited transactions which go uncorrected.

In general, prohibited transactions are those which involve a relationship between "interested parties" where there is a potential for gain—whether economic or otherwise. "Interested parties" include:

• plan administrator;
• plan participant;

- trustee;

- employer;

- plan sponsor;

- "the prohibited group" (highly paid shareholders and other employees);

- salesmen purveying assets to the plan; and

- close relatives of any of the above.

This subject of prohibited transactions is complex and fraught with exceptions. As a general concept, however, you and your client should be aware that small businessmen often wear several "hats" when they set up a pension plan—agent of the plan administrator, trustee, plan sponsor, and plan participant— and that any transaction your client is involved in where he simultaneously wears "two hats" is likely to be problematic. For example, the sale or lease of goods and services by the employer to a plan is typically disallowed. The loaning of money by a plan to the employer or a key man is generally taboo. The use of more than 10% of a plan's assets for the purchase of employer securities is forbidden.

All these transactions have obvious potential for conflict of interest and it is easy to see how the concept of prohibited transactions could apply. However, many more subtle activities are prohibited and your client would be well advised to review the latest regulations before attempting any transaction that involves an interested party.

¶1401   SPECIAL CONSIDERATIONS WHEN CHANGING PLANS MIDSTREAM

What happens if your client adopts the wrong type of qualified plan or "outgrows" one that initially matched his objectives? It's possible to change plans but depending on the circumstances, that can be quite a cumbersome job. In general, it's fairly easy to switch from profit-sharing to money-purchase or from money-purchase to defined-benefit plans, since participants theoretically have more determinable and secure benefits under the latter. However, going from defined-benefit to money-purchase or profit-sharing certainly constitutes a formal plan termination which triggers some onerous liabilities and responsibilities.

Good advance planning and design work usually precludes the need for a substitute change in approach. For example, your client's financial situation may change on a year to year basis as well in more permanent terms. The use of defined-benefit pension plans with Entry Age Normal/FIPSL, as well as profit-sharing plans, "builds in" a substantial amount of flexibility for your client in terms of contributions. But in a rapidly growing and changing business, even this might not be enough. But, if the facts dictate a restructuring, here are some of the issues you and your client should address.

¶1401.1   Is The Change A Termination?

Virtually, any significant change in the format of a qualified plan will constitute a termination. Depending upon the severity of the termination (is it a complete termination or does it reduce benefits for participants, and are all benefits preserved under the new plan?) and the nature of the successor plan, a termination will result in one or more of the following events:

1. Participants will have to be guaranteed that their accrued benefits (in the case of defined-contribution plan, that means account balance) will never be less than their accrued benefits at the time the plan was changed.

2. Participants' accrued benefits will not only have to be guaranteed but also 100% vested at the time of transition.

3. Participants' accrued benefits will not only have to be 100% vested but also "frozen."

Terminating a defined-benefit plan has extremely complicated and far-reaching effects, including potential employer liability. A complete discussion of defined-benefit termination is far beyond the scope of this book, but you should be aware of its substantive impact. The degree to which vesting and benefit freezing are required depends on how similar the successor is to the predecessor plan.

Example: Change-of-Heart Company establishes a profit-sharing plan integrated with Social Security. Five years later, increased profit stability leads Change-of-Heart's owner to the conclusion that his employees would be more highly motivated by the security offered by a money-purchase plan. Therefore, Change-of-Heart amends and restates his profit-sharing plan to an integrated money-purchase plan. In all likelihood, 100% immediate vesting wouldn't be required in this case.

Example: Turnaround, Incorporated implements a defined-benefit plan primarily for the benefit of its 55-year-old owner. One week after the owner retires at age 65, the company's successor managers amend and restate the defined-benefit to a profit-sharing plan. That would constitute the most onerous form of termination, with 100%

vesting of accrued benefits and employer liability up to 30% of net worth for unfunded accrued benefits.

Observation: Despite volumes of case histories, rulings, and regulations, the severity of the ramifications of plan termination is largely a judgmental issue. Be prepared to discuss the issue with the IRS when you submit an amended and restated plan. Emphasize how the new plan improves participants' benefits, discuss the issues with the IRS *prior* to submitting the new plan. An adverse response may have impact on your decision to move forward with your restatement.

¶1401.2   How To Avoid Hidden Problems With Defined-Benefit Terminations

Defined-benefit plan terminations create special problems. The principal upon which these problems are built is that defined-benefit plans in small businesses are generally constructed for the benefit of some older key men. The IRS is justifiably concerned that once the benefits for these older key men are funded, the company will abandon the plan. That means younger participants, whose benefits are actuarially funded over a longer working life, will suffer. To preclude that result, the IRS and the Pension Benefit Guarantee Corporation, *particularly* in the first ten plan years, have considerable power. The two most onerous solutions are:

1. imposition of the 10-year early termination rule; and
2. reallocation of assets.

Under the 10-year early termination rule, the IRS may require that members of the "prohibited" (higher-paid) group may not receive any distributions from the plan unless they post security far in excess of that distribution until such time as all obligations for regular employees are met.

Example: King-Pin, Incorporated adopted a defined-benefit plan eight years ago for the benefit of its owner-president, Charles Blake. Charles Blake retires with fully funded benefits and asks for his $500,000 lump sum. Fine, says the IRS, as long as you provide collateral in the amount of $600,000.

Reallocation of assets may be far worse. In situations where the IRS feels that the plan was not "for the exclusive benefit of employees" but rather discriminated highly in favor of one or more key men, the agency may act to protect the benefits of rank-and-file employees by reallocation of assets.

Example: Dr. Platt sets up an integrated defined-benefit pension plan that nets him 96% of the total contribution. The 58-year-old doctor has six rank-and-file employees in their mid-twenties and early thirties. Several years later he decides to close up his practice and take his pension benefits with him. However, the IRS does some surgery and cuts out what it feels is a malignant part of his contribution. Assets are reallocated to rank-and-file employees.

What To Do: If there is a significant chance for a plan termination within the first ten years, consider using an *insured* plan. If a plan qualifies as being "fully insured" (all benefits quaranteed by level premium contracts issued by an insurance company) then it isn't subject to ERISA's minimum funding standard *or* to Pension Benefit Guaranty Corporation (PBGC) supervision. Furthermore, accrued benefits under fully insured plans are defined as the reserve of the contracts providing the insured benefits. Many annuity contracts, with various expense factors, qualify under the fully insured definition and the expenses associated with the contracts may well be justified if:

1. the plan needs to be terminated; and
2. the servicing agent can provide ancillary services such as plan administration as a part of his coverage.

¶1401.3   Step-By-Step Termination Procedures

If you have to deal with a *formal* termination procedure, such as the suspension of a defined-benefit plan, here are the steps to follow:

1. *Discuss* the circumstances of termination in advance with the IRS and the PBGC;
2. Fully *report* the termination to the PBGC and request a *letter of sufficiency;*
3. Request a letter of determination from the IRS stating that the termination will not have adverse tax consequences. Your letter must include the PBGC letter of sufficiency;
4. *Communicate* to participants their options under the terminated plan, i.e.:
   a) rollover to I.R.A.;
   b) cash distributions;
   c) nontransferable annuity contract; or
   d) "frozen" account left at interest.

¶1402   AN EASY GUIDE TO THE QUALIFICATION OF PLANS

Qualification of pension or profit-sharing plans is a routine process which, with proper supervision, can be effectively delegated to upper-level clerical employees. The process needs control from two perspectives:

- Chronological; and
- Qualitative.

Effective plan qualification involves step-by-step chronological activities. Generally, one activity or sequence of events must be completed before another is begun. Therefore, your profit potential is largely dependent upon your planning.

Example: Attorney Reed spent eight weeks preparing the plan and trust documents for XYZ's pension plan. Then he realizes he has forgotten to post the "Notice of Submission" for XYZ's employees. He'll have to wait several weeks to submit the plan to the IRS, a wait he could have avoided if he'd done first things first.

Qualification also involves a mechanical or qualitative checklist of specific *items* which must be submitted or prepared at some point during the lengthy process. Since most of the items will be required again and again, it's a good idea to develop a list.

Example: Attorney Scatter submits an integrated defined-benefit plan to his regional IRS office. Several months later, he's informed that the designated reviewer has put his plan in a suspense file awaiting receipt of background materials showing how integrated benefits were calculated.

¶1402.1   Step-By-Step Chronological Checklist For Controlling The Qualification Process

The form (Exhibit A) on the next page includes all the items in chronological order, plus columns to designate whether a particular item is applicable to the plan being qualified, whether it has been completed, when follow-up was accomplished, and when the answer or information necessary arrived from the respondent. The chart is followed with a line by line explanation of how it is used in the author's office. It will be easy for you to adapt the form to your own office, procedures and responsibilities.

Exhibit A

QUALIFICATION STATUS/CONTROL

Plan Name: _____ Yr. End. _____
Route Through _____
CC: _____

Function	Req.	Completed	Followup	Rec'd	Comments
Signature Materials:					
Administration Control Card	Yes		■		
Contract	Yes				
Bill - ½ fee	Yes				
*Plan & Trust	Yes				
*5300/5301/5307	Yes				
*Clerk's Certificate					
*SPD	Yes				
*Notice of Plan	Yes		■		
Census Request	No	■	■		
Cover letter	Yes	■	■		
*Power of Attorney	Yes				
Signature Meeting:			■		
Vesting/funding			■		
Include Attorney			■		
Complete Plan Checklist	Yes		■		
Final Prop. & Val.			■		
Add to Package	■		■		
*5302	Yes		■		
*Sample Calculation		(Integrated Plans Only)			
*Notice of Submission	Yes		■		
*Package Completed			■		
*Package to Attorney					
*Package to IRS**	Yes			■	
Amendments for IRS				■	
Determination Letter	Yes			■	
SPD to Labor	Yes		■		
Bill—fee balance	Yes				

*Items needed for complete package.
**Only these items go to IRS.:   1. Plan & Trust (copy)
                                2. 5300/5301/5307 (orig. & copy)
                                3. 5302 (2)
                                4. 2848 (orig.)
                                5. Sample Calculation (when required)

Here's a line by line discussion of the first segment of the chart. In the breakdown of the chart that follows, let's assume you are responsible for qualifying a corporate integrated profit-sharing plan for a company whose fiscal year (and plan year) ended December 31, 1979.

Function	Req.	Completed	Followup	Rec'd	Comments
Signature Materials:					
Administration Control Card	Yes	12/15/79			
Contract	Yes	12/15/79	12/26 ⅓ 1/3	1/9/80	
Bill - ½ fee	Yes	12/15/79	12/26	1/2/80	check "in the mail"
*Plan & Trust	Yes	12/17/79	12/26	1/9/80	
*5300/5301/5307	Yes	12/17/79	12/26	1/9/80	
*Clerk's Certificate	Yes	12/17/79	12/26	1/9/80	

☐ *Signature materials:* First, in sequence, appear those items which require client, trustee, or the plan administrator's signature

☐ *Administration Control Card:* The author's office establishes a "fail-safe" control card for each case which is coded with key recurring administrative dates. For any of the work that is done on a particular client, we establish this 3 × 5 card and insert it in the proper sequence in a chronological filing system. Since the card does not leave our office, the columns "follow-up" and "rec'd" are not applicable and therefore they are filled in. Let's assume the 3 × 5 card is prepared on December 15, 1979.

☐ *Contract:* Most pension consulting firms use a service contract or engagement letter to specify the services and limitations applicable to the qualification process. Since the job originates in the service provider's office, the column "Completed" is left blank. When the responsible person in the office has prepared the service contract, it is forwarded with the other materials to the client. The "follow up" column provides space for noting dates when our office pursued the matter. When the item is finally received, the "rec'd" (received) column is dated. Now since the entire line is filled in, the person responsible for following through with the process can move on to the next chronological item. In this case, we have assumed that the contract was completed and sent December 15, followed up on December 23 and January 3, and finally received January 8, 1980.

☐ *Bill—½ fee:* Standard practice at the author's firm involves obtaining one-half the estimated qualification fee prior to commencement of the work. The illustration shows that we sent our bill December 15, followed up on December 23 at which time we were told that a check was "in the mail" (this should sound familiar), and finally received payment for one-half our fee on January 20, 1980.

☐ **Plan and Trust:* Plan and Trust documents must also be prepared and submitted to the client, trustees, and plan administrator for signature. The asterisk indicates that this is an item that ultimately will be submitted to the Internal Revenue Service. The illustration assumes that all plan materials were completed by our office on December 17 and mailed.

☐ *5300/5301/5307:* One of these "Application For Determination" forms must generally be submitted with any type of qualified plan.

☐ *Clerk's Certificate:* You should obtain a sealed copy of the clerk's/secretary's certificate showing that the plan has been adopted and that formal adoption has been entered into the minutes of the corporation.

*SPD	Yes	12/17	12/25	1/9/80	
*Notice of Plan	Yes	12/17			
Census Request	No				
Cover letter	Yes	12/17			
*Power of Attorney	Yes	12/17	12/25	1/9/80	

☐ *SPD:* Ultimately you will have to provide each plan participant with a summary plan description. Furthermore, IRS usually requires a general description of a plan's terms and operating procedures. Thus, it is the author's practice to prepare a SPD draft as a part of the initial "package."

☐ *Notice of Plan:* Participants should be notified by letter or by clear posting that a plan has been adopted and that they will be given more details soon. Since no response from participants is required at this point, the follow-up and received columns are inapplicable.

☐ *Census Request:* Preliminary proposals are based on estimated census information. Since IRS uses the data you supply, it is important to make sure census data is updated and accurate prior to submission. This example assumes, however, that our office already had accurate, up-to-date census information on hand. Therefore, the preparer of the form wrote "no" in the "req." column and crossed out the balance of the columns as not applicable.

☐ *Cover letter:* You will want to prepare a standard cover letter for submitting the qualification letter to IRS.

☐ *Power of Attorney:* To preclude the IRS from calling your client and asking questions about the plan (questions your client will not be able to answer) you should include a Power of Attorney to "field" IRS inquiries.

Signature Meeting:

Vesting/funding	465	12/21		discuss 4-40 and 5-15
Include Attorney	465	12/21		

☐ *Signature Meeting:* Once the above materials are complete you should plan a meeting with your client, including all parties to the plan. The meeting will serve to:

   a) iron out any last minute difficulties;

   b) reiterate relative responsibilities; and

   c) obtain signatures.

☐ *Vesting/Funding:* One subject for this meeting might be a last minute analysis of the plan's vesting or funding provisions. Often decisions about where to invest plan assets is held off till the last possible moment. The illustration assumes our office wishes to discuss two alternative vesting schedules—IRS 4-40 and the 5 to 15 schedule.

☐ *Include Attorney:* Generally, your client's attorney should be present at this signature meeting. The balance of illustrative form will be left blank so you can think through the chronological process by yourself.

Complete Plan Checklist	Yes		███████	
Final Prop. & Val.				
			███████	
Add to Package	████		███████	
*5302	Yes		███████	
*Sample Calculation		(Integrated Plans Only)		
*Notice of Submission	Yes		███████	

☐ *Pending Correct:* Before submitting the plan to the IRS make any last minute changes occasioned by:

   a) the census information you get back from your client; or

   b) points raised at the signature meeting.

☐ *Complete Plan Checklist:* At this point, with all data in hand, you're in the best position to transfer plan data to the administrative system which will be used for ongoing reporting and disclosure. It's important at this point to coordinate plan provisions with administrative functions.

☐ *Final Prop. and Val.:* If you're using computer-generated reports to illustrate plan parameters and benefits, now is the best time to prepare a finalized version for use in the first plan year reporting and disclosure process.

☐ *Add to Package:* Now you should have the information necessary to prepare the remaining items for your IRS submission package.

☐ **Form 5302:* Form 5302 applies the plan's provisions to current census information to show the IRS reviewer benefits and/or contributions under the plan.

☐ ***Sample Calculation:** If the plan is integrated you must include a sample calculation to show how the plan's integrated provisions work.

☐ ***Notice of Submission:** Prior to IRS submission, you must notify plan participants of the submission and give interested parties an opportunity to be heard.

*Package Completed			███		
*Package to Attorney					
*Package to IRS**	Yes		███		

☐ **Package Completed:** A supervising party should review all of the above before forwarding to the IRS.

☐ **Package to Attorney:** Your client's attorney should have one last chance to review the completed package.

☐ **Package to IRS:** With approval of counsel, you are ready to forward plan, trust, and associated materials to the IRS.

Amendments for IRS				███	
Determination Letter	Yes			███	
SPD to Labor	Yes		███		
Bill—fee balance	Yes				

☐ **Amendments for IRS:** Presumably, the IRS will require some amendments to plan language. This line provides for that contingency.

☐ **Determination Letter:** Ultimately, the IRS (hopefully) will issue a favorable determination letter regarding the qualification of the plan.

☐ **SPD to Labor:** The initial draft of the SPD should be amended to reflect the changes resulting from IRS amendments and that should be forwarded to the Department of Labor.

☐ **Bill—Fee Balance:** It is the practice of the author's firm to bill for the balance of the qualification fee when all tasks are completed.

You will have to experiment with your own chronological checklist. The key is, with adequate planning, qualification is a simple, routine function. Your problems will be commensurate with your ability to organize, delegate, and supervise this process.

¶1402.2   When And Where To Use Prototype Plans

Supervised by qualified counsel, prototypes provide an efficient, cost effective alternative to individually designed plans. However, counsel should view the prototype primarily as a starting point only and evaluate its provisions as if they were rough drafts. Here are some questions to ask about any prototype:

1. What limitations does the instrument place on plan investments?

2. What limitations does the instrument place on distribution alternatives?

3. Does the prototype allow the death beneficiary an opportunity to choose between estate tax exemption or ten-year income averaging?

4. Do the plan's eligibility requirements maximize the legal waiting period without creating undue administrative burdens?

5. Who is responsible for insuring that the prototype will remain consistent with changing IRS rules and regulations?

6. Does the instrument restrict actuarial methodology?

Although this list is by no means complete, it should serve as a reminder that use of a prototype requires professional supervision. (You will find in Appendix B, a sample IRS approved prototype plan.)

Planning Tip: Always keep in mind that prototypes, with amendments, may be submitted as individually designed plans. If you want to make certain changes to a prototype instrument, the qualification instrument will still be dramatically simplified and expedited because the reviewer will feel comfortable with virtually all the plan provisions not affected by your amendments. Too often, prototypes are "sold" as inexpensive, "take-it-or-leave-it," no changes necessary substitutes for good legal advice. Your constant vigilance against that attitude will make prototypes an effective tool without sacrificing your client's best interests.

¶1403   **HOW TO CONTROL PLAN ADMINISTRATION
            AND AVOID PROBLEMS**

The ongoing liability and responsibility for timely and complete reporting and complete disclosure to the government, interested parties, active plan participants, and the employer certainly contributed to the massive number of plan terminations after ERISA. Now that the dust has settled, the functions included in plan administration are more clearly defined. Administration requires constant oversight by a qualified individual or organization to insure that:

1. Administrative practices reflect the latest IRS and Department of Labor requirements;

2. Chronological deadlines are met; and

3. Distributions of information and benefits to plan participants are accurate.

Since the components of plan administration extend beyond the ability of one individual or organization to provide everything, the real role of the plan administrator is to "captain" the team of plan advisors who monitor the plan's performance.

¶1403.1   The Functions And Liabilities Of The Plan Administrator

The administrator is the individual or organization charged with primary responsibility for carrying out the operational requirements of the plan documents. In addition, ERISA specifies certain specific functions that fall within the plan administrator's province. In short, the plan administrator is charged with the day to day responsibility for "running" the plan. That includes a lot of diverse elements such as:

1. obtaining information from various plan service providers (i.e., asset information from the trustee);

2. computing accrued and vested accrued benefits for active and retired participants;

3. authorizing payouts to terminated or retired plan participants;

4. filing various reporting and disclosure forms with the IRS, the Department of Labor, and the PBGC;

5. distributing summary plan descriptions and summary annual reports to plan participants;

6. arbitrating claims that may arise because of ambiguity or disagreement over the terms of the plan.

The nature and extent of the above enumerated responsibilities obviously casts the plan administrator in a fiduciary capacity. In fact, ERISA specifies that the plan administrator is a fiduciary. As such, he is liable for discharging his responsibilities in a prudent manner and can be sued for a breach of his fiduciary capacity.

Because it's impossible for most small firms to assign an employee the task of monitoring ERISA's rules and regulations to insure ongoing plan administrative compliance, many of these small firms rely on a "ministerial assistant" who provides most of the back-up reports necessary to complete the job. For example, a life insurance agent may sell a plan to your client on the assumption that his home office will provide most of the ancillary plan administrative services required. However, the agent would undoubtedly *not* agree to act as the named plan administrator, and in fact, is probably precluded from doing so by ERISA's ban on performing multiple services for a qualified plan.

¶1403.2   Choosing The Right Administrator

Probably over 75% of the small business clients are named in their plan documents as the plan administrator. This is fine, *as long as* your client understands the ongoing responsibilities associated with maintaining a plan and the potential liability for problems.

Many firms that provide prototype, master, or specimen pension plan materials have excellent back-up capability for plan administration. The key is for your client to insure that, in fact, these services are available from the individual or organization who provided the plan, that they can be expected to have substantial continuity, and in the absence of those circumstances that your client have a specific service provider available to perform the necessary services.

Presuming the plan has been initiated and largely set up by a sponsoring organization (such as an insurance or mutual fund company which is providing these services in order to sell some assets to the plan), you should obtain a letter from the representative's home office detailing the ancillary services regularly provided, their costs, and the commitment the company has made to long-term involvement in the pension industry.

You should also discuss the effect of your client's decision to buy other assets in the future. In other words, if the basis for setting up the plan was the sale of a particular type of plan asset, what will happen to administrative services if there is a change in your client's investment philosophy that precludes his dealing with the original asset providers?

The ministerial assistant should be able to provide substantial details about his own involvement, historically and educationally, in the pension field. You should query as to the number of qualified plans he currently maintains and obtain three references. Discuss with these references the ongoing plan administrative services you foresee and find out whether the individual has received adequate service relative to those items. You should also be concerned about the nature of the organization providing the ancillary services. You should ask:

1. What computer capacity does it have?
2. Does it have administrative personnel beyond the salesman or key man that is "selling" the services?
3. How long has it been in the pension business?

Do not let your client underestimate the time and financial expense that can occur if diligent plan administrative services are not provided on a timely, expeditious basis.

Many small to medium-size pension consulting and actuarial firms have sprung up since ERISA. Your client's best bet may be the use of such a firm. As a disinterested third party specializing in qualified plan administration, such a consulting firm may be well worth the price.

¶1403.3   A Chronological Checklist For Controlling
                      Administrative Functions

The plan administrator has two major concerns:

1. That he does everything; and
2. That he does everything on time.

Those concerns lend themselves well to the use of the chronological checklist described at ¶1402.1. The use of a chronological checklist also has the advantage of allowing delegation of most of the administrative process to a lower level and less expensive person. On the following page is the form (Exhibit B) used in the author's office. This form allows for the initial review of the plan to determine *what* functions must be performed. Further, these functions are listed in the order they must proceed and are "fail-safed" at various points at chronological deadlines that must be met.

Following the complete checklist you will find a breakdown with explanations showing step by step instructions on how each item is prepared.

Job Description refers to an item that may or may not be applicable to a particular plan administrative cycle.

Yes/No queries whether or not a particular item is applicable.

Exhibit B

CHRONOLOGICAL PLAN ADMINISTRATIVE CHECKLIST

Job Description		Y/N	?	Completed	Followup	Received	Comments
Tag to Info. Cycle		Yes	C				Deadline-Fye-60 / /
Special Letterhead			O				
Annv. Notice Cover Letter		Yes	M				
Notice of Val/ or Census Sheet		Yes	M				
Contract			U				
Change Schedule			N				
Deposit Schedule			I				
Insurance Fund Values/w/Auth			C				
Side-Fund Values w/Auth			A				Go on to Prop I/A
			T				
Package to Employer			I	Tag "Deposit" Deadline - FYE - 10 / /			
			O				
			N				
Prepare Prop I/A		Yes	I				
Run Prop I A		Yes	N				
Prepare Actuarial Request			T				
Cont. Let. cc: Advisors		Yes	E				
Prep and Run Pending Corrects			R				
New Contrib. Let. cc: Advisors			N	Tag "Finalize" Deadline - FYE + 60 / /			
			A				
			L.				
Prepare Cash Flow Summary		Yes					
Prepare: Prop. Final		Yes	I				
Eliab			N				
Val		Yes	T				
Run: Prop Final		Yes	E				
Eliab			R				
Val		Yes	N				
Prepare Vested Payment Sched			A				
			L				
Report Cover Letter Advisor	A	Yes	C				
5500 C/K	D	Yes	O				
Schedule A	V		M				
Schedule B	I		M				
PBGC-1/Instruct/Bill	S		U				
Cash Flow Summary	O	Yes	N				
Termination Summary	R		I				
Cover Letter-Employer		Yes	C				
Bill		Yes	A				
Amendments			T				
Participants			I				
Cover Letter		Yes	O				
Termination Ltr/1099			N				
Accounting		Yes	S				
Summ. Ann. Report		Yes	T				
Benf. Design New Parts		Yes	A				
Ins. Policies			F				
SPD's New Parts		yes	F	Tag "Gov't" Deadline - FYE + 120 / /			
Report Delivery		Yes					
Forms to Goverment		Yes					
Prepare Amendments cc: Advisor							
Amendments to IRS							
PBGC-1 to Labor				Tag "Garbage" Deadline - FYE +180 / /			

The following is a line-by-line discussion of Exhibit B. You ought to do one like it for your own office. Headings on the form are self-explanatory.

Job Description	Y/N	?	Completed	Followup	Received	Comments
Tag to Info. Cycle	Yes	C		████	████	Deadline-Fye-60 / /
Special Letterhead		O		████	████	
Annv. Notice Cover Letter	Yes	M		████	████	
Notice of Val/or Census Sheet	Yes	M				
Contract		U				
Change Schedule		N				
Deposit Schedule		I				
Insurance Fund Values/w/Auth		C				
Side-Fund Values w/Auth		A				Go on to Prop I/A
		T				
Package to Employer		I	Tag Deposit Deadline - FYE - 10 / /			

? indicates whose responsibility a particular function is.

Completed asks for the date an applicable job was completed.

Followup refers, if applicable, to any follow up made on a particular date to obtain information or materials requested.

Received provides an opportunity for the responsible party to note the date that requested material was received.

☐ *Tag to info. cycle* indicates that the first job in the administrative cycle is to put the name of the plan on a card which we maintain as a visual display in our office.

☐ *Deadline—FYE-60* indicates that our procedure dictates that the plan be reviewed jointly by the administrative staff and the partner assigned to the plan 60 days prior to the end of the plan year.

☐ *Special letterhead* refers to our obtaining from the client a supply of his letterhead so that employee letters and communications can be prepared on a more personalized basis.

☐ *Annv. notice cover letter* reminds staff members that a package of materials goes to each client prior to the end of plan year with a cover letter detailing each component of the package.

☐ *Notice of val.* is the first item in the package and includes census information about prior plan participants. When our office has completed that, the *completed* column is filled in and we await receipt of the requested employee information.

☐ *Contract* means our annual service contract which is renewed each year and includes the fees that will be applicable to the administration for that particular plan.

☐ *Change schedule* means that if, in the review cycle, the responsible partner determines a particular change in the plan document (i.e., increase integration level) it is essential that the client be notified of the change and what it will cost prior to our implementing the administrative process.

☐ We also ask clients to complete a *deposit schedule* reconciling the dates, amounts, and recipients of checks they have drawn during the plan year on the account of the plan. This deposit schedule is checked against a similiar one that is requested from the trustees or funding institution to make sure that all deposits are properly accounted for.

☐ *Insurance fund values/w/auth.* and *side-fund values w/auth.:* If there are any "other" materials that should be included in the employer information request package they would be itemized on this line. Simultaneously sending the information requests to clients, funding letters with "authorization" go to those institutions or agents who, as of the end of the last plan year, held or administered assets subject to the plan.

☐ The notation *Go on to Prop. I/A* indicates to the administrator responsible for completion of the form, that the administrative process need not be held up on account of lack of asset information at this point

When all the above materials are prepared, you should send the package to employer. At that point, the "ball will be in his court" and, other than follow-ups, there is nothing more to be done for that particular plan.

Prepare Prop I/A	Yes	I		■	
Run Prop I/A	Yes	N		■	
Prepare Actuarial Request		T			
Cont. Let. cc: Advisors	Yes	E		■	
Prep and Run Pending Corrects		R			
New Contrib. Let. cc: Advisors		N		Tag "Finalize"	Deadling - FYE + 60 / /

When the information comes back, we:

☐ *Prepare Prop. I/A* which means input necessary for the computer to generate contributions for the plan year being administered.

☐ That complete, we *Run Prop. I/A* to generate a computer report of increases and additions for the plan year.

☐ Immediately, we send a *contribution letter, cc. the client's tax advisor,* to ensure that all parties are aware of the deposit that has been or will be made for the plan year.

☐ *Prepare & run pending corrects* and *New contribution letter, cc: advisors:* Frequently, when the client reviews this contribution letter, he finds that some of the information he provided was in error requiring that we prepare and run "pending corrects"—generate a new computer report, and then send out a new contribution letter "cc. advisors" to finalize everyone's understanding of the amount of and deadline for plan contributions.

Prepare Cash Flow Summary	Yes			
Prepare: Prop. Final	Yes	I		
Eliab		N		
Val	Yes	T		
Run: Prop Final	Yes	E		
Eliab		R		
Val	Yes	N		
Prepare Vested Payment Sched		A		

☐ At that point, said information should be available and you can develop a *cash flow summary* showing beginning of year assets, contributions, earning and ending assets. That cash flow statement allows preparation of computer input for various final reports that will be part of the administrative package.

☐ The notations *Prop. final, ELIAB* and *Val.* represent our names for the computer reports prepared at this point.

☐ Based on the census information finally returned from your client, you should be able to prepare a *vested payment schedule* indicating distribution amounts for terminated vested or retired participants.

☐ Finally, with cash flow, computer reports and vested payment schedule in hand, the responsible partner will have fresh in his mind any specific matters that should be addressed and he can dictate a *cover letter.*

Report Cover Letter Advisor	A	Yes	C			
5500 C/K	D	Yes	O			
Schedule A	V		M			
Schedule B	I		M			
PBGC-1/Instruct/Bill	S		U			
Cash Flow Summary	O	Yes	N			
Termination Summary	R		I			
Cover Letter-Employer		Yes	C			
Bill		Yes	A			
Amendments			T			

☐ With all of the above done, your administrator can prepare the mundane forms that should fulfill the government's requirements for reporting and disclosure. You may find it convenient to break the standard items down to employer and employee components. Since it is very important for various advisors of the plan to be constantly informed of activity, a special report *cover letter for the advisor* ought to be prepared at this point.

☐ Certain components of the client's annual report should be sent to the advisor as well as the client. The *5500-C, Schedule A, Schedule B, PGBC 1* with instructions about payment amounts, fund cash flow summary and participant termination letter (with 1099s) would clearly be of interest to your client's accountant.

☐ Other materials that are employer-related but not necessarily of interest to advisors include a special *cover letter to the employer,* your *bill* for services rendered and copies of *amendments* drafted pursuant to the change schedule discussed above.

Participants: Cover Letter	Yes	O			
Termination Ltr/1099		N			
Accounting	Yes	S			
Summ. Ann. Report	Yes	T			
Benf. Design New Parts	Yes	A			
Ins. Policies		F			
SPD's New Parts	yes	F		Tag "Gov't"	Deadline - FYE + 120 / /
Report Delivery	Yes				
Forms to Government	Yes				
Prepare Amendments cc: Advisor					
Amendments to IRS					
PBGC-1 to Labor				Tag "Garbage" Deadline - FYE +180 / /	

☐ Participants may or may not need certain materials as well. Most of your clients will wish to provide them with a *cover letter* which provides an *accounting* of their accrued and estimated retirement benefits to date, the *summary annual report* required by government regulations, *beneficiary designations* if the plan has an insured benefit of some type and *summary plan descriptions* for new plan participants.

☐ The deadline for completion of all those materials included in the employer's annual report ought to be four months (120 days) after finalized amendments can be prepared for submission to counsel and the IRS.

That should complete the administrative process for virtually any type of qualified plan within the restraints of chronology and completeness mandated by regulation and common sense.

¶1404   CHOOSING THE RIGHT INVESTMENTS AND MONITORING THEIR PERFORMANCE

One of, if not the prime, advantage of qualified retirement programs is the tax-free accumulation of funds they offer. Furthermore, investment performance will have a dramatic effect upon plan costs and funding stability. It is important that you help your client choose the right investments to fulfill his objectives. The key is evaluating and setting these objectives. Your client must understand the consequences of this investment philosophy and, once he has established it, set up a procedure to monitor how closely the philosophy fulfills his expectations.

"Right" is a subjective term. The same "right" won't apply to each client or to each type of qualified plan. However, there can be more or less "right" decisions depending upon the characteristics of your client and your client's plan.

¶1404.1   Actuarial Method Only A Model

Keep in mind that interest assumptions in defined-benefit plans are just that—assumptions. Sooner or later, actual investment performance must be recognized and will eventually control plan costs. Furthermore, the interest assumptions in defined-benefit plans assume earnings stability which never occurs. Since your client can, by his investment decisions, control to a considerable extent yield stability, some investment options may be "more right" than others with defined-benefit plans.

> *Example:* Go-Get-Them, Incorporated and Take-It-Easy Company establish defined-benefit plans with 6½ percent interest assumptions. Go-Get-Them, Incorporated invests all its money in bonds rated B or lower at a time when long-term interest rates are averaging 6 to 7 percent. Take-It-Easy, Company invests half its money in certificates of deposit and half in long-term guaranteed investment contracts with major insurance companies. Two years later, long-term interest rates have risen to the 9 to 10 percent level. Go-Get-Them, Incorporated—according to fair market value—has sustained a paper loss of 40 percent on its bonds and must increase its annual plan contribution by almost 25 percent. The change in interest rates hardly affects Take-It-Easy, Company and their funding remains constant.

Observation: It's generally agreed that defined-benefit funding ought to be in more conservative than defined-contribution.

¶1404.2   The Prudent Man Rule Is Always In The Background

ERISA requires fiduciaries to act in the highest and best interest of plan participants (note the emphasis on participants as opposed to employer). That dictates caution for the investment manager. Since the named fiduciary can be sued for a breach of this Prudent Man Rule, it is incumbent upon your client not to be too aggressive *or* conservative in his investment approach but rather follow a middle-of-the-road course with aggressive investments tempered by more conservative ones to provide a balanced portfolio.

¶1404.3   The Advantages Of Conservatism

No matter what type of plan your client adopts, a conservative investment posture will be rewarded. The effect of "overshooting" investment objectives could create either:

- lower contributions for your client in a defined-benefit plan; or
- a bigger "pot" for participants in a defined-contribution plan.

However, the consequences of *undershooting* investment goals would be the converse and each would have a negative impact such as:

- higher employer costs in a defined-benefit plan; or

  lower participant accumulations in a defined-contribution plan.

> *Example.* Mason Company sets up a profit-sharing and defined-benefit plan with which it hopes to achieve spectacular investment results by investing exclusively in the solar energy industry. Three years later, scientists discover a simple way to convert coal to a readily usable liquid form. All of Mason Company's stocks plummet. Participants find that their profit-sharing account balances have been slashed and several consider suing the company for failure to meet the prudence requirement. Two older participants are so close to retirement that Mason's defined-benefit funding costs must increase by 40 percent to meet the upcoming actuarial liabilities.

¶1405   ALTERNATIVE INVESTMENTS FOR THE SMALL PLAN

It's traditionally been difficult for small pension plans to obtain high quality investments or investment advice. In recent years, however, the competition for small plan business has led to the development of some really attractive alternatives so that your client should have an excellent opportunity to "shop" among a number of excellent "products." The following is a brief description of four alternatives that you or your client might consider.

¶1405.1   Pooled Investment Funds—A Poor Man's Diversified
                                      Portfolio

Many bank and trust departments currently offer pooled or common funds in which your client could participate. Size of the pooled fund is sufficient to warrant aggressive full-time investment management and thus your client has the advantage of professional money management. Most pooled investment funds have a small custodial or trustee's fee which generally covers some of the ancillary services provided by the funding institution. Usually the pooled funds are quite liquid and most major funding institutions offer the opportunity for switching among several different pooled funds with significantly divergent investment goals.

For example, many trust companies have a pooled fund composed primarily of common stocks with an orientation toward long-term growth, one designed to produce high current yields (a bond fund), or one emphasizing liquidity (for example, a money market instrument fund). The investment expense associated with these funds is so low that they generally aren't the basis for decision making.

Observation: Mutual funds offer a comparable opportunity with similiar "portfolio-hopping" potential. Make sure you compare pooled funds on the basis of reasonable long-term investment performance rather than the short-term investment achievements that are often so highly touted.

¶1405.2   Guaranteed Investment Contracts: The Perils, Pitfalls
                                      And How They Work

Major insurance companies have been creatively responsive to investment fears engendered by the stockmarkets and other traditional investment media's poor consistency of the last decade. The response has been guaranteed investment funds alternatively known as group deposit administration contracts, group annuities or, simply, DAs. These insurance contracts can, at their best, provide virtually an ideal small plan funding vehicle; at their worst, they can be an expensive trap that locks your client into a long-term commitment.

A. How Government Investment Contracts Work

Most GICs share a common format. Your client commits either an initial lump-sum or a series of payments to an insurance company which, in turn, invests those funds, either as part of its general assets or in a segregated fund. Generally, the underlying investments are mortgages, private placements, or other long-term debt instruments. In exchange for the use of your clients funds, the insurance company shares "the portfolio investment returns," usually providing a relatively long-term guarantee of interest and principal.

> *Example:* One major company offers a five-year guarantee of interest and principal. It will set up a guaranteed rate of interest on all deposits received during the five-year period, with the interest rate renegotiated at the end of that time frame.

> *Example:* Another company uses a declining balance format. Under this approach, the company guarantees a specific rate of interest for each year's "new" money. The interest guarantee lasts fifteen years and is payable on a declining balance. Each year, the company returns to your client 1/15th of his principal with "no strings attached." The guaranteed rate of interest is payable on the remaining balance. Assuming a series of deposits over a period of years, the combination of changing "new money" rate, plus rollovers effectively gives your client a "rolling interest rate" that simultaneously protects him from being "locked in" and offers substantial principal and interest stability.

B. Getting Out Can Be Costly

DAs boast relatively nominal expense factors. They are generally applicable either to:

- deposits; or
- accumulated assets.

Typical charges include the following:

1. *Sales Charge:* Some DAs have a specific sales charge, usually expressed as a percentage of each deposit (i.e., two percent of contributions). Frequently, the sales expense is graded downward for a larger deposit. For example, it might be two percent of the first $25,000 of an annual contribution and one percent of the balance.

2. *Investment Charge:* A number of DAs apply an investment or "management" charge against the accumulated assets in the contract. This charge, usually ranging from .5 to 1% covers some of these

issuing companies' expenses for maintaining the contract. It, too, is frequently graded downward for larger asset accumulations.

3. *Contract Charges:* A number of GICs have an annual "contract charge." Generally the charge is between $100 and $500.

Given the high long-term interest guarantees associated with DAs the above expenses aren't onerous. The real problems and expenses usually relate to contract termination provisions. Since the issuing insurance company uses long-term investments to fulfill the commitments it makes to your client, it is only fair that contractholders should be discouraged from jumping in and out of DAs. The resultant portfolio instability would adversely affect all contractholders. However, it is *extremely* important for your client to request specific illustrations of the application of the contract's termination provisions to hypothetical scenarios in which interest rates are assumed to rise or fall after the contract is purchased. Typically, a DA offers two "escape valves"—market value withdrawal and book value withdrawal.

C. How Market Withdrawal Works

GIC market value withdrawal formulas usually "pretend" that the contract is an intermediate maturity bond. The purpose of the market value withdrawal formula is to determine what the principal value of a bond issued with the same "coupon rate" (e.g., long-term interest guarantee) would be at the time your client elects to terminate his DA.

If long-term interest rates have risen since issue, then the principal value of a bond, and therefore, the GIC will have declined. If interest rates have fallen, then the converse is true. "Pure" market value withdrawal formulas do nothing more than complete this exercise and a check goes to your client. However, some or all of the following penalties and charges may apply to the contract you are considering:

- *Termination Charge:* Some issuers take a flat percentage of the contract's accumulated value (sometimes as high as five percent) before applying the market value withdrawal formula. That can be worse than an initial sales charge since it is applied to total accumulated value (principal *plus* interest) as opposed to deposits (principal only).

- *Ceiling On Profit:* A "pure" market value withdrawal formula gives your client an opportunity to make a substantial profit if long-term interest rates decline after he purchases the DA. Many insurance companies issue DAs which, although they happily allow your client to share in a *loss,* will not allow him to receive more than accumulated principal plus guaranteed interest. In effect, under one of those contracts, your client has no downside limit on his potential loss but has a cap on his potential profit.

- *Interest Differentials:* A few GIC's, when comparing the hypothetical "coupon rates" of bond equivalents, *subtract* one or two percentage points. The upshot of that is that your client can't make a profit unless long-term interest rates have moved downward at least as many percentage points. While that's not really a penalty, it does tend to preclude investment decisions based on short-term changes and interest rates. In fairness, that may be a legitimate and sensible approach for an issuer of GICs to take.

D. Book Value Withdrawals

Usually, GIC contract issuers will allow contractholders to take an "installment payout." By spreading the payout over several years' time, the company avoids portfolio disruption and can better anticipate its cash flow requirements. Typically, the payout period will be four to seven years. Installments are paid without applying the market value formula. The two questions to ask about a GIC's book value termination provision are

1. *What is the interest rate on the unpaid balance?* Some issuers pay their normal guaranteed interest rate on any unpaid balance. Others apply a substantially reduced rate. The reduction, if severe, is a form of penalty.

2. *What contractual expenses continue during the payout period?* Frequently, annual contract charges and investment management fees (described above) continue during the installment period. Since your client may have comparable charges in his successor funding medium, he may be paying double expenses during the payout period.

¶1405.3   Annuity Contracts—Are The Guarantees Worth The Costs?

Much of the marketing of small pension plans is accomplished through insurance agents. Frequently, individual annuity contracts are recommended as a funding vehicle. Individual annuity contracts have theoretical advantages:

1. *They automatically provide participant recordkeeping.* Since participant assets are segregated in individual contracts, financial reporting and disclosure is simplified.

2. *Compensation:* Commissions from contracts provide a source of compensation for the agent and the insurance company for which they may be able to provide ancillary plan services such as prototypes, administration and reporting and disclosure.

3. *Annuity Guarantees:* The issuing insurance company usually *guarantees* the minimum payout rate applicable to distributions many years down the road. Therefore, the insurance company assumes the risk that future changes in mortality and morbidity will increase longevity so significantly that participants will outlive their annuities.

4. *Principal and Interest:* Annuity contracts generally specify guarantees of principal and periodic interest rates. Quite often the interest guarantee will take the form of a minimum with excess earnings credited at the option of the company. Historically, credited interest rates have been higher than guaranteed ones.

In a very small plan, these advantages can be quite persuasive. However, consider them in conjunction with the following potential disadvantages.

- *Are the commissions for sales or service?* Absent a commitment from an insurance agent and his company, the commission may turn out to be nothing more than a reward for the agent's *sales* effort. Because of the necessity of ongoing reporting and disclosure inherent in qualified plans, that's not enough. Someone needs to perform the ancillary functions associated with the plan. Make sure there is an understanding that the commissions will support this service aspect.

- *How meaningful are the annuity guarantees?* The annuity rates guaranteed in most annuity contracts are so conservative as not to be relevant. In other words, the insurance company really is not assuming a substantial risk. If that's the case on the contracts you are looking at, there may be no justification for using the annuity structure as opposed to, for example, long-term certificates of deposit comparable in safety of principal and interest.

- *How is your client's investment freedom affected?* Using a particular insurance company's ancillary services—prototypes, for example— may carry with it an obligation to continue using that company's products forever. It is often difficult to predict what the investment environment will be like ten or fifteen years from now or that today's "products" will fulfill future corporate objectives. Make sure you consider the potential costs of amendment and transition that will occur with a change in investment orientation and philosophy.

¶1405.4   Life Insurance—The Great Debate

More time and energy has been expended arguing the merits of including an insured death benefit in small pension plans than virtually any other subject. Arguments on each side are powerful and sophisticated. Probably more important than these arguments is the quality and continuity of the life insurance salesman.

The value of ancillary pension services available through a qualified and conscientious insurance underwriter is immeasurable; conversely, the problems and expense that can result from the improper use of life insurance by a short-sighted or inexperienced life insurance salesman can be overwhelming. In any event, here are some of the major arguments in favor of using life insurance in qualified plans.

1. *Services available:* As discussed above, the potential value of ancillary services available from a major insurance company is a substantial cost saver.

2. *Premiums are deductible:* The funds used to pay premiums than are part of a qualified trust or deducted by the corporation and thus, the premiums are, effectively, tax-deductible.

3. *Estate Tax Benefit:* Life insurance proceeds like other qualified plan proceeds can be structured to avoid federal estate taxes, thereby, providing immediate 100 percent liquidity.

4. *Policy Tax Matters:* Since reserves held by qualified insurance pursuant to qualified plans receive more favored tax treatment than do reserves held for other business, many companies pass these savings on to policyholders in the form of increased dividends, cash values or settlement option rates.

5. *Conservatism:* Life insurance provides one of the safest and most conservative of all investments and using it as a component in the plan's portfolio justifies more aggressive investments for the balance of plan funds.

The above arguments are persuasive. However, consider the arguments marshalled *against* including life insurance in the plan.

1. *PS-58 Costs:* Life insurance protection is construed to be a current economic benefit. Participants must report as taxable income the value of this economic benefit at the time it is received (e.g., the year of premium payment). Since a major incentive of small businessmen

for establishing qualified plans is to defer income taxation, PS–58 costs may seem counterproductive. However, note that a taxable income charge for PS–58 costs is credited against the taxable income occasioned by later plan distributions (e.g., at retirement).

2. *Rate of Return:* Many opponents argue that the major advantage of qualified plans is the tax-free accumulation of investment income. They contend that putting life insurance, which has a very low return when viewed as an investment, in a plan in effect "robs" the plan of substantial compound interest potential.

3. *Public Relations:* Normally it is the key men of the organization who, because of large estates and estate taxes, are motivated to include a large death benefit in the plan. Regular participants, if asked, tend to say "no, thank you" if given a choice about an insured death benefit. Is it advisable to "saddle" all employees with an insured death benefit ultimately to fulfill the estate planning objectives of one or two key principals?

4. *Alternatives:* Opponents point out that, for example, group term life insurance, can provide the same death benefit with *no* tax liability on the first $50,000 of coverage and only a reduced tax liability on the balance. Futher, they point out group term life is one of the least expensive forms of death protection available.

5. *Transience of Most Insurance Agents:* The insurance industry has historically high levels of turnover among its agents. Since qualified plans need to be attended with continuity, it's possible to argue that some insured plans will be "sold," high front-end commissions paid, and then plans—no longer profitable—abandoned. However, most insurance companies are diligently working to create "quality control" at the field agent level to preclude this scenario.

Ultimately, an insurance sales organization with a good history of continuity and proven experience in the qualified plan field, can pay its way for a small plan. Further, to avoid many of the potential negatives, your client might consider issuing only term insurance to plan participants during the first three years, only switching to permanent forms of insurance after that period of uncertainty about their employment longevity is past. The cost of cancelled term insurance policies is substantially less than for permanent plans.

In the final analysis, your client's decision about an insured death will be more a qualitative than a quantitative evaluation. Just make sure you inform him of the quantitative pluses and minuses discussed above.

¶1406   CHOOSING A FIDUCIARY—COST VERSUS INVESTMENT EXPERIENCE

Someone needs to be trustee of the plan you implement. The trustee's duties are primarily investment and protection of plan assets for the benefit of participants. Responsibilities must be carried out under the guidance of various federal and local requirements for prudence and diversification. In addition, the trustee of most larger plans will be under considerable pressure to increase investment performance since any yield in excess of assumptions will reduce employer costs.

Trustees can be sued personally for a breach of their fiduciary capacities and therefore their job should not be taken lightly. As a practical matter, many small plans opt for an "in house" trustee—e.g., the company president—and invest plan assets so conservatively as to fall within the safe harbor provisions of the law. There are a number of reasons for that. Consider both sides.

¶1406.1   Advantages And Disadvantages Of Self-And-Corporate Trusteed Plans

Here are the widely acknowledged advantages of self-trusteed plans:

1. Using a corporate officer or other employee close to the situation allows him to be more responsive to the individual needs of the small plan;

2. The company president, by acting as his own trustee, can avoid the expenses of a full-fledged corporate trustee (e.g., a bank);

3. By investing on the most conservative levels, the company president can fulfill the obligations imposed by the prudent man and diversification rules.

However, use of an individual trustee, such as the company president, has several inherent or potential drawbacks. These include:

1. He may die or be disabled thereby leaving the plan in a turmoil;

2. He probably lacks the investment experience of a corporate trustee;

3. He probably can't diversify his assets as a corporate trustee which pools the assets of a number of clients; or

4. He may not have a good enough accounting or recordkeeping system to keep proper track of investment performance and account allocations.

Those are persuasive arguments both for and against an individual trustee. To further complicate the issue, consider the advantages of a corporate trustee:

1. A bank (assuming that is the most typical form of corporate trustee) spends most or all of its time depositing and monitering investments; it therefore, has more experience;

2. A bank has continuity that extends beyond the life of individuals;

3. Naming a corporate trustee transfers a substantial part of the fiduciary liability associated with investment and pension funds;

4. A corporate trustee's charges are generally not substantial;

5. The bank will typically have extensive computer capacity that can be used both for recordkeeping and participant allocation;

6. Because of its larger size and the pooling of its customers funds, the bank can typically purchase investments for lower expenses, and, in addition, buy larger "blocks" of investment—with higher rates of return—than generally available to the small (e.g., individual trustee) investor.

Offsetting these advantages are the following potential problems:

1. Banks can't guarantee principal and interest;

2. Trustee's fees, even nominal ones, can represent a substantial amount to small plans. This is particularly so assuming the corporate trustee has a *minimum* account charge;

3. Investment performance over the last several years has been subject to substantial fluctuation;

4. Many owners of small businesses prefer either:

    a) investments so conservative (e.g., Treasury obligations or Certificates of Deposit) as to preclude a persuasive argument in favor of a corporate trustee; or

    b) to invest their own plan funds, reasoning (probably incorrectly) that their success in running their business presupposes general investment skill.

In general, the arguments in favor of a corporate trustee seem more powerful than those against, except for the smallest or most conservatively-invested plans.

¶1407   MONITORING INVESTMENT COST AND PERFORMANCE

The first step for your client to take is to set his own investment objectives, including the risks he is willing to take. Some of those variables will be affected by the type of plan he has chosen; others are purely subjective. These are the components of a successful investment program.

¶1407.1   Self-Prompting Questionnaire For Critical Investment Choices

Partly to focus your client's attention on the critical issues he must address, and partly to eliminate various alternative investment choices, your client ought to address the following questions:

1. *How important are the pension assets to the long-term financial health of your client?* With some wealthy small businessmen, funds accumulated in a qualified plan, no matter how well invested, aren't essential. In some cases, a qualified plan is almost a "toy" which allows tax-free investment. Other resources may be so substantial that they could fulfill your client's financial objectives in and of themselves.

2. *Does your client's company have substantial profits above beyond those deposited in the plan?* Depending on the availability of surplus cash in the business, your client may be tempted to take a more or less aggressive posture with relative regard to investments. Less conservative assets with their attendant risks of fluctuation could lead to instability in pension funding. Some clients can tolerate that; others can't.

3. *What type of plan has your client elected?* Choice of a defined-benefit plan carries with it an implication of greater conservatism, both to avoid funding fluctuation and the potential financial liability that could result from a substantial drop in portfolio value. Alternatively, plans that promise nothing more than account balances (e.g. profit-sharing, money-purchase and target benefit plans), might warrant a more aggressive investment.

¶1407.2   Measuring Costs Of Alternative Choices

Having narrowed the field of acceptable investment choices, your client should further cull the group by comparing external and internal costs and contract features. Here are some obvious items to compare

- What is the current rate of return?
- Is it guaranteed?
- If so, for how long?
- Is there a long-term floor on investment returns?
- What minimum settlement option rates (annuity rates) does the contract *guarantee?*
- What annuity rates does the company *currently* pay?
- What are the sales charges for years one through ten assuming a constant investment?
- What are the investment or management charges for years one through ten assuming a level deposit and a constant rate of return?
- Is there an annual contract charge?
- Are market value withdrawals available?
- If so, are they "pure" e.g., is there an adjustment to interest rates or holdback?
- Is there a ceiling on the profit your client can make on a market value transfer?
- What is the interest rate payable on the unpaid balance if a book value installment withdrawal is chosen?
- Which contract or investment charges continue during a book value withdrawal?
- If participants who reach retirement take annuity contracts as their distribution form, are there any contract charges?
- Do the assets used to purchase annuity contracts for participants come out at book or market value?
- What are the trustee or custodial fees if applicable?
- Are there any other termination charges?
- What happens if your client chooses to deposit next year's allocation elsewhere?
- What ancillary services (e.g., qualification or administration) are available given the purchase of a particular asset?

- How many pension accounts does the asset-supplier actually manage—obtain three names and call them.
- How long has the supplier been in the pension business?
- Who will be the trustee if the particular investment is chosen?

Some or all of those questions may be applicable. They are all potentially important since alternative funding media vary so widely in their provisions. Even if your client is "sold" on a particular type of investment, make him aware of the alternatives.

¶1407.3   Evaluating Performance—Setting Goals

Ultimately, a particular investment will be chosen because its attributes most closely fulfill your client's objectives. However, objectives and investment products change. It is important to commit to writing the reasons a particular choice was made. Then, after a reasonable time, it is easy to compare actual performance with original objectives. And, periodically, you will want to go through the investment alternative exercise to make sure that your client's

- objectives haven't changed; or
- investment products still represent the most efficient method of attaining the objectives set out.

Above all, be sure your client's plan allows for flexibility to accommodate changing times.

¶1408   **REVIEWING THE EXTRAORDINARY
            OPPORTUNITIES FOR THE SMALL BUSINESS
                            EMPLOYER**

Few areas of financial planning and consulting offer the same level of rewards for both practitioner and client as the qualified retirement plan area. Because of changing regulations and the otherwise sophisticated nature of qualified plans, involvement in the retirement plan area can be intellectually stimulating and fulfilling. Likewise, a small business that finds itself in a position to afford to implement a plan has probably been successful enough in its own right to form an interesting story.

Finally, small businessmen who implement qualified plans, *enjoy* working on their programs. That's because, as opposed to estate planning, with its concommitant discussion of death and mortality, retirement plans offer *current* economic benefits in the form of tax relief. Small businessmen are likely to be frustrated. They are caught by their own productivity—further profits are so eroded by oppressive taxation that they seem pointless.

In spite of all the intricacies, expenses, reporting and disclosure liabilities, and complex regulations, don't let your client lose sight of these advantages:

1. Contributions are deductible—they therefore conserve for your client money that would otherwise have been shipped off to Washington;

2. Tax-free accumulation—without application of immediate taxation to their yield, pension plan assets can compound at least twice the rate of more traditional alternatives. Over a twenty year period, the effect of 9 percent gross as opposed to 4½ percent net interest can achieve remarkable results;

3. Distribution taxation—your clients' key men will be able to choose among a group of attractively-taxed distribution options. In the event of death, benefits can be distributed free of estate tax. In the event of disability, accrued benefits can be utilized without *any* tax whatsoever. And in the event of normal retirement, lump-sum distributions are accorded extremely favorable taxation on a par, in many cases, with long-term capital gains.

Your client won't find a package like that elsewhere within the investment domain.

Appendix

HOW TO USE THIS SECTION

So far, this book has described all the factors to be considered prior to designing a pension plan. It also examined the planning opportunities available in alternative formats for designing the plan most advantageous to the owner and key men. Finally, it set forth the administrative and investment aspects of plan design and ongoing maintenance. This section of the book outlines:

Appendix A: The Actuarial Methods Commonly Used in Small Plans

The complexity and sophistication of actuarial methodology associated with defined-benefit plans has been the largest single "fly in the ointment" preventing practitioners from using the plan more frequently. Appendix A is an article describing in layman's terms the mechanical aspects of several popular actuarial methods. While it will not make you an actuary, it will give you sufficient insight into the language and concepts of these popular actuarial methods to allow you to participate in a meaningful way in planning sessions that involve actuarial choices.

Appendix B: IRS-Approved Prototype Plan

An IRS-approved prototype plan—for a defined-benefit plan is reprinted in its entirety in Appendix B. A prototype offers a broad spectrum of choices both for formulas and investment media. The adoption of any qualified plan, even one approved by IRS, is a serious matter with significant legal and business consequences. It should only be contemplated in conjunction with close association and communication with clients' counsel whose broader knowledge of a client's personal and business affairs puts him in the best position to weigh repeating and alternative suggestions.

305

Appendix A
Actuarial Cost Methods and the Small Plans*

INTRODUCTION

In this paper, we will explain in detail six actuarial cost methods which are most popular with small plans, particularly the small split-funded plans. Three of the six we will cover are among the "acceptable six" as enumerated in ERISA. The other three are variations of the "acceptable" cost methods, and these evolved because of some shortcomings inherent with the traditional cost methods especially when applied to small plans.

The following discussion will be geared to the cost methods when applied to split-funded plans. However, by simply ignoring references to the policy cash values, the principles will apply to uninsured plans as well. By the way, a split-funded plan is one which is funded by cash value life insurance or annuity contract which is allocable to each participant, and an auxiliary fund. The cash value at retirement supplemented by the auxiliary fund should provide the monthly pension. (See Chapter 2, paragraph 204.8.)*

---

*This article has been reprinted with the kind permission of Datair, a Chicago, Illinois purveyor of pension consulting software programs and ancillary services.

OVERVIEW

Here are six more popular actuarial cost methods:

PTAX or Direct Code	Actuarial Cost Method
A	Individual Level Premium Cost Method
B	Entry Age Normal with Frozen Initial Liability Cost Method
C	Aggregate Cost Method
E	Modified Aggregate Cost Method
K	Modified Entry Age Normal with Frozen Initial Liability Cost Method
P	Modified Individual Level Premium Cost Method

Note that the first three cost methods are among the "acceptable" actuarial cost methods enumerated in ERISA. All the above cost methods, except the traditional individual level premium cost method, automatically spread gains and/or losses.

WHAT IS AN ACTUARIAL COST METHOD?

Section 3(31) of ERISA defines actuarial cost method as "... a recognized actuarial technique utilized for establishing the amount and incidence of the annual actuarial cost of pension plan benefits and expenses." The same section also gives examples of acceptable actuarial cost methods:

> Acceptable actuarial cost methods shall include the accrued benefit cost method (unit credit method), the entry age normal cost method, the individual level premium cost method, the aggregate cost method, the attained age normal cost method, and the frozen initial liability cost method. The terminal funding cost method and the current funding (pay-as-you-go) cost method are not acceptable actuarial cost methods. The Secretary of the Treasury shall issue regulations to further define acceptable actuarial cost methods.

A cost method, for purposes of the minimum funding rules, must be systematic and consistent in its allocation of expected cost. The objective is to allocate the expected cost of the plan to the years of service that give rise to the benefit and, hence, cost.

ESTIMATING THE MONTHLY PENSION AT RETIREMENT

In most small plans, the monthly pension is estimated with the assumption that the current salary remains the same until retirement age. Therefore, it is a simple matter to apply the benefit formula to the current salary. Where the final pension is based on some averaged salary, some averaging procedure may be used. For example, where the plan provides for 50% of average salary based on the highest 5 consecutive salaries on or before age 59 and the participant is 57 years old, the current salary may be assumed to remain the same to age 59. The monthly pension may be based on the average monthly salary using actual salaries at ages 55 to 57, and projected salaries at ages 58 and 59, e.g.:

55	850	actual
56	935	actual
57	1000	actual
58	1000	projected
59	1000	projected

$$4785 \div 5 = 957 \text{ averaged salary}$$
$$\times\ .50$$

478.50 estimated monthly pension

On the other hand, you may wish to take into consideration a salary scale. Consider the case of A. Smith who is 47 years old and is currently earning $55,000 per year. The final pension is based on averaged salary as described above. The salary scale is based on 3% per year, and from a table of Sx we can find the projected salary.

Projected
Averaged

$$\text{Salary} = 55{,}000 \times \frac{(S55 + S56 + S57 + S58 + S59) \div 5}{S47}$$

$$= 55{,}000 \times \frac{(.7440939 + .7664167 + .7894092 + .8130915 + .8374843) \div 5}{.5873946}$$

$$= 55{,}000 \times 1.3450909$$

$$= 73{,}980 \text{ projected averaged salary}$$

Now, look for the factor MZR/Sx for age 47. (The table based on R = 60 may be obtained by using the "VALFAC" program.) Note that this is the same averaged salary projection factor we just calculated.

SOME NOTATIONS AND FORMULAE

A. Ages

1. a = Attained age as of valuation date (assuming this date to be as of the beginning of a plan year).

2. e = Entry age: for plan members who were such as of the plan effective date, the age they would have become eligible had there always been a plan; for other plan members, their age as of actual participation in the plan. For simplicity, most practitioners (including Datair) assume that e = employment age.

3. r = Retirement age.

4. p = Participation age: age at which plan member actually became eligible.

5. i = Issue age when dealing with split-funded plans which use an incremental approach in cost calculations. This is the age at which a particular benefit increase was recognized, the normal cost attributable to the "new" benefit is calculated from "issue" age to retirement age.

6. f = Age as of the beginning of the first plan year.

B. Benefits

1. B = Total projected benefit. When salary scale is used, the benefit formula is applied to the salary projected according to the salary scale assumed.

2. ΔB = Incremental benefits for plans described in A5 above.

C. Salaries

1. CS = Current salary: the plan member's annual salary used in the current year's valuation.

D. Cost of Benefits at Retirement

1. MV = Maturity value: the total lump sum required at retirement to provide the project benefit.
2. CV@NRD = The total cash value at normal retirement date of all policies held to partially fund the projected benefit.
3. COC = Cost of conversion: the amount required to convert the policies at normal retirement date to an annuity which will provide the projected benefit.

$$COC = MV - CV@NRD$$

E. Present Values

1. $(PVB)_x$ = Present value of the projected benefit as of age x, *net* of the cash value at normal retirement.

$$(PVB)_x = (MV - CV@NRD)\ \frac{Dr}{Dx} = COC \cdot \frac{Dr}{Dx}$$

2. $(PV\triangle B)_x$ = Present value of the *increase* in benefit as of age x, net of cash values at normal retirement of any policy attributable to the increase.

$$(PV\triangle B)_x = (MV\ for\ \triangle B - CV@NRD\ attributable\ to\ \triangle B) \cdot \frac{Dr}{Dx}$$

3. $(PVFS)_x$ = Present value of future salaries. This is lump sum equivalent at age x of all salaries payable from age x until retirement. Or, it may be regarded simply as the product of the current salary and a temporary annuity factor. As we shall see later, this latter concept is important in understanding the aggregate cost method.

$$(PVFS)_x = CS \cdot \ddot{a}_{x\ :\ r-x}$$

$\ddot{a}_{x\ :\ \overline{r-x}}$ is the value at age x of a temporary annuity of $1 payable from age x and every year thereafter until retirement age when the payment stops. It is therefore payable immediately at age x for a total of $r - x$ years. And if a salary scale is involved, an increasing annuity factor is used which is denoted by ${}^s\ddot{a}_{x\,:\,\overline{r-x}|}$

F. Normal Costs and Their Present Values

1. $(PVFNC_e)_x$ = Present value of normal cost based on total projected benefits as of age x where the normal costs themselves are calculated as of entry age.

$$(PVFNC_e)_x = \frac{(PVB)_e}{{}^s\ddot{a}_{e\,:\,\overline{r-e}|}} \bullet {}^s\ddot{a}_{x\,:\,\overline{r-x}|} \text{, where x is greater than e.}$$

(Note that the "s" in the temporary annuity is optional, i.e., a salary scale may be used.)

2. $(PVFNC_i)_x$ = Present value of normal costs based on the incremental benefit as of age x where the normal costs themselves are calculated as of the *issue* age.

$$(PVFNC_i)_x = \frac{(PV\triangle B)_i}{\ddot{a}_{i\,:\,\overline{r-i}|}} \bullet \ddot{a}_{x\,:\,\overline{r-x}|} \text{, where x is greater than i.}$$

(Note that salary scale is not permissible here.)

3. $(PVFNC_p)_x$ = Present value of normal costs based on the total projected benefit as of age x where the normal costs themselves are calculated as of the *participation* age.

$$(PVFNC_p)_x = \frac{(PVB)_p}{{}^s\ddot{a}_{p\,:\,\overline{r-p}|}} \bullet {}^s\ddot{a}_{x\,:\,\overline{r-x}|} \text{, where x is greater than p.}$$

(Note that salary scale is permitted here.)

G. Fund Offset

As we shall soon see, the modified individual level premium cost method requires an artificial allocation of assets among the plan members. The fund offset is the term we use to refer to this asset allocated to each employee.

The way this is calculated is given by the following formula:

$$\text{Fund Offset} = \frac{(PVB)_a \bullet \dfrac{\mathring{a} - p}{r - p}}{\sum \left[(PVB)_a \bullet \dfrac{a - p}{r - p} \right]} \bullet \text{Total Assets}$$

H. Remaining Initial Accrued Liability

$$(RIAL)_x = \left[(RIAL)_{x-1} + (NC)_{x-1} \right] \bullet (1+i) - C_{x-1} - I_c$$

where $(RIAL)_x - 1$ = Last year's remaining initial accrued liability

NC_{x-1} = Last year's normal cost for the plan as a whole

C_{x-1} = Actual contribution towards last year's cost

I_c = Interest attributable to the contribution

i = Interest rate

I. Gains (Losses) for the Year

Gain (Loss) = EUF − AUF

where EUF = Expected unfunded liability

AUF = Actual unfunded liability

$(EUF)_x = \left[(AUF)_{x-1} + (NC)_{x-1} \right] \bullet (1+i) - C_{x-1} - I_c$

$(AUF)_x = (\text{Accrued Liability})_x - \text{Assets}$

INDIVIDUAL LEVEL PREMIUM COST METHOD (A METHOD)

This cost method originated at the time when plans were entirely funded by retirement income or annuity contracts. As increases in pensions due to increases in salaries are recognized, they are funded by new contracts. Hence, when split-funded plans came into vogue, auxiliary fund deposits were calculated for each increment of benefit from the time the increase in benefit is recognized until retirement date. The total of all the auxiliary fund deposits and the life insurance premiums is the normal cost. Under this method, gains and losses are determined each year and separately amortized and added (or subtracted) as adjustments to the level deposits (normal costs).

Note that the method does not lend itself to the use of a salary scale, since by its very nature salary increases are taken into account at the time of occurrence.

The advantage of this method, however, is that it is very easy to explain to the client, his accountants, or even his attorney. The client knows exactly to what each dollar of cost is attributable. It is especially important in situations where a breakdown of cost per participant is required by the accountant.

MODIFIED INDIVIDUAL LEVEL PREMIUM COST METHOD (P METHOD)

The disadvantages associated with the traditional individual level premium cost method led to this modification. Let's review these disadvantages:

First, the record keeping associated with the incremental approach is a definite shortcoming of the method. An old plan with a multitide of policies yet with very few participants may involve a lot of records, since information is kept on each increase in benefit. It makes it almost impossible to take over an existing plan using this method because of the need to have a history of all previous increases and corresponding fund deposits.

Second, since the method by its very nature takes into account salary increases as they occur, changes in actuarial assumptions involving salary scales cannot be accommodated under the individual level premium cost method.

Third, gains and/or losses are not automatically spread out. Therefore, each year's gain (or loss) must be calculated and noted. Every year all previous year's components of gains (or losses) must be taken into consideration for the minimum funding standards.

The modification to this cost method eliminated the need to keep track of each increment of benefit while maintaining the capability to automatically provide a breakdown of cost per participant.

The procedure involves an allocation of the assets as of each valuation date. It is most important, however, that the participants are not led to believe that the asset allocation is in any way a measure of what they are vested in . Hence, the term "fund offset" is used to refer to this figure. Here is a step-by-step procedure:

1. Calculate the present value of benefits for each participant by determining the discounted value of the amount required from the fund to provide the expected retirement benefits. (For split-funded plans the amount required is the cost of conversion.) Note that this is the present value of each participant's *total* benefits as of the valuation date. The benefits may be calculated with or without salary scale. $(PVB)_a$

2. Multiply each participant's present value of benefits by a fraction, the numerator of which is the number of years he has participated in the plan as of the valuation date, and the denominator the total projected number of years of participation to normal retirement date. Let's call this the "fund liability." $\dfrac{a - p}{r - p} \bullet (PVB)_a$

3. Allocate the total assets to each participant in proportion to his fund liability. Call this the "fund offset."

4. Subtract the fund offset from the present value of benefits to arrive at the present value of future normal cost.

5. Finally, the normal cost for each participant is determined by dividing the present value of future normal cost by the value of a temporary annuity with payments commencing at the participant's attained age and ending at his normal retirement age. Of course, if a salary scale is utilized, the present value of an increasing annuity should be used.

Note how gains and losses are automatically spread over the anticipated working lifetime of each participant.

Let us summarize the advantages of this modified ILPC method:

1. It greatly simplifies the entire valuation process because it does not require the calculations associated with each incremental benefit.

2. Since gains and/or losses are automatically spread over the anticipated working lifetime of each employee, the funding standard account is simplified. There is no need to keep track of each year's actuarial gain (or loss) for separate amortization. Furthermore, the annual contribution may be based on market value valuation of assets without resulting in violent fluctuations in contributions.

3. The method is a natural for take-over cases.

4. If the case becomes such that the actuary finds a need to use a salary scale, unlike the traditional ILPC method, he does not have to change actuarial cost methods. As you know, changes in actuarial cost methods require prior IRS approval.

AGGREGATE COST METHOD (C METHOD)

The actuarial cost methods we just discussed involve the calculation of cost on an individual-by-individual basis. Under the traditional individual level premium cost method, for example, we calculate the cost attributable to an increment of benefit by spreading it over a period of time from the date the increase was realized to retirement date. The actual mathematical procedure is to divide the present value of benefit (PVB_x) by the temporary annuity of $1.00 payable from the "issue" age to a year prior to retirement date.

For large plans, this becomes very cumbersome. So, why not determine the *average* number of years applicable to the group over which cost must be spread, i.e., find the average temporary annuity factor for this group. And to find this average, we can simply add each member's temporary annuity factor and divide by the number of plan members:

$\ddot{a}_a : \overline{r - a}\rceil$ is the symbol for the present value of $1.00 per year beginning at age a and payable for $\overline{r-a}\rceil$ years. This is the temporary annuity factor.

$$\text{Averaged Temporary Annuity Factor (ATAF)} = \frac{\Sigma \ddot{a}_a : \overline{r-a}\rceil}{\text{No. of Participants}}$$

Therefore, if we divided the present value of benefits for all participants by this average factor, we should come very close to approximating the cost for this plan.

$$\text{Normal Cost} = \frac{\Sigma(PVB)a}{ATAF}$$

Well, in some cases, yes. If all plan members' benefits are the same, then this method is appropriate and easy to use. However, most benefits are tied to the plan members' salary, e.g., benefit is 50% of salary. In this case, wouldn't it be better to give more weight to the temporary annuity factors of the plan members with higher salaries and less for those with lower salaries in the averaging process? Of course! We accomplish this by multiplying each plan member's temporary annuity factor by his current salary. (PVFS$_a$) Calculate the present value of future salary for the whole group and divide it by the total current salary.

$$\text{Weighted Ave. Temporary Annuity Factor (WATAF)} = \frac{\Sigma(PVFS)a}{\Sigma CS}$$

The normal cost can then be determined by dividing the present value of benefits for all participants by the weighted factor. Now, this is what the traditional aggregate cost method is about. (C Method):

$$\text{Normal Cost} = \frac{\Sigma(PVB)a}{WATAF}$$

This formula is good for the first plan year, but must be adjusted for existing assets in subsequent years. Therefore, in subsequent years,

$$\text{Normal Cost} \ = \ \frac{\Sigma(PVB)a - \text{Assets}}{WATAF}$$

Therefore, under this method, we are amortizing the benefits still to be funded (after reduction for amounts already in the fund) over the averaged future working lifetime of the group with such average weighted by salary.

Some people might be more familiar with the following formula:

$$\text{Normal Cost} \ = \ \frac{\Sigma(PVB)a \ - \ \text{Assets}}{\Sigma(PVFS)a} \quad \bullet \quad CS$$

Through algebra, the above can easily be shown as another way of writing:

$$\text{Normal Cost} \ = \ \frac{\Sigma(PVB)a \ - \ \text{Assets}}{\dfrac{\Sigma(PVFS)a}{\Sigma CS}}$$

The aggregate cost method, therefore, is a neat and easy way of calculating plan cost. Its advantages are:

1. It is one of the 6 "acceptable" actuarial cost methods.
2. It is quite easy to calculate and very little record keeping is involved when compared to the individual level premium cost method.
3. It can be used with salary scales. This is done by calculating benefits based on projected salaries. The present value of benefits are in turn calculated with salary scales taken into account. An increasing temporary annuity is then used in the denominator so that a cost based on a *level* percentage of payroll is expected instead of a level dollar amount.
4. The spread gain feature of the method makes the funding standard account easier to maintain.

MODIFIED AGGREGATE COST METHOD (E METHOD)

When ERISA's provisions on minimum funding standards became effective, the pension actuaries were faced with the problem of choosing the "acceptable" actuarial cost method. A great many of them were most concerned with using a cost method that automatically spread gains and losses. Others liked the aggregate concept which kept the funds unallocated and helped to keep the concept of vested accrued benefits from the "my account balance" concept.

The problem with the aggregate cost method, however, lies in the fact that many plans are integrated, and the use of salaries as weights distorted the cost. A few young employees with minimum benefits can increase the average temporary annuity factor and decrease the cost particularly when the highly paid principal is quite old. Therefore, modified aggregate cost methods became popular. Quite a few variations emerged, but they all seem to have one thing in common—the use of a weight based on "tabular normal costs". Some actuaries used the incremental normal costs as calculated in the individual level premium cost methods as weights. Therefore, such normal costs were referred to as tabular normal costs to distinguish them from the normal costs. In cost method E, we have adopted the simpler version of calculating a tabular normal cost for each plan member as of his original participation age. This tabular normal cost is recalculated every year based on the then total projected benefit.

And this is what we use as the weight in arriving at the average temporary annuity factor. Following is a step-by-step procedure of this method:

1. Calculate the tabular normal cost for each active plan participant. This is the level annual payment, calculated from each participant's date of participation in the plan, which will accumulate to the amount required in the auxiliary fund at retirement to provide the projected benefits. (NCp)

2. Determine the present values of future tabular normal costs by multiplying each participant's tabular normal

cost by the temporary annuity due factor from attained age to normal retirement age.

$$(\text{PVFNCp}) \, a = (\text{NC}_p) \bullet \ddot{a}a : \overline{r - a}$$

3. Determine the weighted average temporary annuity by dividing the total present value of future tabular normal cost for the group by the total tabular normal costs. Note that the weights used for this average annuity are the individual level amounts required from entry age for each participant's total projected benefit on the valuation date.

$$\Sigma_{(\text{PVFNCp})a} \div \Sigma_{(\text{NCp})}$$

4. The normal cost is determined in the aggregate for the group by dividing the present value of benefits less assets by the weighted temporary annuity for the group.

$$\text{NC} = \cfrac{\Sigma \text{PVBa} - \text{Assets}}{\cfrac{\Sigma_{(\text{PVFNCp})a}}{\Sigma \text{NCp}}}$$

Note that at the time of plan inception, the first plan year normal cost is equal to the sum of the individual tabular normal costs required to fund for the initial benefit.

ENTRY AGE NORMAL WITH FROZEN INITIAL LIABILITY COST METHOD (B METHOD)

This actuarial cost method allows for funding flexibility. The result is to offer a range of contribution for the year. The flexibility is accomplished by establishing a past service liability which may be amortized over 10 or 30 years (40 for multi-employer plans).

This liability attributable to prior years, called the frozen initial past service liability, is calculated at the plan's inception. The excess of contributions for each plan year over the Normal

Cost for that year, is allocated toward funding this frozen liability. Once the initial past service liability is established, the procedure involved is very much similar to the aggregate cost method. In fact, after this past service liability is completely amortized, it reverts to the aggregate cost method.

Following is a step-by-step procedure of how the initial past service liability is calculated:

1. Calculate the tabular normal cost from entry age for each plan member. This is the annual payment, calculated from each participant's date of employment (his entry age), which will accumulate to the amount required in the auxiliary fund at retirement to provide the projected benefits (NCe).

2. Determine the present value of future tabular normal costs by multiplying each participant's tabular normal cost by his temporary annuity factor from attained age to normal retirement age.

$$(PVFNCp)a = NCe \cdot \ddot{a}a:\overline{r - a}|$$

3. Calculate the present value of benefits for each participant by determining the discounted value of the amount required from the fund to provide the projected benefits at retirement (PVBa).

4. The initial past service liability is equal to the difference between the present value of all benefits and the present value of future normal costs:

$$IPSL = \Sigma(PVB)a - \Sigma(PVFNCe)a$$

The normal cost is calculated by using an average temporary annuity factor weighted by salaries, i.e.

$$NC = \frac{\Sigma(PVB)a - Assets - RIAL}{\frac{\Sigma(PVFS)a}{\Sigma CS}}$$

Rial is the remaining initial accrued liability. It originated from the initial past service liability:

$$(RIAL)n = (RIAL)n - 1 + (NC)n - 1 + I - (C)n - 1$$

where n = this year
   n−1 = last year
     I = interest attributable to each component
    C = last year's contribution

Therefore, this cost method has not only all of the advantages of the aggregate cost method which includes "spread" gain technique and ease of calculation and recordkeeping, but in addition it provides for flexibility in contribution.

MODIFIED ENTRY AGE NORMAL COST METHOD WITH FROZEN INITIAL LIABILITY COST METHOD (K METHOD)

The modification to this cost method is in the use of "tabular" normal cost, calculated from entry age, as weights in determining the averaged temporary annuity factor for the group. It is, therefore, nothing more than a fine tuning of the traditional entry age normal with FIPSL.

The initial past service liability is determined as in the traditional version.

The normal cost is determined in the aggregate for the group using the following procedure:

1. Calculate the tabular normal cost for each active plan participant. This is the level annual payment, calculated from each participant's date of employment (entry age), which will accumulate to the amount required in the auxiliary fund at retirement to provide the projected benefits (NCe).

2. Determine the present value of future tabular normal costs by multiplying each participant's tabular normal

cost by the temporary annuity due from attained age to normal retirement age.

$$(\text{PVFNCe})a = \text{NCe} \bullet \ddot{a}a:\overline{r - a|}$$

3. Determine the weighted average temporary annuity by dividing the total present value of future tabular normal cost for the group by the total tabular normal costs. Note that the weights used for this average annuity are the individual level amounts required from entry age for each participant's total projected benefit on the valuation date.

$$\frac{\Sigma(\text{PVFNCe})a}{\Sigma\text{NCe}}$$

4. The normal cost is determined in the aggregate for the group by dividing the present value of benefits less remaining frozen initial liability less assets by the weighted average temporary annuity for the group.

$$\frac{\Sigma(\text{PVB})a \ - \ \text{Assets} \ - \ \text{RIAL}}{\dfrac{\Sigma(\text{PVFNCe})a}{\Sigma\text{NCe}}}$$

Note that at the time of plan inception, the first plan year normal cost is equal to the sum of the individual tabular normal costs required to fund for the initial benefit.

Further, note that under this method the accrued liability can easily be determined should it be needed; i.e.

$$\text{AL} = \Sigma(\text{PVB})a - \Sigma(\text{PVFNCe})a$$

SUMMARY

There you have it. The 6 more popular actuarial cost methods. The following two pages show all the formulae discussed. Have fun!

ACTUARIAL COST METHODS FOR SPLIT-FUNDED PLANS
MODIFIED METHOD

Actuarial Cost Method	Initial Accrued Liability	Normal Cost	Accrued Liability
1. Modified Individual Level Premium (P Method)	none	$\sum\left(\dfrac{(PVB)a - \text{Fund Offset}}{{}^{s}\ddot{a}\,:\,r-a}\right)$	$\sum\left((PVB)a \cdot \dfrac{a - :p}{r - p}\right)$
2. Modified Entry Age Normal w/Frozen Initial Liability (K Method)	$\sum(PVB)_r - \sum(PVFNC_e)_r$	$\dfrac{\dfrac{\sum(PBV)_a - \text{Assets} - \text{Rial}}{\sum(PVFNCe)a}}{\sum(NC)e}$	$\sum(PBV)a - \sum(PVFNCe)a$
3. Modified Aggregate (E Method)	none	$\dfrac{\dfrac{\sum(PVB)a - \text{Assets}}{\sum(PVFNCp)a}}{\sum NCp}$	$\sum(PVB)a - \sum(PVFNCp)a$

ACTUARIAL COST METHODS FOR SPLIT-FUNDED PLANS
TRADITIONAL METHOD

Actuarial Cost Method	Initial Accrued Liability	Normal Cost	Accrued Liability
1. Individual Level Premium (A Method)	none	$\displaystyle\sum\left(\frac{(PV\Delta B)\ I}{\ddot{a}:\overline{r-i}}\right)$	$\sum(PVB)a - (PVFNCi)a$
2. Entry Age Normal w/Frozen Initial Liability (B Method)	$(PVB)_f - (PVFNCe)_f$	$\dfrac{\dfrac{\sum(PVB)a - Assets - Rial}{\sum(PVFS)a}}{\sum CS}$	none
3. Aggregate (C Method)	none	$\dfrac{\dfrac{\sum(PVF)a - Assets}{\sum(PVFS)a}}{\sum CS}$	none

Appendix B
IRS-Approved Prototype Plan

DEFINED-BENEFIT PLAN

Following is an IRS approved defined-benefit pension plan written for and used by Future Planning Associates, Inc., the author's firm. The plan allows the use, by a choice of different adoption agreements, of six different common defined-benefit plans (integrated and nonintegrated), such as:

- flat-benefit plans;
- unit-benefit plans; and
- offset plans.

Further, it is not restrictive as to investments, preserving as much flexibility as possible for clients. Various options appear in the plan. Most notable of which are:

1. allowance for benefit reductions occasioned by service less than "x" years

2. alternative choices for "normal form of benefit"/life only or joint and full survivor—allowing for aggressive and conservative funding rules.

Notwithstanding the "everything but the kitchen sink" approach, this prototype offers, it does not diminish the need to involve client counsel to make decisions about the adoption of a qualified plan.

Future Planning Associates, Inc.
Corporate Defined-Benefit Prototype Plan

FUTURE PLANNING ASSOCIATES, INC.
CORPORATE DEFINED BENEFIT PROTOTYPE PLAN

TABLE OF CONTENTS

FUTURE PLANNING ASSOCIATES, INC.
CORPORATE DEFINED BENEFIT PROTOTYPE PLAN

Whereas the Employer designated in the Adoption Agreement constituting a part of this Plan wishes to provide retirement benefits for its Employees, the Employer hereby establishes this plan and trust, hereinafter called the Plan, to be administered pursuant to the terms set forth in the Adoption Agreement and hereinafter below.

Article I
Definitions

As used in this plan and trust instrument, the following words and phrases shall have the following meanings, unless a different meaning is clearly required by the context:

1.01 ACCRUED BENEFIT shall be the sum of the following:

(a) the present value of the participant's projected normal retirement benefit multiplied by a fraction, the numerator of which is the participant's actual years of participation in the plan and the denominator of which is the number of years of participation which the participant would have as of his normal retirement date. For purposes of this paragraph a participant's normal retirement benefit shall be calculated as if the participant's annual pay remained constant from the date of such calculation until his normal retirement date; and

(b) the balance of the separate account, if any, maintained for voluntary employee contributions under Section 3.02.

If this plan constitutes an amendment or restatement of a preexisting plan, then a participant's accured benefit under this plan will be at least equal to his accrued benefit under the predecessor plan. If this plan is insured, then the Accrued Benefit shall be the reserve carried for a participant by the Insurer under the insurance and annuity contracts issued on the life of a participant.

1.02 ADOPTION AGREEMENT means the agreement which is signed by the Employer, Trustee(s) and Plan

Administrator, and which sets forth the elective provisions of this Plan and Trust designated by the employer.

1.03 AGE means the chronological attained age, in years, of the employee as of the last anniversary of his date of birth.

1.04 ANNIVERSARY DATE means the last day of the Plan Year, as of which day assets and liabilities of the plan will be valued and contributions determined.

1.05 ANNUAL PAY means the remuneration paid or accrued during a plan year as salary or wages, including overtime, bonuses, commissions and any other compensation subject to tax under Section 3101(a) of the Internal Revenue Code, as certified to the Plan Administrator by the employer. The Plan Administrator may rely on such certification for his computation of benefits. Annual Pay may be limited as specified in the Adoption Agreement.

1.06 ANTICIPATED NORMAL RETIREMENT BENEFIT means a participant's projected retirement benefit calculated in accordance with the provisions of Article IV.

1.07 AVERAGE ANNUAL PAY means, unless the Employer elects a different averaging period in Item 19(c) of the Adoption Agreement, the participant's annual pay averaged over the final 5 years of his employment with the employer. If a participant has less than 5 years of employment, the average annual pay shall be averaged over the participant's total period of service.

1.08 BENEFICIARY shall mean the person or entity designated by a participant in accordance with this Agreement to receive benefits upon the death of said participant. If a participant does not designate a beneficiary or if the designated beneficiary predeceases the participant, benefits payable to a beneficiary shall be payable to the first of the following who is living at the participant's death:

(a) the participant's spouse;

(b) the participant's children, per stirpes;

(c) the participant's parents;

(d) the participant's grandparents;

(e) the participant's brothers and sisters; or

(f) the participant's estate.

1.09 BREAK IN SERVICE means a Plan Year in which the employee or participant fails to complete more than 500 hours of service.

1.10 CODE means the Internal Revenue Code, As Amended.

1.11 COVERED COMPENSATION means an amount indicated in the Adoption Agreement determined by the following tables, based on one of the following amendments to the Social Security Act:

1968

Calendar Year of 65th Birthday	Amount	Calendar Year of 65th Birthday	Amount
1968 or earlier	$4,800	1979–1993	$6,600
1969–1971	5,400	1994–2000	7,200
1972–1978	6,000	2001 or later	7,800

1971

Calendar Year of 65th Birthday	Amount	Calendar Year of 65th Birthday	Amount
1971 or earlier	$5,400	1992–1998	$7,800
1972–1975	6,000	1999–2003	8,400
1976–1981	6,600	2004 or later	9,000
1982–1991	7,200		

1973

Calendar Year of 65th Birthday	Amount	Calendar Year of 65th Birthday	Amount
1974 or earlier	$6,600	1990–1994	$10,200
1975–1976	7,200	1995–1997	10,800
1977–1978	7,800	1998–1999	11,400
1979–1981	8,400	2000–2002	12,000
1982–1984	9,000	2003–2006	12,600
1985–1989	9,600	2007 or later	13,200

1976

Calendar Year of 65th Birthday	Amount	Calendar Year of 65th Birthday	Amount
1976	$ 7,200	1995–1996	$12,000
1977	7,800	1997–1998	12,600
1978–1979	8,400	1999–2000	13,200
1980–1981	9,000	2001–2003	13,800
1982–1983	9,600	2004–2006	14,400
1984–1987	10,200	2007–2010	15,000
1988–1991	10,800	2011 or later	15,300
1992–1994	11,400		

1977

Calendar Year of 65th Birthday	Amount	Calendar Year of 65th Birthday	Amount
1977 or earlier	$ 7,800	1995–1996	$12,600
1978–1979	8,400	1997–1998	13,200
1980	9,000	1999–2000	13,800
1981–1982	9,600	2001–2002	14,400
1983–1985	10,200	2003–2004	15,000
1986–1987	10,800	2005 –2006	15,600
1988–1991	11,400	2007–2011	16,200
1992–1994	12,000	2012 or later	16,500

1978

Calendar Year of 65th Birthday	Amount	Calendar Year of 65th Birthday	Amount
1978 or earlier	$ 8,400	1997–1998	$13,800
1979–1980	9,000	1999	14,400
1981	9,600	2000–2001	15,000
1982–1983	10,200	2002–2003	15,600
1984–1986	10,800	2004–2005	16,200
1987–1988	11,400	2006–2007	16,800
1989–1992	12,000	2008–2012	17,400
1993–1994	12,600	2013 or later	17,700
1995–1996	13,200		

Alternatively, Covered Compensation may be a uniform dollar amount selected in the Adoption Agreement for all participants, or such other Table as may be published from time to time by the Internal Revenue Service and specified in the Adoption Agreement.

1.12 DISABILITY means the inability to substantially perform the functions of employment by reason of physical or mental impairment which can be expected to result in death or to be of long-continued and indefinite duration. With mutual agreement of the Participant and the Trustee(s), disability shall be determined by a licensed physician. However, if either the Participant or the Trustee(s) desire, Disability shall be determined by a majority of three licensed physicians, two selected by the Participant and the Trustee(s) individually and one selected by their mutual agreement.

1.13 EFFECTIVE DATE shall mean the first day of the period for which the terms of this Plan and Trust Agreement are effective, as indicated in the Adoption Agreement.

1.14 EMPLOYEE means any person employed by the Employer, but shall not mean any person as defined in Code Section 401(c)(1) or any person as defined in Code Section 1379(d).

1.15 EMPLOYER: The employer who adopts this plan as indicated in the Adoption Agreement.

1.16 EMPLOYMENT DATE means the date on which an employee is first credited with an hour of service. For a Participant who has incurred a Break-In-Service, Employment Date shall be the date after the Break-In-Service on which the employee is first credited with an hour of service.

1.17 ENTRY DATE means the first day of the Plan Year, as specified in the Adoption Agreement, on which an eligible employee becomes an active participant under the plan.

1.18 ERISA means the Employee Retirement Income Security Act of 1974 as amended.

1.19 The term "Fiduciary" shall mean and include the Trustee, Plan Administrator, Plan Sponsor, Investment Manager, and any other person who:

(a) Exercises any discretionary authority or discretionary control respecting management of the Plan or exercises any authority or control respecting management or disposition of its assets;

(b) Renders investment advice for a fee or other compensation, direct or indirect, with respect to any moneys or other property of the Plan, or has any authority or responsibility to do so;

(c) Has any discretionary authority or discretionary responsibility in the administration of the Plan; or

(d) Is described as a "fiduciary" in Section 3 (14) or (21) of ERISA or is designated to carry out fiduciary responsibilities pursuant to this Agreement to the extent permitted by Section 405(c)(1)(b) of ERISA.

1.20 The term "Hour of Service" is defined as:

(a) Each hour for which an employee is directly or indirectly paid or entitled to payment by the employer for the performance of duties. These hours shall be credited to the employee for the computation period or periods in which the duties are performed; and

(b) Each hour (up to a maximum of 501 hours in a single continuous period) for which an employee is directly or indirectly paid or entitled to payment by the employer on account of a period of time during which no duties are performed (irrespective of whether the employment relationship has terminated) due to vacation, holiday, illness, incapacity, disability, layoff, jury duty, military duty or leave of absence. These hours shall be credited to the employee for the computation period or periods in which the duties were to be performed in accordance with Section 2530.2006-2(b) and (c) of the Department of Labor Regulations.

(c) Each hour for which back pay irrespective of mitigation of damages, has been either awarded or agreed to by the employer. The same hours of service shall not be credited to the employee under paragraph (a) or paragraph (b) as the case may be, and under this paragraph (c). The hours under this paragraph (c) shall be credited to the employee for the computation period or periods to which the award or agreement pertains rather than the computation period in which the award, agreement, or payment was made.

1.21 Insurer(s) means any legal reserve life insurance company licensed to do business in the state where this plan is adopted.

1.22 The term "Investment Manager" shall mean any Fiduciary (other than a Trustee or named Fiduciary) who:

(a) Has the power to manage, acquire or dispose of any asset of the Plan;

(b) Is a registered investment advisor, bank, or insurance company; and

(c) Has acknowledged in writing that he is a fiduciary with respect to the Plan.

1.23 JOINT AND SURVIVOR ANNUITY means an annuity for the life of the participant with a survivor annuity for the life of his spouse which is equal to not less than 50% and not more than 100% of the annuity payable during the joint lives of the participant and the participant's spouse and which is the actuarial equivalent of a single life annuity, in the case of an item 16(a) Adoption Agreement election or a joint and 100% survivor annuity in the case of an item 16(b) Adoption Agreement election in either case determined by reference to the 1971 Group Annuity Table, 6% interest.

1.24 LIMITATION YEAR means the 12 consecutive month period considered for determining a participant's maximum normal retirement benefits under Code Section 415 under all plans of the employer. The Limitation Year shall be the Plan Year.

1.25 NORMAL RETIREMENT AGE means the age specified in Section 11 of the Adoption Agreement. Anything in the Plan to the contrary notwithstanding, a Participant's right to his normal retirement benefit shall be non-forfeitable upon the earlier of (a) his attainment of normal retirement age or (b) his 70th birthday, or (c) any mandatory retirement age consistently enforced by the Employer.

1.26 NORMAL RETIREMENT DATE means the first day of the first month following attainment of Normal Retirement Age.

1.27 NORMAL FORM OF RETIREMENT BENEFIT means a single life or joint and 100% survivor annuity as selected in the Adoption Agreement.

1.28 PARTICIPANT means an Employee who has met the requirements of Article II.

1.29 PLAN, TRUST, OR PLAN AND TRUST mean this Pension Plan, Trust and Adoption Agreement.

1.30 PLAN ADMINISTRATOR means the person designated in the Adoption Agreement or any duly appointed successor. If no designation is effective at any time, the Plan Administrator shall be the employer. The Plan Administrator shall also be the named fiduciary. When the designated Plan Administrator is the Employer, an authorized delegate of the Plan Administrator shall be named in the Adoption Agreement.

1.31 PLAN YEAR means the 12 consecutive month or other period of time adopted by the employer and his fiscal year for Federal Income Tax reporting purposes and specified in the Adoption Agreement.

The Plan Year shall also be coincident with the Limitation Year and shall be the period used to measure years of service for purposes of the vesting and break-in-service provisions of this plan.

1.32 PREDECESSOR EMPLOYER means the employer as he may have operated prior to his present business form, assuming that the nature and character of his business before and after any change in status or structure was substantially similar. At the election of the Employer in the Adoption Agreement, subject to Section 1.33, hours of service and years of service performed by Employees of the Employer or Predecessor Employer may be counted for purposes of eligibility and vesting, but not benefit accrual, under this plan.

1.33 PREDECESSOR PLAN means any plan formerly maintained by the Employer or Predecessor Employer which is subsumed, restated or amended in its entirety by this plan and specified in the Adoption Agreement. In such event, Years of Service under this Plan shall include service with the Predecessor Employer. The foregoing notwithstanding, there shall be no duplication of benefits between those provided by this Plan and those provided by the Predecessor Plan.

1.34 SEPARATION FROM SERVICE means cessation of employment with the employer.

1.35 TRUSTEE(S) means the trustees designated in the Adoption Agreement and any duly appointed successor trustees.

1.36 TRUST FUND means the assets of this Trust.

1.37 VESTING SCHEDULE means the vesting schedule elected in the Adoption Agreement.

1.38 YEAR OF SERVICE shall mean, for eligiblity purposes, a 12 consecutive month period during which an employee is credited with 1000 hours of service as further provided in Section 2.02. YEAR OF SERVICE shall mean, for vesting and benefit accrual purposes, a Plan Year during which the participant is credited with 1000 hours of service, except that if

(a) an employee's period of service for determining his eligibility to participate in this plan overlaps two plan years; and

(b) Such employee is credited with a Year of Service during such period for eligibility purposes but does not complete a year of service in either Plan Year in which such period occurs; and

(c) The employee becomes a participant in the plan; the Year of Service for eligibility purposes shall also be credited as a year of service for vesting purposes.

YEAR OF SERVICE shall mean, for benefit accrual purposes, a Plan Year during which a participant is credited with 1000 hours of service.

The foregoing notwithstanding, service with any employer which together with the Employer constitute a controlled group as defined in Section 11.16 hereof shall be credited as service with the Employer for purposes of eligibility and vesting.

Article II
Eligibility

2.01 Participation in this Plan is limited to Eligible Employees, as defined in the Employer's Adoption Agreement. An Eligible Employee shall become a Participant on an Entry Date as specified in the Employer's Adoption Agreement.

2.02 For the purpose of determining Years of Service and Breaks in Service for purposes of eligibility, the initial 12 month period shall commence on the date the Employee first performs an Hour of Service. The second 12 month period shall be the Plan Year which commences prior to the end of the initial 12 month period.

In the event that the Employer elects 100% Immediate Vesting, the second and subsequent 12 month periods shall commence on the anniversary of the employment commencement date. However, if, in such case, the Employee fails to complete a Year of Service in the initial 12 month period, all subsequent periods shall be Plan Years beginning with the Plan Year that includes his first anniversary of employment.

In the event that the Employer elects 100% Immediate Vesting, for the purpose of eligibility all Years of Service prior to a Break in Service shall be disregarded.

2.03 Within 90 days after the execution of this Agreement, the Trustees shall notify each eligible Employee and give the Employee an opportunity to become a Participant. At least 15 days but not more than 60 days after each Anniversary Date, the Plan Administrator shall notify each Employee eligible to become a Participant.

2.04 Each eligible Employee who desires to become a Participant shall: (1) execute any application(s) for insurance or annuities on the forms provided for that purpose; (2) submit such evidence of insurability as may be required by an insurer; and (3) execute an agreement to make required contributions, if any.

2.05 In the event an Employee fails or refuses to participate on the date the Employee first becomes eligible, the Employee may participate on any subsequent Anniversary Date upon fulfilling the requirements of this Article.

2.06 A former Participant shall become a Participant immediately upon his return to the employ of the employer.

2.07 In the event a Participant becomes ineligible to Participate because he is no longer a member of an eligible class of Employees, such Employee shall participate immediately upon his return to an eligible class of Employees.

2.08 In the event an Employee who is not a member of the eligible class of Employees becomes a member of the eligible class such Employee shall participate immediately if such Employee has satisfied the minimum age and service requirements and would have previously become a Participant had he been in the eligible class.

2.09 If the Employer maintains a Predecessor Plan of a Predecessor Employer, service as a common law employee for such Predecessor Employer shall be treated as service with the employer. If the Predecessor Employer was not a corporation, Years of Service shall include service with the Predecessor Employer as a Partner or Sole Proprietor, unless the employer shall designate otherwise in the Adoption Agreement. If the Predecessor Employer did not maintain a Plan, or maintained a Plan that has been terminated, years of service under this plan shall include service with the Predecessor Employer unless the Employer shall designate otherwise in the Adoption Agreement.

Article III
Contributions

3.01 The Employer shall pay to the Trustees each Plan Year the funds necessary to provide the benefits of this Plan and Trust as may be determined by an enrolled actuary. No contribution shall be required of any person other than the Employer. Any payments from this Plan and Trust shall be made by the Trustees or the Insurer. Contributions will be made and benefits accrued for Active Participants only.

3.02 In addition to those contributions required to be made by the Employer, if the Voluntary Contribution option has been elected in the Adoption Agreement, each Participant may each year voluntarily contribute to this Plan and Trust an amount which together with amounts so contributed to all other qualified plans of the Employer, if any, shall not exceed 10% of his compensation. Such contributions must be made to the Trustees intermittently or by regular payroll deductions in a manner designated by the Employer. The right to make such contributions shall be cumulative and a Participant who has failed or been unable to make the maximum voluntary contributions permitted under this Plan and Trust in any year may make such contributions in any subsequent year as shall be permitted to fully utilize his right. Furthermore, the amount which a Participant may voluntarily contribute may be limited by the limitations placed on the annual additions to defined contribution plans.

       Such contributions shall be credited to a voluntary contribution account established for the Participant. The Trustees may comingle such voluntary contributions with those contributions of the Employer; however, the Plan Administrator shall keep separate records of the Participant's voluntary contributions. The Trustees may apply such voluntary contributions to pay premiums on insurance as may be requested by the Participant, or the Trustee may invest such voluntary contributions in the same manner as provided for the Employer's contributions in Article V.

       Upon written notice to the Plan Administrator, a Participant shall be entitled to withdraw at any time the lesser of the aggregate amount of such voluntary contributions or the current value of such voluntary contributions. Any earnings and gains on such contributions cannot be withdrawn or distributed until the Participant's death, disability, retirement or termination. The Participant shall be fully vested and have a nonforfeitable interest in the value of his voluntary contributions at all times. In determining the benefits or interest of any Participant or Beneficiary under this Plan, no account shall be taken of any amounts attributable to the Participant's voluntary contributions and any such amounts shall be in addition to the benfits or interest of the Participant or Beneficiary as otherwise determined.

       3.03 The Trustees may receive and invest the assets from any other plan previously maintained by the Employer or other entity so long as each Participant would (if the prior plan terminated) receive a benefit immediately after the receipt of the assets from the prior plan equal to or greater than the benefit he would have been entitled to receive before the receipt of the assets from the prior plan. Such amounts shall be held for the benefit of the Participant but shall be accounted for separately in an individual account maintained for him. All such amounts shall be fully vested and shall be paid to the Participant in the manner he elects at his retirement, termination or death.

3.04 The Trustees may receive and invest any amounts received by a Participant from a qualified plan, either directly within the time prescribed by law for such rollover or through an individual retirement account or individual retirement annuity. The foregoing notwithstanding, in no event shall the Trustees receive and invest any amounts which at any time were accumulated under a plan which provided benefits for persons defined in Code Section 401(c)(1). Such amounts shall be held for the benefit of the Participant but shall be accounted for separately in an individual account maintained for him. All such rollover amounts shall be fully vested and shall be paid to the Participant in the manner he elects at his retirement, termination or death.

3.05 The Trustees may, at the election of a terminated Active Participant, pay the value of the Participant's Vested Interest to the Trustees of the Qualified Plan of the Participant's successor employer, provided such plan is authorized to receive such rollover amounts, or to a Qualified Individual Retirement Account.

3.06 Any forfeitures occasioned by the termination of an Active Participant who was not fully vested shall be used to reduce Employer Contributions required under this section. If the amount of such forfeitures exceeds the contributions required for the year, then the excess shall be used to reduce employer contributions in the next succeeding Plan Year.

Article IV
Benefits

4.01 Each participant shall be entitled to receive a retirement benefit commencing at his Normal Retirement Date determined in accordance with the normal retirement benefit formula designated in the Adoption Agreement with the following limitations:

(a)   to avoid duplication of benefits, if any participant ceases to be employed for any reason other than retirement and is reemployed, his retirement benefit as a new participant shall be reduced by any benefit vested in him on account of his previous participation in the plan;

(b) no participant may receive a retirement benefit more than the lesser of:

(i) $98,100 (or such larger amount as may be prescribed by the Secretary of the Treasury or his delegate); or

(ii) 100% of the Participant's average compensation over the five plan years preceding retirement.

Notwithstanding the foregoing, the limitation described in Article 4.01(b) shall be deemed satisfied as to any participant if the Annual Benefit otherwise payable under this plan to such participant does not exceed $1,000 multiplied by such participant's Years of Service (not to exceed 10) with the Employer.

The Normal Retirement Benefit designed in the Adoption Agreement shall be adjusted to the actuarial equivalent (using the 1971 Group Annuity Table, 6% Interest) of the normal retirement benefit under either of the following cases:

(i) if the Participant selects an optional form of distribution other than the Normal Form of Retirement Benefit as selected in the Adoption Agreement; or

(ii) if retirement is earlier than age 55.

4.02 If the Employer also maintains a qualified defined contribution plan, then the sum of the fractions provided under each plan for any participant may not exceed 1.4, determined as follows:

(a) Defined Benefit Fraction:

$$\frac{\text{projected annual benefit of the participant under the plan for the current year}}{\text{projected annual benefit of the participant under the plan if the plan provided for maximum benefit allowable under Article 4.01(b)}} = X$$

(b) Defined Contribution Fraction:

$$\frac{\text{sum of the annual additions to the participant's account for the current year under all defined contribution plans}}{\text{sum of the maximum amount of annual additions to the participant's account which could have been made under Section 4.02(c)(i) for the current and each prior year of service with the employer}} = Y$$

X plus Y may not exceed 1.4

(c) For purposes of Section 4.02(b), the following definitions shall apply:

  (i) Maximum Amount—for a limitation year, the maximum permissible amount with respect to any participant shall be the lesser of (1) $32,700 (or such larger amount as may be prescribed by the Secretary of the Treasury or his delegate) or (2) 25 percent of his compensation for the limitation year.

  (ii) Annual Additions—with respect to any participant, an annual addition shall be the sum for the limitation year, of (1) all employer contributions allocated to his account; (2) all forfeitures allocated to his account; and (3) the lesser of (i) one-half of the employee contributions allocated to his acount, or (ii) the amount of employee contributions allocated to his account in excess of 6 percent of his compensation for the limitation year.

In the event that the sum of the aforesaid fractions for any participant does exceed 1.4 then the Employer shall cause said sum to be reduced to 1.4 by reduction of the Annual Additions applicable to the participant under the qualified defined contribution plan.

4.03 For purposes of this Article, "Employer" means the employer that adopts this Plan. In the case of a group of employers which constitutes a controlled group of corporations [as defined in

Section 414(b) of the Internal Revenue Code as modified by Section 415(h)] or which constitutes trades or businesses (whether or not incorporated) which are under common control [as defined in Section 414(c) as modified by Section 415(h)], all such employers shall be considered a single employer for purposes of applying the limitations of this Article.

4.04 A participant may withdraw from his voluntary account an amount not to exceed the lesser of the amount of voluntary contributions, or the value of his account, made under Section 3.02 at any time. Such a withdrawal, however, shall prevent such participant from making further voluntary contributions during the 2 plan years succeeding the date of withdrawal.

4.05 A participant who is married and

(a) begins to receive payments under the plan on or after his Normal Retirement Date; or

(b) dies on or after his Normal Retirement Date while still employed by the Employer; or

(c) begins to receive payments on or after the Qualified Early Retirement Age; or

(d) terminates employment on or after his Normal Retirement Date (or the Qualified Early Retirement Age) and after satisfying the eligibility requirements for the payment of benefits under the Plan and thereafter dies before beginning to receive such benefits;

shall receive payments under this Plan in the form of a Joint and Survivor Annuity, unless the Participant has elected otherwise during the election period which shall begin on the Participant's Entry Date and ends on the date benefits commence. Any election hereunder shall be in writing and may be changed at any time.

The Qualified Early Retirement Age shall be the latest of:

(a) The early retirement date under the plan as designated in the Adoption Agreement; or

(b) the first day of the 120th month beginning before the Participant's Normal Retirement Date; or

(c) the Participant's Entry Date.

4.06 A Participant who is employed after attaining the Qualified Early Retirement Age shall be given the opportunity to elect, during the election-period, to have a survivor annuity payable upon his death. If the Participant elects the survivor annuity, payment under such annuity shall be the greater of:

(a) the survivor annuity provided under the Joint and Survivor Annuity, or

(b) the death benefit otherwise payable under the Plan.

Any election under this provision shall be in writing and may be changed at any time. The election period shall begin on the later of (1) the 90th day before the Participant attains the Qualified Early Retirement Age, or (2) his Entry Date, and ends on the date the Participant terminates employment.

4.07 The normal form of Retirement Benefit under this Plan shall be as designated in the Adoption Agreement unless the Participant elects an optional form of distribution as provided in this Article 4.07, or a Joint and Survivor Annuity is elected, or is mandatory as provided in Article 4.05 and the Participant has not elected otherwise. With the approval of the Plan Administrator, a Participant may elect in writing an optional form of distribution other than either the normal form of distribution or the Joint and Survivor Annuity. When considering the election, the Plan Administrator shall act in a consistent and nondiscriminatory manner, treating Participants in similar circumstances in a similar manner.

The optional forms of distribution that may be elected by the Participant are as follows:

(a) A lump sum cash distribution;

(b) A distribution of a non-transferable annuity contract;

(c) A distribution of any combination of the above over 2 taxable years, with the annual installments elected by the participant or his beneficiary.

However, no Participant shall make an election the effect of which would be to have all or part of his nonforfeitable interest paid only to his designated Beneficiary after his death if such interest would otherwise have become available to the Participant during his lifetime. This limitation shall not prevent the election of an annuity or an annuity for life with survivorship, refund or period certain options provided that (1) the certain period does not extend beyond the normal life expectancy of the Participant or the Participant and his spouse, and (2) the present value of the payments to be made to the Participant during his normal life expectancy exceeds 50% of the present value of the total payments expected to be made under the form of distribution elected. No elections shall be made for the periodic payments of interest and the deferred payment of principal after a Participant has actually retired. Any optional form of payment of benefits must be the actuarial equivalent of the Normal Form of Retirement Benefit elected in the Adoption Agreement.

4.08 Unless otherwise elected by the Participant in writing, payment of benefits to the Participant must begin not later than the 60th day after the close of the Plan Year in which the latest of the following occur:

(a) he attains Age 65;

(b) he completes ten years of participation in the Plan; or

(c) he terminates his employment with the Employer.

4.09 If the Employer has designated in the Adoption Agreement requirements for early retirement, each Participant who meets such requirements may elect to retire on any date thereafter which is prior to his Normal Retirement Date. Each Participant who retires on an early retirement date shall be entitled to receive a monthly retirement benefit commencing on his Normal Retirement Date in an amount equal to his Accrued Benefit as of his early retirement date. In lieu of such benefit, the Participant may elect, by written notice to the Plan Administrator, that his monthly retirement benefit commence at some time on or after his early retirement date but not later than his Normal Retirement Date in which event such monthly retirement benefit shall be equal to his Accrued Benefit as of his early retirement date, reduced by 1/15 for each of the first five years, 1/30 for each of the next five years and reduced actuarially for each additional year by which the starting date of his retirement benefit precedes his Normal Retirement Age.

4.10 A Participant may, with the consent of the Employer, postpone his actual retirement to some date after his Normal Retirement Date. A Participant shall be entitled to actual retirement on the first day of any month thereafter upon at least 15 days' written notice to the Plan Administrator and the Employer. The Employer may, by giving not less than 15 days' written notice to the Plan Administrator and Participant, withdraw its consent to further postponement of the actual retirement of a Participant in which event such Participant's actual retirement shall be on the first day of the month following the expiration of the 15 day period. Payment of the Participant's monthly retirement benefit will be postponed until he actually retires and shall be in an amount determined in accordance with the designation in the Adoption Agreement.

4.11 A Participant whose employment is terminated due to disability shall receive the present value of his accrued benefit in a lump sum cash distribution or non-transferable annuity contract not later than 60 days after the close of the Plan Year in which disability occurs. Any disability benefit payable under this section shall be subject to the same reductions as provided for early retirement under Section 4.09.

4.12 In the event of the death of a Participant, his beneficiary shall be entitled to a benefit equal to either (a) or (b), whichever shall be applicable, where

(a) is any death benefits payable under any contract of life insurance on the life of the Participant issued pursuant to Section 5.08 hereof plus any post mortem dividends; and

(b) is, in the absence of any contract of life insurance on the life of the participant an amount equal to the present value of any "side fund" or "fund offset" maintained for the Participant pursuant to the actuarial method employed by the enrolled actuary to satisfy the Funding Standard Account Requirements of ERISA.

Benefits under this Section shall be payable as a lump sum unless the Participant's Beneficiary elects an alternate mode of distribution under Article 4.07.

4.13 Upon Separation of Service, a Participant will presumptively incur a break-in-service and will be entitled to receive the Present Value vested accrued benefit in a lump sum within 60 days following the close of the plan year in which the separation occurs. In the event that the Employee is reemployed before a break-in-service actually occurs, and he repays to the Trustees the amount previously distributed to him, plus 5% interest for the period commencing upon distribution and ending upon repayment, then the employee's full benefits under the plan will be reinstated. If the employee is reemployed after a break-in-service he shall have the same repayment option described above and his benefits under the plan shall be either:

(a) if repayment is not made, then the participant's retirement benefits shall be reduced by the actuarial equivalent of the normal retirement benefit that could have been provided by the amount distributed on the prior termination; or

(b) if repayment is made, then the participant's full benefits under the plan will be reinstated.

Whether a reemployed participant's benefits are reinstated or not pursuant to Articles 4.13(a) or (b) above, no credit shall be given under this plan for purposes of benefit accrual for any full plan year during which a break-in-service occurred.

Subject to the provisions of this Article IV a terminated Participant who is reemployed shall receive full credit for each Year of Service before any Break-in-Service for purposes of vesting.

The foregoing notwithstanding, if the Present Value of the vested accrued benefit exceeds $1,750, the distribution can only be made with the consent of the Participant.

4.14 Subject to the provisions hereof limiting the benefits of the 25 most highly compensated Employees whose annual benefit exceeds $1,500, but notwithstanding any other provisions hereof, upon the complete or partial termination of this Plan and Trust, the rights of each Participant to his Accrued Benefit as of the date of such complete or partial termination shall become nonforfeitable.

Article V
Provisions Relating To The Trust And Trustees

5.01 The Employer has established a Trust Fund under the terms of this Plan with the Trustee to hold the funds necessary to provide the benefits set forth in this Plan.

The Trust Fund shall be received, held in trust, and disbursed by the Trustee in accordance with the provisions of the Trust Agreement and this Plan. No part of the Trust Fund shall be used for or diverted to purposes other than for the exclusive benefit of Participants, retired Participants, disabled Participants, or their Beneficiaries under this Plan. No person shall have any interest in, or right to, the Trust Fund or any part thereof, except as specifically provided for in this Plan and/or the Trust Agreement.

5.02 The Employer may remove the Trustee at any time upon the notice required by the terms of the Trust Agreement, and upon such removal or upon the resignation of a Trustee, the Employer shall appoint a successor Trustee.

5.03 The Trustee shall have the power to invest and reinvest the Trust Fund and shall serve as "Investment Manager" of the Plan as provided in ERISA. Such investments and reinvestments may include, but not be limited to the following: any type of security including but not necessarily limited to, common stocks or preferred stocks; open-end or closed-end mutual funds; corporate bonds, debentures, convertible debentures, commercial paper; bankers' notes and bonds; improved or unimproved real estate located in the United States; participations in any common trust fund or commingled fund for the investment of Qualified Pension and Profit Sharing Plan Assets which may be established and maintained from time to time by a bank which might become a party to this agreement; and to lend the funds of the Trust to others, except as prohibited by ERISA or the provisions of the Plan, upon receipt of adequate security, including chattel mortages, first and second loan deeds, at a reasonable rate of interest. Such loans may be made to parties in interest as defined by ERISA Section 4975.

The Trustees shall have full power to do all such acts, take all such proceedings and exercise all such rights and privileges, whether herein specifically referred to or not, as could be done, taken or exercised by the absolute owner thereof, including, but without in any way limiting or impairing the generality of the foregoing, the following powers and authority:

(a) To retain the same for such period of time as the Trustee in its sole discretion shall deem prudent;

(b) To sell the same, at either public or private sale, at such time or times and on such terms and conditions as the Trustee shall deem prudent;

(c) To consent to or participate in any plan for the reorganization, consolidation or merger of any corporation, the security of which is held in the Trust, and to pay any and all calls and assessments imposed upon the owners of such securities as a condition of their participating therein. In connection therewith, to consent to any contract, lease, mortgage, purchase or sale of property, by or between such corporation and any other corporation or person;

(d) To exercise or dispose of any right the Trustees may have as the holder of any security to convert the same into another or other securities, or to acquire any additional security or securities, to make any payments, to exchange any security or to do any other act with reference thereto which the Trustee may deem prudent;

(e) To deposit any security with any protective or reorganization committee, and to delegate to such committee such power and authority with relation thereto as the Trustee may deem prudent, and to agree to pay and to pay out of the Trust such portion of the expenses and compensation of such committee as the Trustees may deem proper;

(f) To renew or extend the time of payment of any obligation due or becoming due;

(g) To grant options to purchase any property;

(h) To compromise, arbitrate or otherwise adjust or settle claims in favor of or against the Trust, and to deliver or accept in either total or partial satisfaction of any indebtedness or other obligation any property, and to continue to hold same for such period of time as the Trustees may deem appropriate;

(i)   To exchange any property for other property upon such terms and conditions as the Trustees may deem proper, and to give and receive money to effect equality in price;

(j)   To execute and deliver any proxies or powers of attorney to such person or persons as the Trustees may deem proper, granting to such person such power and authority with relation to any property or securities at any time held for the Trust and the Trustees may deem proper;

(k)   To foreclose any obligation by judicial proceeding or otherwise;

(l)   To sue or defend in connection with any and all securities or property at any time received or held for the Trust, all costs and attorney's fees in connection therewith to be charged against the Trust;

(m)   To manage any real property in the same manner as if the Trustee were the absolute owner thereof;

(n)   To cause any securities held by the Trust to be registered and to carry any such securities in the name of a nominee or nominees;

(o)   To hold such portion of the Trust as the Trustees may deem necessary for the ordinary administration of the Trust and disbursement of funds as directed in Section 5.04 in cash, without liability for interest, by depositing the same in any bank, including a successor Trustee's bank, if any, subject to the rules and regulations governing such deposits, and without regard to the amount of any such deposits; and

(p)   To invest in life insurance contracts on the lives of key employees of the Employer, payable on death to the Trustees as beneficiaries. (Such insurance contracts shall be vested exclusively in the Trustees for the benefit of the Trust as a whole and shall not be distributed in kind to a Participant in satisfaction of any interest he may have in the Trust fund.)

5.04 Dealings with Plan Administrator: The Trustees shall, from time to time, on the written direction of the Plan Administrator, make distribution from the Trust to such persons, in such manner, in such amounts and for such purposes as may be specified in such directions. The Trustees shall be under no liability for any distribution made by it pursuant to the directions of the Plan Administrator, and shall be under no duty to make inquiry as to whether any distribution directed by the Plan Administrator is made pursuant to the provisions of the related Plan and this Section, except to the extent required of a prudent Co-fiduciary under ERISA. The Trustees shall not be liable for the proper application of any part of the Trust if distributions are made in accordance with the written directions of the Plan Administrator as herein provided, nor shall the Trustees be responsible for the adequacy of the Trust to meet and discharge any and all payments and liabilities under the related plan.

5.05 Prohibited Transactions: The Trustees shall not accept or act upon direction from the Plan Administrator or any other person to engage in a transaction known by the Trustees to be a "prohibited transaction" under ERISA. In the event of any uncertainty or dispute respecting any such proposed transaction, the Trustees shall not be required to act or be liable to any person for failing to act on such direction unless and until a final administrative or judicial determination shall be obtained by any person interested in such transaction and duly served upon the Trustees and the Trustees shall thereafter have had a reasonable opportunity to comply with such direction if it is determined to be lawful under the terms of the Plan and ERISA, in the opinion of legal counsel. The Trustees are hereby expressly authorized to engage in any transaction not expressly prohibited by ERISA or the terms of this Trust Agreement or the Plan, and properly directed by a Fiduciary with respect to the Plan.

5.06 Manner of Payment: The Trustees may make any payment required to be made by it hereunder, by mailing to the person or entity a check or delivering the property directed to be distributed by the Plan Administrator, at the last known address as may have last been furnished the Trustees.

5.07 Restriction on Exercise of Powers; Prudent Man Rule: The Trustees, Plan Administrator and all other Fiduciaries with respect to the Plan are required to discharge their duties solely in the interests of Participants and Beneficiaries, with the care, skill, prudence and diligence, under the circumstances then prevailing, that a prudent man acting in a like capacity and familiar with such matters would use in the conduct of an enterprise of like character and with like aims; by diversifying the investments so as to minimize the risk of large losses unless under the circumstances it is clearly prudent not to do so; and in accordance with the Plan, this Trust Agreement, the rules and directions of the Plan Administrator and the provisions of Title I of ERISA. Furthermore, the Trustees shall at all times consider the funding policy of this Plan and Trust which shall be the orderly and conservative accumulation of funds to provide Participants and their Beneficiaries under this Plan the benefits hereunder.

5.08 Life Insurance: As directed in writing by the Plan Administrator, the Trustees shall have the following powers and duties with respect to any life insurance policy held in Trust for the benefit of a Participant:

(a)   To apply in writing for insurance to be issued on the life of any insurable Participant in the Plan in an amount to be determined by the Plan Administrator, not to exceed 100 times the Participant's anticipated monthly normal retirement benefit. Any such policy shall be issued by any legal reserve life insurance company authorized to sell such policy in the state of issue and selected by the Plan Administrator. Each such policy shall be a contract between the insurer and the Trustees, and shall be held by the Trustees for the benefit of the insured Participant. Any other provision to the contrary notwithstanding, the Trustee shall convert the entire value of any life insurance contract held for the benefit of a Participant at or before such Participant's retirement into cash or shall provide periodic income so that no portion of such value may be used to continue life insurance protection beyond retirement, or shall distribute such contracts to the Participant.

(b)   To exercise all rights, options and benefits provided by any policy or permitted by any insurer with respect to any policy issued by it, including the right to change any provision which shall become inoperative upon the retirement of any Participant.

(c) To pay premiums on any policy held in the Trust; accumulate dividends and apply dividends in reduction of premiums. Any dividends payable with respect to any policy as to which there shall be no further premiums due shall be paid in cash to the Trustees and added to the Trust Fund.

(d) To name the beneficiary of any such policy and change such beneficiary from time to time and to select the method of settlement to be effective upon the maturity of any such policy and change any such method of settlement. No Participant shall have the right to direct the Trustees with respect to any of such matters without the consent of the Plan Administrator.

No insurance company which shall issue any policy, as hereinabove provided, shall be a party to this Trust Agreement. The liability of any such insurance company shall be only as provided in any policy which it may issue and such company shall not be considered a Named Fiduciary hereunder, provided, however, that if such insurance company shall undertake to invest Plan assets in an unallocated investment medium, such insurance company shall also be considered a Named Fiduciary hereunder.

In the event of any conflict between the terms of the Plan and any policy, the terms of the Plan shall control.

5.09 Third Parties: All persons dealing with the Trustee are released from inquiring into the decision or authority of the Trustees and from seeing to the application of any monies, securities or other property paid or delivered to the Trustees.

5.10 Co-Fiduciaries: Anything in the Trust Agreement or the Plan to the contrary notwithstanding, each Fiduciary with respect to the Plan acknowledges, by participating in the execution of this Plan and Trust Agreement or by consenting directly or indirectly, orally or in writing, to act as a Fiduciary with respect to the Plan, that he is responsible for carrying out his own duties in accordance with the standards set forth under ERISA and all regulations promulgated thereunder. Each Fiduciary shall be responsible for the actions or failure to act of all other Fiduciaries with respect to the Plan if he participates, approves, acquiesces in or conceals a breach committed by another such Fiduciary; or if his failure to exercise reasonable care in the administration of his own duties enables the breach to be committed. Each Fiduciary is required to act prudently in the delegation or allocation of responsibilities to other persons. In the event that there are Co-Trustees acting hereunder, each Trustee will be responsible for participating in the administration of the Plan and for exercising reasonable care to prevent the other from committing a breach. If the Plan or the Trust Agreement or any written rule or direction of the Plan Administrator shall by agreement allocate responsibilities among Co-Trustees, only the Trustee to whom the responsibilities are delegated will be responsible for the breach unless the other Trustee or Trustees knowingly participate therein. Nothing herein shall relieve any Trustee from his duty to conduct a periodic review to assure that delegated duties and responsibilities are being properly carried out by all persons to whom any such duties and responsibilities have been delegated. In the event that an Investment Manager other than a Trustee is appointed, pursuant to this Trust, no Trustees shall be liable for the acts or omissions of such Investment Manager, or under any obligation to invest or manage the assets of the Plan which are subject to management by an Investment Manager as such term is defined in ERISA Section 3(38). Nothing in the Plan or Trust Agreement shall be deemed to enlarge the responsibilities or liabilities of any Trustee or Co-Trustee or any other Fiduciary with respect to the Plan beyond those imposed by ERISA and all regulations promulgated thereunder.

5.11 General Records: The Trustees shall maintain accurate records and detailed accounts of all investments, receipts, disbursements and other transactions hereunder. Such records shall be available at all reasonable times for inspection by the Plan Administrator, the Employer or any Fiduciary, Participant or Beneficiary or authorized representative of such persons. The Trustees shall submit or cause to be submitted in a timely manner to the Plan Administrator such information as the Plan Administrator may reasonably require in connection with the preparation of the various reports required to be made in ERISA to various regulatory agencies and to Plan Participants and Beneficiaries. In the absence of fraud or bad faith, the valuation of the Trust by the Trustees shall be conclusive on all parties affected by this Trust.

5.12 Annual Accounting: Within sixty (60) days following the close of each Plan Year, the Trustees shall file with the Plan Administrator a written accounting setting forth a description of all property purchased and sold and all receipts, disbursements, and other transactions effected by it at the end of such period and such list shall include a valuation of each asset at its fair market value as determined at the close of the Plan Year. The Plan Administrator may approve such accounting by written notice of approval delivered to the Trustees or by failure to object in writing to the Trustees within sixty (60) days from the date upon which the account was delivered to the Plan Administrator. Upon receipt of written approval of the account, or upon passage of said period of time without written objections having been delivered to the Trustees, such accounting shall be deemed to be approved and the Trustees shall be released and discharged as to all items, matters and things set forth in such accounting as if such accounting had been settled and allowed by a decree of a court of competent jurisdiction.

5.13 Agents: The Employer or the Plan Administrator, or both, at any time may employ any person or entity as an agent to perform any act, keep any records or accounts or make computations which are required of them under the Code or ERISA. Such employment shall not be deemed to be contrary to or inconsistent with the provisions of this Trust Agreement. Nothing done by such person or corporation as agent for the Employer or the Plan Administrator shall change or increase in any manner the responsibility or liability of the Trustee hereunder, unless such agent shall be deemed to be a Fiduciary with respect to the Plan, and the Trustees shall have failed to meet the standards imposed by Section 5.07 and 5.10 hereof.

5.14 Resignation or Removal of the Trustees: The Trustees may resign or may be removed by the Employer. The resignation or removal shall be effective thirty (30) days after receipt of written notice of such resignation or removal. Upon such resignation or removal, Employer shall appoint a Successor Trustee to whom the resigning or removed Trustees shall transfer all of the assets of the Trust Fund then held by it as expeditiously as possible. Such Successor Trustee shall thereupon succeed to all of the powers and duties given to the Trustee by this Trust

Agreement. Within sixty (60) days of such transfer of the Trust assets, the resigning or removed Trustee shall render to the Employer an accounting in the form and manner prescribed in Section 5.11. Unless Employer shall within sixty (60) days after the receipt of such accounting file with the resigning or removed Trustees written objections thereto, the accounting shall be deemed to have been approved, and the resigning or removed Trustees shall be released and discharged as to all items, matters and things set forth in such accounting, as if such accounting had been settled and allowed by a decree of a court of competent jurisdiction subject, however, to the rights of participating Employees or Beneficiaries to appropriate notice as provided in Section 104(b) of ERISA.

5.15 Taxes: The Trustees shall deduct from and charge against the Trust Fund any taxes paid by it which may be imposed upon the Trust Fund or income thereon which the Trustees are required to pay with respect to the interest of any person therein. The Trustees are not authorized to pay any excise or other tax levied upon any disqualified person imposed by reason of such person's engagement in any prohibited transaction. The Trustees are also not authorized to purchase any errors and omissions insurance for Fiduciaries not permitted by Section 410(b)(3) of ERISA.

5.16 Trustees' Compensation: Employer shall pay to the Trustee reasonable compensation for its services as Trustees hereunder at the rate to be agreed upon from time to time and reimburse the Trustees for their reasonable expenses. The Trustees shall have a lien on the Trust Fund for such compensation and for any reasonable expenses, including the attorney's fees and the same may be withdrawn from the Trust Fund if not paid within a reasonable time by the Employer. No compensation (other than reasonable expenses) shall be paid to a Trustee who is a full-time employee of the Employer.

5.17 Spendthrift Provision: No Participant or Beneficiary entitled to any benefits under this Trust Agreement shall have any right to assign, pledge, transfer, hypothecate, encumber, commute or anticipate his interest in any benefits under this Trust. Such benefits shall not in any way be subject to any legal process or levy of execution or attachment or garnishment proceedings in connection with the payment of any claim against any such person.

Article VI
Claims Procedure

6.01 A Plan Participant or Beneficiary shall make a claim for Plan Benefits by filing a written request with the Plan Administrator upon a form to be furnished to him for such purpose.

6.02 If a claim is wholly or partially denied, the Plan Administrator shall furnish the Participant or Beneficiary with written notice of the denial within sixty (60) days of the date the original claim was filed. This note of denial shall provide (1) the reason for denial, (2) specific reference to pertinent plan provisions on which the denial is based, (3) a description of any additional information needed to perfect the claim and an explanation of why such information is necessary, and (4) an explanation of the Plan's Claim Procedure.

6.03 The Participant or Beneficiary shall have sixty (60) days from receipt of denial notice in which to make written application for review by the Plan Administrator. The Participant or Beneficiary may request that the review be in the nature of a hearing. The participant or Beneficiary shall have the rights (1) to representation, (2) to review pertinent documents, and (3) to submit comments in writing.

6.04 The Plan Administrator shall issue a decision in writing on such review within sixty (60) days after receipt of an application for review as provided in Section 6.03.

Article VII
The Plan Administrator

7.01 The Plan Administrator as named in the Adoption Agreement, will administer the Plan, keep records, and notify Participants and Beneficiaries annually of the amount of their benefit. The Plan Administrator may name a delegate to act on its behalf for performance of routine duties.

The Plan Administrator shall serve until his resignation or dismissal by the Employer and a vacancy shall be filled in the same manner as the original appointment. No compensation shall be paid to the Plan Administrator from the Trust Fund for his services. The Plan Administrator shall keep a permanent record of his actions with respect to the Plan which shall be available for inspection by appropriate parties as provided in the Code and ERISA. The Plan Administrator or his delegate shall be entitled to reasonable compensation which shall be paid by the Employer. However, no compensation will be paid to the Employer if he is acting as the Plan Administrator.

7.02 Subject to the limitations of the Plan, the Plan Administrator shall from time to time establish rules for the administration of the Plan and transaction of its business. The records of the Employer, as certified to the Plan Administrator, shall be conclusive with respect to any and all factual matters dealing with the employment of a Participant. The Plan Administrator shall interpret the Plan and shall determine all questions in the administration, interpretation, and application of the Plan, and all such determinations by the Plan Administrator shall be conclusive and binding on all persons subject, however, to the provisions of the Code and ERISA.

7.03 The Plan Administrator shall direct the Trustee in writing to make payments from the Trust Fund to Participants who qualify for such payments hereunder. Such written order to the Trustee shall specify the name of the Participant, his Social Security number, his address, and the amount and frequency of such payments.

7.04 the Plan Administrator shall not take action to direct the Trustee to take any action with respect to any of the benefits provided hereunder or otherwise in pursuance of the powers conferred herein upon the Plan Administrator which would be discriminatory in favor of Participants who are officers, shareholders or highly compensated employees, or which would result in benefiting one Participant, or group of Participants, at the expense of another or in discrimination between Participants similarly situated or in the application of different rules to substantially similar sets of facts.

7.05 The Trustee may request instructions in writing from the Plan Administrator on any matters affecting the Trust and may rely and act thereon.

7.06 The Plan Administrator shall be responsible for the determination of benefits, and the Trustee need not segregate accounts either among Participants or among Employers for investment purposes.

Article VIII
Prevention of Discrimination On Early Termination

8.01 Notwithstanding any provisions hereof to the contrary, during the first ten years after the Effective Date or during a period in which the full current costs of the Plan for the first ten years after the Effective Date have not been met, the benefits provided by the Employer contributions for Participants whose annual benefits provided by such contributions will exceed $1,500 but applicable only to the twenty-five highest paid Employees as of the time of establishment of this Trust (including any Employees who are not Participants at that time but may later become Participants) shall be subject to the following conditions:

(a) Such benefits shall be paid in full which have been provided by the Employer's contributions not exceeding the larger of the following amounts: (1) $20,000; or (2) an amount equal to 20% of the first $50,000 of the Participant's average regular annual compensation multiplied by the number of years between the date of establishment of the Plan and (a) the date of the termination of the Plan or (b) the date on which benefits become payable to the Participant, if such date precedes the date of termination of the Plan, or (c) the date of the failure to meet the full current costs of the Plan.

(b) If the Plan is terminated within ten years after the Effective Date or terminated during a period in which the full current costs of the Plan for the first ten years have not been met, the benefits which any of the Participants described in the first paragraph of this Article 8.01 may receive from the Employer's contributions shall not exceed the benefits set forth in paragraph (a) above. Any distribution under this Article shall be subject to the provisions for adequate security for repayment as provided under Revenue Ruling 61-10.

(c) If a Participant described in the first paragraph of this Article 8.01 leaves the employ of the Employer or withdraws from participation in the Plan when the full current costs have been met, the benefits which he may receive from the Employer's contributions shall not at any time, within the first ten years after the Effective Date, exceed the benefits set forth in paragraph (a) above.

(d) These conditions shall not restrict the full payment of any insurance, death or survivor's benefit on behalf of a Participant who dies while the Plan is in full effect and its full current costs have been met.

(e) These conditions shall not restrict the current payment of full retirement benefits called for by the Plan for any retired Participant while the Plan is in full effect and its full current costs have been met.

(f) In the event of the termination of the Plan within ten years after the Effective Date, distributions to then unretired Participants other than the Participants described in the first paragraph of this Article 8.01 shall be made in accordance with Article 4.07.

(g) If the Plan has been amended so as to increase substantially the extent of possible discrimination as to contributions and as to benefits actually payable in event of the subsequent termination of the Plan or the subsequent discontinuance of contributions thereunder, then the provisions of this Article 8.01 shall be applied to the Plan as so amended, with respect to the increased contributions or benefits resulting from such amendment, as if it were a new plan established on the date of such amendment.

Article IX
Termination of Plan

9.01 While it is the intention of the Employer that this Plan shall be permanent, the Employer reserves the right to terminate it. Termination shall be effective upon receipt by the Trustees of a written instrument of termination signed by the Employer.

9.02 In the event that the Employer is declared bankrupt or insolvent, dissolved or merger or consolidation with another entity, and no provisions for the continuation of the Plan is made, the Plan shall terminate.

9.03 Upon termination or partial termination of the Plan, each Participant whose interests are affected shall have a nonforfeitable interest in his entire Accrued Benefit.

9.04 Upon termination of the Plan the Trustees shall distribute to each Participant the total value of his Accrued Benefit in any manner described in Section 4.07 or transfer any assets held in trust for the Participant to a successor trust.

Article X
Amendment of Plan

10.01 Except as provided in Section 11.01, this Plan may be amended by the sponsoring organization in writing at any time. The employer may amend any option in the Adoption Agreement. An amendment may not increase the duties of Trustees without their written consent nor may it reduce the vested interest of any Participant or Beneficiary.

10.02 Any amendment necessary for the qualification of the Plan under the Code or necessary to meet the requirements of any other applicable law may be made without regard to the limitation of Sections 10.01 or 11.01.

10.03 Neither the consent of any Participant nor any other payee is required for any amendment to the Plan.

10.04 Any amendment to the Plan which alters the vesting schedule of the Plan shall not reduce the Vested Accrued Benefit of any Participant on the effective date or adoption date of such amendment.

10.05 In the event the vesting schedule of this Plan is amended or the vesting schedule of any preceding Plan is amended by adoption of this amendment and restatement, any Participant who has completed at least five (5) Years of Service, may elect to have his vested interest in Employer Contributions determined without regard to such amendment by notifying the Plan Administrator in writing during the election period as hereafter defined. The election period shall begin on the date such amendment is adopted and shall end no earlier than the latest of the following dates:

(a) the date which is 60 days after the date the amendment is adopted;

(b) the date which is 60 days after the date the plan amendment becomes effective; or

(c) the date which is 60 days after the date the Participant is issued written notice of the amendment by the Employer or Plan Administrator. Such election shall be available only to an individual who is a Participant at the time such election is made and such election shall be irrevocable.

10.06 If the Employer amends any provision of the Trust other than an elective provision, said amendment shall terminate the Employer's status as a participating Employer under a Prototype Plan approved as to form by the Internal Revenue Service. This agreement including any amendments thereto shall then be considered as "individually designed plan" as referred to in Section 7.06 of Revenue Procedure 72-8, I.R.B. 1972-1.

10.07 Future Planning Associates, Inc., as the sponsoring organization has the authority to amend this Prototype in order to conform to any applicable law, regulation, ruling or procedure including Revenue Procedure 72-8, I.R.B. 1972-1 or any future similar procedure. Furthermore, Future Planning Associates, Inc. as the sponsoring organization has the authority to amend this Prototype in order to include additional elective provisions in Prototype Plans under Revenue Procedure 72-8 or any future similar procedure. Future Planning Associates, Inc. as the sponsoring organization shall not, however, have any duty to exercise the authority granted to it by this paragraph.

10.08 Each Employer who adopts this Prototype prior to the execution of any amendment referred to in paragraph 10.07 shall be deemed to have consented to such amendment and furthermore, shall be deemed to have delegated the authority to Future Planning Associates, Inc. as the sponsoring organization to execute such amendment.

Article XI
Miscellaneous Provisions

11.01 Prior to the satisfaction of all liabilities with respect to Participants and Beneficiaries, no part of the corpus or income shall revert to the Employer or be used for or diverted to any purpose other than the exclusive benefit of Participants and Beneficiaries. This section may not be altered or amended.

11.02 No Employee of the Employer nor anyone else shall have any rights whatsoever against the Employer or the Trustee(s) as a result of this agreement except those expressly granted to them hereunder, or under any applicable law. Nothing herein shall be construed to give any Participant the right to remain an Employee of the Employer.

11.03 For purposes of this agreement, the masculine shall be read for the feminine and the singular shall be read for the plural, whenever the person or context shall plainly so require.

11.04 Subject to the provisions herein contained with respect to earlier termination, the Trust created hereunder shall continue in existence for the longest period permitted by law.

11.05 In case any provisions of this agreement shall be held illegal or invalid for any reason, said illegality shall be construed and enforced as if said illegal and invalid provisions had never been inserted therein.

11.06 In the event of any merger or consolidation with, or transfer of assets or liabilities to, any other plan, each Participant shall be entitled to receive a benefit immediately after the merger, consolidation or transfer if the plan were then terminated, which is at least equal to the benefit he would have been entitled to receive immediately before the merger, consolidation or transfer if the plan had then terminated.

11.07 Any contribution or part thereof which is made by the Employer by a mistake of fact as defined in section 403(c)(2)(A) of ERISA, may be returned to the Employer within one year after the payment of the contribution.

11.08 Each contribution to the Plan is contingent upon the continued qualification of the Plan under Section 401(a) of the Code and upon the deductibility of the contribution under Section

404 of the Code. Upon denial of qualification, all contributions made by the Employer within the year preceding the date of denial shall be repaid to the Employer. Contributions for which deductions are disallowed shall be repaid to the Employer to the extent deductions are disallowed.

11.09 The Employer shall submit the Plan to the appropriate office of the Internal Revenue Service for an initial letter of determination within a reasonable time after the Plan is adopted. Prior to the issuance of a letter of determination stating that the Plan meets the requirements of section 401(a) of the Code, no Participant shall have a nonforfeitable right to any Employer contributions. If such a letter of determination is not obtained the Employer may recover all amounts held in trust attributable to Employer contributions, and the Plan shall terminate. The value of any Employee contributions shall be returned to the Participant upon termination of the Plan.

11.10 The Employer shall notify each Employee and other person who is an Interested Party within the meaning of section 747(b)(1) of the Code of any request for a letter of determination, in a manner consistent with section 7476 of the Code.

11.11 Failure to retain qualification of the Trust under section 401(a) of the code shall terminate the Employer's status as a participating Employer under a Prototype Plan approved as to form by the Internal Revenue Service.

11.12 Payments to Minors, etc. In making any distribution to or for the benefit of any minor or incompetent Beneficiary, or any other Beneficiary who, in the opinion of the Plan Administrator, is incapable of properly using, expending, investing or otherwise disposing such distribution, then the Plan Administrator, in his sole, absolute and uncontrolled discretion may, but need not, order the Trustee to make such distribution to a legal or natural guardian or other relative of such minor or court appointed committee of any incompetent, or to any adult with whom such person temporarily or permanently resides; and any such guardian, committee, relative or other person shall have full authority and discretion to expend such distribution for the use and benefit of such person; and the receipt of such guardian, committee, relative or other person shall be on a complete discharge to the Trustee, without any responsibility on its part or on the part of the Plan Administrator to see to the application thereof.

11.13 Unclaimed Benefits: Any benefits payable, to or on behalf of, a Participant or former Participant or beneficiary which are not claimed shall not bear interest, but shall be deemed abandoned and relinquished only if such person cannot be located after reasonable efforts at the time of payments of such benefits become due. If, subsequent to relinquishment, the Participant, former Participant or Beneficiary to whom payment is due shall make valid claim for his benefits under the Plan, then these benefits shall be reinstated and distributed to said Participant in accordance with the provisions of this Plan.

11.14 Governing Law: This Plan shall be administered in the United States of America, and its validity, construction and all rights hereunder shall be governed by the laws of the United States under ERISA. To the extent that ERISA shall not be held to have pre-empted local law, the Plan shall be administered under the laws of the state in which the Plan is adopted. If any provision of the Plan shall be held invalid or unenforceable, the remaining provisions hereof shall continue to be fully effective.

11.15 Indemnification: The Employer hereby agrees to indemnify the Plan Administrator and any other Employee of the Employer to the full extent of any expenses, penalties, damages or the pecuniary loss which such Employee or Plan Administrator may suffer as a result of his responsibilities, obligations or duties in connection with the Plan or fiduciary activities actually performed in connection with the Plan. Such indemnification shall be paid by the Employer to the Employee or the Plan Administrator to the extent that fiduciary liability insurance is not available to cover the payment of such items, but in no event shall such items be paid out of Plan assets.

Notwithstanding the foregoing, this indemnification agreement shall not relieve any Employee or Plan Administrator serving in a fiduciary capacity of his fiduciary responsibilities and liabilities to the Plan for breached of fiduciary obligations, nor shall this agreement violate any provision of Part 4 of Title I of ERISA as it may be interpreted from time to time by the U.S. Department of Labor and any courts of competent jurisdiction.

11.16 Employees of Controlled Groups: Except as provided in Section 4.03 of Article IV, all Employees of all corporations which are members of a controlled group of corporations as defined in Section 414(b) of the Code and all Employees of all trades or businesses (whether or not incorporated) which are under common control [as defined in Section 414(c)] shall be treated as employed by a single Employer.

FUTURE PLANNING ASSOCIATES, INC.
CORPORATE PROTOTYPE PENSION PLAN NO. 1
(DEFINED BENEFIT)
APPROVAL DATE: SERIES NUMBER:
ADOPTION AGREEMENT
FLAT BENEFIT INTEGRATED PENSION PLAN

Whereas the Employer desires to:
□ establish a pension plan and trust; or
□ restate in its entirety its existing plan and trust for the purpose of providing pension benefits for its eligible Employees in accordance with the terms and conditions set forth herein, and

Whereas, the Board of Directors of the Employer has approved and adopted the plan embodied herein,

Now, Therefore, in consideration of mutual covenants herein contained it is agreed by and between the Employer and the Trustees as follows:

(1) Employer Name (Article 1.05): _____
     Address: _____   Tax ID #: _____
                                      Phone #: (   ) _____
(2) Name of Plan (Article 1.29); _____
(3) Predecessor Plan (Article 1.33): _____
(4) Predecessor Employer (Article 1.32): _____
(5) Name of Trustees (Article 1.35): _____
(6) Name of Plan Administrator (Article 1.30): _____
     Authorized Delegate of Plan Administrator: _____

(7) (A) If this is a restatement of an existing Plan and/or Trust in its entirety

    (1) The original effective date of the Plan and/or Trust was: _____

    (2) The effective new date of the restatement is:

_____

(B) If this is a new Plan and Trust, the effective date is:

_____

(8) The Plan Year (Article 1.31) is: _____

(9) The Entry Date (Article 1.17) is: _____

(10) Eligibility Provisions (Article II)

    (A) Eligible Classes

        ☐ All employees

        ☐ All employees except those:

            ☐ compensated on an hourly basis

            ☐ compensated on a salaried basis

            ☐ whose employment is covered by a collective bargaining agreement under which retirement benefits were the subject of good faith bargaining between the Employer and the collective bargaining agent.

            ☐ other _____

(10) (B) Service with Predecessor Employer (Article 2.09):

    ☐ If the Predecessor Employer was not a corporation, Years of Service under this Plan shall include service with the Predecessor Employer as a partner or sole proprietor.

    ☐ If the Predecessor Employer did not maintain a Plan or maintained a Plan that has been terminated, Years of Service under this Plan shall include service with the Predecessor Employer.

(10) (C) Participation of Eligible Employees

    ☐ An Employee will be eligible to participate in the plan on the Entry Date nearest, forward or backward to the completion of one Year of Service and attainment of age   (not to exceed 25).

    ☐ An Employee shall be eligible to participate in the Plan on the Entry Date preceding the date the Employee completes the later of   Years of

Service (not to exceed 3. If more than one Year of Service is required, 100% immediate vesting must be elected); or attainment of age   (not to exceed 25).

☐ An Employee hired within   (not to exceed 5) years of his Normal Retirement Age when first employed by the Employer shall not be eligible to participate. *NOTE:* DO NOT CHECK THIS BOX IF YOU ALSO CHECK BOX (11)(B).

(11) Normal Retirement Age (Article 1.25):
   (a) ☐ Age   (not less than 55 or more than 65)
   (b) ☐ Age   or the   Anniversary of the time he commenced participation in this Plan, whichever is later (not less than age 55 or more than 70 or more than the 10th anniversary of the time he commenced participation in this Plan).

(12) Annual Pay (Article 1.05):
   ☐ Total Annual Pay (Must be selected for an integrated plan.)
   ☐ Annual Pay, Excluding
      ☐ Bonuses
      ☐ Overtime
      ☐ Commissions

(13) Early Retirement Requirements (Article IV):
   To retire prior to his Normal Retirement Age, a Participant must meet the following requirements: (Check and complete all requirements which apply.)
      ☐ Minimum Age of   . (Not less than 50.)
      ☐ Completion of   Years of Service. (Not more than the maximum number of Years of Service for 100% vesting.)
      ☐ Completion of   Years of Participation. (Not more than 10.)
      ☐ No provision for early retirement is made under the Plan.

(14) Deferred Retirement (Article IV):
   ☐ No further benefits accrue after a Participant's Normal Retirement Age and the deferred retirement income is the actuarial equivalent of his monthly Normal Retirement Benefit.

☐ No further benefits accrue after a Participant's Normal Retirement Age and the deferred retirement income shall be equal to his Normal Retirement Benefit.

☐ Benefits continue to accrue until the Participant's deferred retirement date.

(15) Vesting Requirements (Article 1.37):

(1) Vesting Schedules:

☐ 100% vesting immediately upon participation

☐ 100% vesting upon the completion of ____ Years of Service (Not to exceed 10).

☐ _____% for each Year of Service up to a maximum of 100% (Not to be less than 16.7% per Year of Service).

☐ 25% upon the completion of 5 Years of Service plus 5% for each of the next 5 years, plus 10% per Year of Service for each of the next 5 years.

☐ 40% upon the completion of 4 Years of Service, plus 5% per Year of Service for each of the next 2 years, plus 10% per Year of Service for each of the next 5 years.

☐ The schedule set forth as follows, provided that the vesting percentage at every duration must be at least as great as that provided under one of the schedules listed above:

Years of Service	Percentage	Years of Service	Percentage
1	_____%	9	_____%
2	_____%	10	_____%
3	_____%	11	_____%
4	_____%	12	_____%
5	_____%	13	_____%
6	_____%	14	_____%
7	_____%	15 or more	_____%
8	_____%		

(2) Service excluded for vesting purposes only:

☐ No Years of Service are excluded. (This must be checked if the 4-40 vesting schedule has been elected.)

☐ Years of Service which end before a Participant reaches Age 22

☐ Years of Service during any period in which the Employer did not maintain any plan.

(3) Immediate distribution of a Participant's vested benefit is permitted prior to an actual Break in Service.

(16) Normal Form of Retirement Benefit (Article IV):

☐ Straight Life annuity

☐ Joint and 100% Survivor annuity

(17) Voluntary Contributions (Article 3.02):

☐ shall be   ☐ shall not be permitted.

(18) Forms of Investment (Article V):

☐ Combination Funding. The Trustees shall fund the benefits to be provided under the Plan by applying a sufficient portion of the Employer's contribution to the purchase of Life Insurance policies on the life of each Participant in an amount equal to _____ times (not to exceed 100 X) the monthly retirement benefit under the Plan.

The balance of the Employer's contributions shall be invested in an investment fund to be invested in accordance with the provision of Article V of the Plan.

☐ Investment fund only. The Trustees shall fund the benefits to be provided under the Plan by investing the Employer's contributions in an investment fund to be invested in accordance with the provisions of Article V of the Plan.

(19) Normal Retirement Benefits (Article IV):

(A) Covered Compensation (Article 1.11) shall be:

☐ Table Amount for Year _____ shown in the Plan or such other covered compensation Table as may be published from time to time by the Internal Revenue Service.

☐ Uniform Dollar Amount of $_____ (If the Uniform Dollar Amount exceeds $750 of monthly compensation, then the maximum integration percentage rate shown in the Subsection 18(2)b of this Article must be multiplied by a fraction, the numerator of which is $750 and the denominator of which is the Dollar Amount Integration Level selected).

(B) The Normal Retirement Benefit shall be:

☐ _____% of a Participant's average annual pay, plus

☐ _____% of his average annual pay in excess of the integration level (not to exceed 33.333% if the normal form or retirement benefit is a life annuity or 26.333% if the normal form of retirement benefit is a life and 100% survivor annuity). The percentage of this Subsection must be further reduced, if applicable:

(a) by 1/15 for each year of service less than 15 at normal retirement age; and/or

(b) by 1/15 for each of the first 5 years and 1/30 for each of the next 5 years by which normal retirement age is less than age 65;

☐ Benefits under Section (a) and (b) above shall be reduced pro rata for each year of service less than _____ at normal retirement age.

(C) Average Annual Pay means the Participant's Annual Pay averaged over the _____ highest consecutive earnings during the _____ plan year period prior to Normal Retirement Date.

(20) This Adoption Agreement sets forth the Employer's elections as to the variable provisions contained herein as provided for in the Plan and Trust to which this Adoption Agreement is attached and made a part.

The Employer, by executing this document, acknowledges that he has read this Plan and Trust in its entirety, that he has consulted his legal counsel, and that this Plan and Trust is suitable for his purposes and the Employer accepts full responsibility for his participation hereunder.

Executed at _____ , _____
               City   State

this _____ day of _____ , 19_____

Employer: _____

By: _____
              Name and Title of Authorized Officer

Acceptance By Trustees And Plan Administrator

The Trustees and Plan Administrator hereby accept the Plan and
Trust created by the Employer's adoption of this Plan and Trust
and agree to perform the duties to be performed by them.

Trustees   Plan Administrator

_____   _____

_____   _____

_____   _____

FUTURE PLANNING ASSOCIATES, INC.
CORPORATE PROTOTYPE PENSION PLAN NO. 1
(DEFINED BENEFIT)
APPROVAL DATE: SERIES NUMBER:
ADOPTION AGREEMENT
FLAT BENEFIT INTEGRATED PENSION PLAN

Whereas the Employer desires to:

☐ establish a pension plan and trust; or

☐ restate in its entirety its existing plan and trust for the
purpose of providing pension benefits for its eligible Employees in
accordance with the terms and conditions set forth herein, and

Whereas, the Board of Directors of the Employer has approved
and adopted the plan embodied herein,

Now, Therefore, in consideration of mutual covenants herein
contained it is agreed by and between the Employer and the
Trustees as follows:

(1)   Employer Name (Article 1.05): _____

     Address: _____ Tax ID #: _____

     _____ Phone #: (   )

(2)   Name of Plan (Article 1.29); _____

(3)   Predecessor Plan (Article 1.33): _____

(4)   Predecessor Employer (Article 1.32): _____

(5)   Name of Trustees (Article 1.35): _____

(6) Name of Plan Administrator (Article 1.30): _____

Authorized Delegate of Plan Administrator: _____

(7) (A) If this is a restatement of an existing Plan and/or Trust in its entirety

(1) The original effective date of the Plan and/or Trust was: _____

(2) The effective new date of the restatement is:

_____

(B) If this is a new Plan and Trust, the effective date is:

_____

(8) The Plan Year (Article 1.31) is: _____

(9) The Entry Date (Article 1.17) is: _____

(10) Eligibility Provisions (Article II)

(A) Eligible Classes

☐ All employees

☐ All employees except those:

☐ compensated on an hourly basis

☐ compensated on a salaried basis

☐ whose employment is covered by a collective bargaining agreement under which retirement benefits were the subject of good faith bargaining between the Employer and the collective bargaining agent.

☐ other _____

(B) Service with Predecessor Employer (Article 2.09):

☐ If the Predecessor Employer was not a corporation, Years of Service under this Plan shall include service with the Predecessor Employer as a partner or sole proprietor.

☐ If the Predecessor Employer did not maintain a Plan or maintained a Plan that has been terminated, Years of Service under this Plan shall include service with the Predecessor Employer.

(C) Participation of Eligible Employees

☐ An Employee will be eligible to participate in the plan on the Entry Date nearest, forward or backward to the completion of one Year of Service and attainment of age_____ (not to exceed 25).

☐ An Employee shall be eligible to participate in the
Plan on the Entry Date preceding the date the
Employee completes the later of _____ Years of
Service (not to exceed 3. If more than one Year of
Service is required, 100% immediate vesting must be
elected); or attainment of age _____ (not to exceed
25).

☐ An Employee hired within _____ (not to exceed 5)
years of his Normal Retirement Age when first
employed by the Employer shall not be eligible to
participate. *NOTE:* DO NOT CHECK THIS BOX
IF YOU ALSO CHECK BOX (11)(B).

(11) Normal Retirement Age (Article 1.25):

(A) ☐ Age _____(not less than 55 or more than 65)

(B) ☐ Age _____ or the _____ Anniversary Date as a
Participant under this Plan, whichever is later (not
less than age 55 or more than 70 or more than 10
years' participation).

(12) Annual Pay (Article 1.05):

☐ Total Annual Pay (must be selected for an integrated
plan.)

☐ Annual Pay, Excluding
    ☐ Bonuses
    ☐ Overtime
    ☐ Commissions

(13) Early Retirement Requirements (Article IV):

To retire prior to his Normal Retirement Age, a
Participant must meet the following requirements:
(Check and complete all requirements which apply.)

☐ Minimum Age of _____. (Not less than 50.)

☐ Completion of _____ Years of Service. (Not more
than the maximum number of Years of Service for
100% vesting.)

☐ Completion of _____ Years of Participation. (Not
more than 10.)

☐ No provision for early retirement is made under the
Plan.

(14) Deferred Retirement (Article IV):

☐ No further benefits accrue after a Participant's
Normal Retirement Age and the deferred retirement

income is the actuarial equivalent of his monthly Normal Retirement Benefit.

☐ No further benefits accrue after a Participant's Normal Retirement Age and the deferred retirement income shall be equal to his Normal Retirement Benefit.

☐ Benefits continue to accrue until the Participant's deferred retirement date.

(15) Vesting Requirements (Article 1.37):

   (1) Vesting Schedules:

   ☐ 100% vesting immediately upon participation

   ☐ 100% vesting upon the completion of ____ Years of Service (Not to exceed 10).

   ☐ _____% for each Year of Service up to a maximum of 100% (Not to be less than 16.7% per Year of Service).

   ☐ 25% upon the completion of 5 Years of Service plus 5% for each of the next 5 years, plus 10% per Year of Service for each of the next 5 years.

   ☐ 40% upon the completion of 4 Years of Service, plus 5% per Year of Service for each of the next 2 years, plus 10% per Year of Service for each of the next 5 years.

   ☐ The schedule set forth as follows, provided that the vesting percentage at every duration must be at least as great as that provided under one of the schedules listed above:

Years of Service	Percentage	Years of Service	Percentage
1	_____%	9	_____%
2	_____%	10	_____%
3	_____%	11	_____%
4	_____%	12	_____%
5	_____%	13	_____%
6	_____%	14	_____%
7	_____%	15 or more	_____%
8	_____%		

(2) Service excluded for vesting purposes only:
    ☐ No Years of Service are excluded. (This must be checked if the 4-40 vesting schedule has been elected.)
    ☐ Years of Service which end before a Participant reaches Age 22.
    ☐ Years of Service during any period in which the Employer did not maintain any plan.
(3) Immediate distribution of a Participant's vested benefit is permitted prior to an actual Break in Service.

(16) Normal Form of Retirement Benefit (Article IV):
    ☐ Straight Life annuity
    ☐ Joint and 100% Survivor annuity

(17) Voluntary Contributions (Article 3.02):
    ☐ shall be   ☐ shall not be permitted.

(18) Form of Investment (Article V):
    ☐ Combination Funding. The Trustees shall fund the benefits to be provided under the Plan by applying a sufficient portion of the Employer's contribution to the purchase of Life Insurance policies on the life of each Participant in an amount equal to _____ times (not to exceed 100 X) the monthly retirement benefit under the Plan.
    The balance of the Employer's contributions shall be invested in an investment fund to be invested in accordance with the provision of Article V of the Plan.
    ☐ Investment fund only. The Trustees shall fund the benefits to be provided under the Plan by investing the Employer's contributions in an investment fund to be invested in accordance with the provisions of Article V of the Plan.

(19) Normal Retirement Benefits (Article IV):
    The normal retirement benefit shall be:
(A) ☐ _____% of a Participant's average Monthly Compensation less _____% (not to exceed 74.074%) of the estimated monthly benefit under the Social Security Act in effect at the time the offset is first applied reduced, prorata, by years of service with the Employer less than _____.

    ☐ _____% of a Participant's Average Monthly Compensation for each year of ☐ Service ☐

Participation at his normal retirement age less
_____% (not to exceed 74.074%) of the estimated
monthly benefit under the Social Security Act in
effect at the time the offset is first applied, not to
exceed _____ years (no more than 40 of N/A).

Under either alternative above, the 74.074% shall be
reduced to 58.519% if the normal form of retirement
benefit under this Plan is a Joint and 100% Survivor
annuity.

(B) Average Annual Pay means the Participant's Annual
Pay averaged over the _____ highest consecutive
annual earnings during the _____ plan year period
prior to Normal Retirement Date.

(20) This Adoption Agreement sets forth the Employer's elections
as to the variable provisions contained herein as provided for
in the Plan and Trust to which this Adoption Agreement is
attached and made a part.

The Employer, by executing this document, acknowledges
that he has read this Plan and Trust in its entirety, that he has
consulted his legal counsel, and that this Plan and Trust is
suitable for his purposes and the Employer accepts full
responsibility for his participation hereunder.

Executed at _____ , _____
                  City   State
this _____ day of _____ , 19_____
Employer: _____
By: _____
              Name and Title of Authorized Officer

Acceptance By Trustees And Plan Administrator

The Trustees and Plan Administrator hereby accept the Plan and
Trust Created by the Employer's adoption of this Plan and Trust
and agree to perform the duties to be performed by them.

         Trustees   Plan Administrator
_____   _____
_____   _____
_____   _____

FUTURE PLANNING ASSOCIATES, INC.
CORPORATE PROTOTYPE PENSION PLAN NO. 1
(DEFINED BENEFIT)
APPROVAL DATE: SERIAL NUMBER:
ADOPTION AGREEMENT
UNIT BENEFIT INTEGRATED PENSION PLAN

Whereas the Employer desires to:

☐ establish a pension plan and trust; or

☐ restate in its entirety its existing plan and trust for the purpose of providing pension benefits for its eligible Employees in accordance with the terms and conditions set forth herein, and

Whereas, the Board of Directors of the Employer has approved and adopted the plan embodied herein,

Now, Therefore, in consideration of mutual covenants herein contained it is agreed by and between the Employer and the Trustees as follows:

(1) Employer Name (Article 1.05): _____

Address: _____   Tax ID #: _____

                                     Phone #: (   ) _____

(2) Name of Plan (Article 1.29); _____

(3) Predecessor Plan (Article 1.33): _____

(4) Predecessor Employer (Article 1.32): _____

(5) Name of Trustees (Article 1.35): _____

(6) Name of Plan Administrator (Article 1.30): _____

     Authorized Delegate of Plan Administrator: _____

(7) (A) If this is a restatement of an existing Plan and/or Trust in its entirety

         (1) The original effective date of the Plan and/or Trust was: _____

         (2) The effective new date of the restatement is: _____

    (B) If this is a new Plan and Trust, the effective date is: _____

(8) The Plan Year (Article 1.31) is: _____

(9) The Entry Date (Article 1.17) is: _____

(10) Eligibility Provisions (Article II)

    (A) Eligible Classes

        □ All employees

        □ All employees except those:

            □ compensated on an hourly basis

            □ compensated on a salaried basis

            □ whose employment is covered by a collective bargaining agreement under which retirement benefits were the subject of good faith bargaining between the Employer and the collective bargaining agent.

            □ other _____

(10) (B) Service with Predecessor Employer (Article 2.09):

        □ If the Predecessor Employer was not a corporation, Years of Service under this Plan shall include service with the Predecessor Employer as a partner or sole proprietor.

        □ If the Predecessor Employer did not maintain a Plan or maintained a Plan that has been terminated, Years of Service under this Plan shall include service with the Predecessor Employer.

(10) (C) Participation of Eligible Employees

        □ An Employee will be eligible to participate in the plan on the Entry Date nearest, forward or backward to the completion of one Year of Service and attainment of age   (not to exceed 25).

        □ An Employee shall be eligible to participate in the Plan on the Entry Date preceding the date the Employee completes the later of   Years of Service (not to exceed 3. If more than one Year of Service is required, 100% immediate vesting must be elected); or attainment of age   (not to exceed 25).

        □ An Employee hired within   (not to exceed 5) years of his Normal Retirement Age when first employed by the Employer shall not be eligible to participate. *NOTE:* DO NOT CHECK THIS BOX IF YOU ALSO CHECK BOX (11)(B).

(11) Normal Retirement Age (Article 1.25):
  (a) ☐ Age   (not less than 55 or more than 65)
  (b) ☐ Age   or the   Anniversary of the time he
          commenced participation in this Plan, whichever is
          later (not less than age 55 or more than 70 or more
          than the 10th anniversary of the time he commenced
          participation in this Plan.)

(12) Annual Pay (Article 1.05):
       ☐ Total Annual Pay (Must be selected for an integrated
          plan.)
       ☐ Annual Pay, Excluding
          ☐ Bonuses
          ☐ Overtime
          ☐ Commissions

(13) Early Retirement Requirements (Article IV):
       To retire prior to his Normal Retirement Age, a
       Participant must meet the following requirements:
       (Check and complete all requirements which apply.)
       ☐ Minimum Age of   . (Not less than 50.)
       ☐ Completion of   Years of Service. (Not more than
          the maximum number of Years of Service for 100%
          vesting.)
       ☐ Completion of   Years of Participation. (Not
          more than 10.)
       ☐ No provision for early retirement is made under the
          Plan.

(14) Deferred Retirement (Article IV):
       ☐ No further benefits accrue after a Participant's
          Normal Retirement Age and the deferred retirement
          income is the actuarial equivalent of his monthly
          Normal Retirement Benefit.
       ☐ No further benefits accrue after a Participant's
          Normal Retirement Age and the deferred retirement
          income shall be equal to his Normal Retirement
          Benefit.
       ☐ Benefits continue to accrue until the Participant's
          deferred retirement date.

(15) Vesting Requirements (Article 1.37):
  (1) Vesting Schedules:
       ☐ 100% vesting immediately upon participation

☐ 100% vesting upon the completion of _____ Years of Service (Not to exceed 10).

☐ _____% for each Year of Service up to a maximum of 100% (Not to be less than 16.7% per Year of Service).

☐ 25% upon the completion of 5 Years of Service plus 5% for each of the next 5 years, plus 10% per Year of Service for each of the next 5 years.

☐ 40% upon the completion of 4 Years of Service, plus 5% per Year of Service for each of the next 2 years, plus 10% per Year of Service for each of the next 5 years.

☐ The schedule set forth as follows, provided that the vesting percentage at every duration must be at least as great as that provided under one of the schedules listed above:

Years of Service	Percentage	Years of Service	Percentage
1	_____%	9	_____%
2	_____%	10	_____%
3	_____%	11	_____%
4	_____%	12	_____%
5	_____%	13	_____%
6	_____%	14	_____%
7	_____%	15 or more	_____%
8	_____%		

(2) Service excluded for vesting purposes only:

☐ No Years of Service are excluded. (This must be checked if the 4-40 vesting schedule has been elected.

☐ Years of Service which end before a Participant reaches Age 22.

☐ Years of Service during any period in which the Employer did not maintain any plan.

(3) Immediate distribution of a Participant's vested benefit is permitted prior to an actual Break in Service.

(16) Normal Form of Retirement Benefit (Article IV):

☐ Straight Life annuity

☐ Joint and 100% Survivor annuity

(17) Voluntary Contributions (Article 3.02):
    ☐ shall be   ☐ shall not be permitted.

(18) Forms of Investment (Article V):

    ☐ Combination Funding. The Trustees shall fund the benefits to be provided under the Plan by applying a sufficient portion of the Employer's contribution to the purchase of Life Insurance policies on the life of each Participant in an amount equal to _____ times (not to exceed 100 X) the monthly retirement benefit under the Plan.

    The balance of the Employer's contributions shall be invested in an investment fund to be invested in accordance with the provisions of Article V of the Plan.

    ☐ Investment fund only. The Trustees shall fund the benefits to be provided under the Plan by investing the Employer's contributions in an investment fund to be invested in accordance with the provisions of Article V of the Plan.

(19) Normal Retirement Benefits (Article IV):

  (A) Covered Compensation (Article 1.11) shall be:

    ☐ Table Amount for Year _____ shown in the Plan or such other covered compensation Table as may be published from time to time by the Internal Revenue Service.

    ☐ Uniform Dollar Amount of $_____ (If the Uniform Dollar Amount exceeds 1/12 of the Taxable Wage Base applicable on the Anniversary Date of the Plan Year for which a benefit computation is being made, then the maximum integration percentage rates shown in Subsection 18(2)b of this Article must be multiplied by a fraction, the numerator of which is 1/12 of the Applicable Taxable Wage Base and the denominator of which is the Dollar Amount integrated level selected.)

  (B) The Normal Retirement Benefit shall be:

    ☐ _____% of a Participant's Average Monthly Compensation for each year of   Service

Participation at his Normal Retirement Age, not to exceed _____ years (no more than 40 or N/A); plus

☐ _____% (not more than .889% if the Normal Form of Retirement Benefit is a life annuity or .702% if the Normal Form of Retirement Benefit is a Joint and Survivor Annuity of his Average Monthly Compensation in excess of the integration level for each year of service participation at his Normal Retirement Age, not to exceed _____ years (no more than 40 or N/A). The percentage of this Subsection must be further reduced, if applicable by

    (a) by 1/15 for each year of service less than 15 at normal retirement age; and/or

    (b) by 1/15 for each of the first 5 years and 1/30 for each of the next 5 years by which normal retirement age is less than age 65;

☐ Benefits under Section (a) and (b) above shall be reduced prorata for each year of service less than _____ at normal retirement age.

(C) Average Annual Pay means the Participant's Annual Pay averaged over the _____ highest consecutive earnings during the _____ plan year period prior to Normal Retirement Date.

(20) This Adoption Agreement sets forth the Employer's elections as to the variable provisions contained herein as provided for in the Plan and Trust to which this Adoption Agreement is attached and made a part.

The Employer, by executing this document, acknowledges that he has read this Plan and Trust in its entirety, that he has consulted his legal counsel, and that this Plan and Trust is suitable for his purposes and the Employer accepts full responsibility for his participation hereunder.

Executed at _____ , _____
                 City   State

this _____ day of _____ , 19_____

Employer: _____

By: _____
              Name and Title of Authorized Officer

Acceptance By Trustees And Plan Administrator

The Trustees and Plan Administrator hereby accept the Plan and Trust created by the Employer's adoption of this Plan and Trust and agree to perform the duties to be performed by them.

<table>
<tr><td>Trustees</td><td>Plan Administrator</td></tr>
<tr><td>_____</td><td>_____</td></tr>
<tr><td>_____</td><td>_____</td></tr>
<tr><td>_____</td><td>_____</td></tr>
</table>

Index

Please Return to General Library